The Constitution of Markets

The failures of early "market reforms" in many post-communist countries have refocused attention on the relevance of the institutional framework of market economies – an aspect grossly neglected in orthodox economic theory and often overlooked by Western economists advising transformation governments. By looking at markets as social institutions, the articles collected in this volume seek to fill this void.

Standard economic analysis studies markets as arenas in which demand and supply forces interact. While such analysis presupposes that this interplay of economic forces takes place within a given framework of rules and institutions, the manner in which these framing rules and institutions condition the operation of markets is rarely explored explicitly. The articles in this volume focus on the "constitution of markets" as the rules of the game within which the evolutionary process of market competition unfolds. A central theme is the connection between the nature of the constituting rules and the character of the economic process that emerges within these rules. Particular attention is paid to the relation between the market and the state, specifically the role of governments in shaping and maintaining the economic constitution of their societies.

The theoretical perspective presented in this book draws, in particular, on three sources of ideas: Friedrich A. Hayek's theory of spontaneous order and cultural evolution, James M. Buchanan's constitutional political economy, and the notion of economic policy as *Ordnungspolitik* (politics of constitutional framing) developed by the Freiburg school of law and economics.

Viktor J. Vanberg is Professor of Economics at the University of Freiburg, Germany. He is also the editor of *Constitutional Political Economy* and the author of several books, including *Rules and Choice in Economics* (Routledge 1994).

Foundations of the Market Economy
Edited by Mario J. Rizzo, *New York University*, and
Lawrence H. White, *University of Georgia*

A central theme in this series is the importance of understanding and assessing the market economy from a perspective broader than the static economics of perfect competition and Pareto optimality. Such a perspective sees markets as causal processes generated by the preferences, expectations and beliefs of economic agents. The creative acts of entrepreneurship that uncover new information about references, prices and technology are central to these processes with respect to their ability to promote the discovery and use of knowledge in society.

The market economy consists of a set of institutions that facilitate voluntary cooperation and exchange among indiviudals. These institutions include the legal and ethical framework as well as more narrowly 'economic' patterns of social interaction. Thus, the law, legal institutions and cultural and ethical norms, as well as ordinary business practices and phenomena, fall within the analytical domain of the economist.

The Meaning of Market Process
Essays in the development of modern Austrian economics
Israel M. Kirzner

Prices and Knowledge
A market-process perspective
Esteban F. Thomas

Keynes' General Theory of Interest
A reconsideration
Fiona C. Maclachlan

Laissez-Faire Banking
Kevin Dowd

Expectations and the Meaning of Institutions
Essays in economics by Ludwig Lachmann
Edited by Don Lavoie

Money and the Market
Essays on free banking
Kevin Dowd

Calculation and Coordination
Essays on socialism and transitional political economy
Peter Boettke

Keynes and Hayek
The money economy
Gerry Steele

The Constitution of Markets
Essays in political economy
Viktor J. Vanberg

The Constitution of Markets

Essays in political economy

Viktor J. Vanberg

Routledge
Taylor & Francis Group

LONDON AND NEW YORK

Published 2001 by Routledge
2 Park Square, Milton Park, Abingdon, Oxon, OX14 4RN

Simultaneously published in the USA and Canada by Routledge
52 Vanderbilt Avenue, New York, NY 10017

First issued in paperback 2018

Routledge is an imprint of the Taylor & Francis Group, an informa business

British Library Cataloguing in Publication Data
A catalogue record for this book is available
from the British Library

Library of Congress Cataloging in Publication Data
Vanberg, Viktor J.
    The constitution of markets : essays in political economy / Viktor J. Vanberg.
        p. cm. – (Foundations of the market economy)
    Includes biographical references and index.
        1. Economics. 2. Economic policy. 3. Capitalism. 4. Post-communism. I. Title. II.
Foundations of the market economy series
HB171 .V36 2001
338.9–dc2   00-069038

Typeset in Garamond by
Prepress Projects Ltd, Perth, Scotland

ISBN 13: 978-1-138-86590-7 (pbk)
ISBN 13: 978-0-415-15471-0 (hbk)

To Monika

Contents

Preface

In economics literature, the concept of the market is used with two critically different meanings. On the one hand, it is used as a general label for any kind of social arena in which goods and services are traded and in which the "market forces" of demand and supply tend to bring about equilibrium prices. On the other hand, it is used in a much more specific sense as a name for a particular type of social arrangement that is defined by certain legal–institutional characteristics or, in other words, by certain "rules of the game."

Standard economics textbooks typically emphasize the first of the two notions.[1] Reflecting the dominant neo-classical paradigm, they focus on the mechanics of demand and supply in line with the research program that Leon Walras had laid out in his *Eléments D'Economie Politique Pure* in 1874 for a "science of pure economics," a science that was to explain the operation of market forces in a manner similar to "a physico-mathematical science like mechanics or hydrodynamics" (Walras 1954: 71).

By contrast, the concept of the market is used in the second noted sense when, for instance, modern market economies are contrasted with centrally planned or premodern types of socioeconomic arrangements, when "well-functioning" markets are contrasted with heavily regulated or restricted markets, or when legal markets are distinguished from "black" or "shadow" markets. In such context, the "market" is not simply viewed as an arena of interacting economic forces, but as a social–institutional arrangement with specific institutional characteristics.

To be sure, the two uses of the concept of the market are by no means incompatible with each other. The interplay of the forces of demand and supply on which the first notion concentrates is, of course, at work within the specifically defined institutional arena emphasized by the second notion. Yet, the two notions tend to direct our analytical attention into different directions. The "demand-and-supply" outlook draws attention to the general mechanics of economic forces that can be expected to work wherever people seek to obtain from each other desired goods and services. In a world of scarcity, competition for desired things is omnipresent, and so is the interplay of the forces of demand and supply. This is not only true for "markets" in the above-noted specific sense but it is also true for all kinds of social arenas, whatever their particular institutional characteristics may be. Indeed, "markets" can be considered universal social phenomena if we define them in the general sense as "arenas where the forces of demand and supply meet." Also, an economics that focuses on the mechanics of demand and supply can surely be applied to all kinds of social phenomena outside its traditional domain, as shown by Gary S. Becker's generalized "economic approach to human behavior."[2]

The institutional outlook at markets, on the other hand, draws attention to the particular contingencies that condition the ways in which competition for scarce rewards proceeds, and the manner in which the interaction of economic forces plays itself out. Depending on the nature of the legal–institutional framework within which they take place, competition and the interplay of economic forces can take on quite different characteristics; and it is because of the very ways in which they condition the working of competition and the forces of demand and supply that we attribute particular significance to the kind of institutions that define a "market" in the more narrow, institutional sense of the term.

Certainly, the standard textbook approach does not ignore the fact that markets may exhibit quite different working properties, dependent on particular contingencies that condition the operation of market forces. Yet, in the spirit of the Walrasian research program, it specifies these contingencies not in institutional terms but in terms of variables that directly relate to the mechanics of interacting economic forces, such as the number of firms operating in a market, the homogeneity of products, or the speed of adaptive responses. In fact, in defining the principal subject of its study, the "perfect market," it abstracts entirely from institutional characteristics, following the lead of Walras, whose "pure economics" was to assume a world in which economic forces interact without friction in the same sense in which "in pure mechanics we suppose, to start with, that machines are perfectly frictionless" (Walras 1954: 84).[3]

Neo-classical economics has often been criticized for being "institution blind," for describing the mechanics of demand and supply forces as operating in an institutional vacuum. Such criticism may not be fully justified in the sense that, at least implicitly, neo-classical economists have, of course, always presumed that the interplay of market forces that they study takes place in a world of voluntary exchange, in which property rights are well defined and respected and in which fraud and coercion are absent. In this sense, they cannot be accused of being unaware of the institutional preconditions implied in their model case of perfect competition.[4] Yet, the very fact that the institutional dimension of markets is left implicit indicates that it is not considered an important issue, worthy of analytical attention, or, at least, not the appropriate subject of theoretical economics.

The neo-classical focus on the abstract mechanics of demand and supply and its disinterest in institutional specifics has long been the target of criticism from heterodox approaches, such as the German historical school and American institutionalism. Dissatisfaction with the institutional deficiency of mainstream economics has also been the motivating force behind a number of more recent theoretical developments in economics that can be subsumed under the summary label "new institutional economics." These more recent approaches seek to add an institutional dimension to economics with lesser revisions of the received theoretical and methodological apparatus than the earlier heterodox approaches considered necessary. The papers collected in this volume are meant as a contribution to these theoretical efforts. They explicitly look at markets as *constitutional systems*, as arenas of social interaction that are defined by specific rules of the game. And they examine the role of government, or "the state," in establishing and maintaining the legal–institutional framework within which market forces operate.

More specifically, the perspective adopted in the contributions to this volume is that of *constitutional political economy*, one of the branches of the more inclusively defined new institutional economics, a branch that owes much to the work of James M. Buchanan.[5] Constitutional political economy takes its departure from a fundamental distinction between what Friedrich A. Hayek (1969a) has called the *order of rules* and the *order of actions*, i.e. the distinction between the *rules of the game* that govern human social conduct and the *pattern of actions* that results within these rules. The principal focus of constitutional political economy is on choices among rules and on the question of how such choices affect the ways in which socioeconomic–political "games" are played. It seeks to examine and to compare the working properties of alternative rules, and it explores the question of how persons may come to play a *better game* by agreeing to submit to *better rules*, rules that make the game more desirable for all parties involved.

The analogy with ordinary games, insinuated in the above remarks, is helpful in illustrating the basic concern of the constitutional perspective. In ordinary games, we can clearly distinguish between choices of strategies within a given set of rules, and choices among rules. In playing a game, our principal concern is to play the game well, to choose strategies that promise to serve us well. Yet, beyond our interest in playing a given game successfully, we may also ask the question whether the game itself may not be improved by adopting better rules. Life in society is certainly in many regards different from a game. The interests that bring us together in real social life are much more varied and most often much more serious. Also, we typically cannot as easily, as we can with games, enter and exit the social networks in which we participate. Even so, it is just as true for our "real" social life that we interact within *rules of the game*, the laws, rules, and customs that define the institutional constraints within which we act and interact and which shape, for better or worse, the order of actions that emerges among us. And just as with ordinary games, the principal means by which we can hope to give our socioeconomic–political arrangements a more desirable character is to seek to improve the rules of the game.

Although the contributions to this volume take their principal departure from a constitutional political economy perspective, they also draw on two other principal sources that are usually not counted among the varieties of the new institutional economics, namely F. A. Hayek's social philosophy and the ideas of the Freiburg school of law and economics (see Chapter 3 in this volume).

In fact, a major goal of my own research efforts, here and elsewhere, is to show how these three theoretical approaches in economics can be integrated, with their distinctive characteristics, into a coherent constitutional outlook at markets and politics.

The nature of the market as a spontaneous social order is, of course, the central theme in Hayek's work, and Hayek has left no doubt that he regards the institutional framework as the essential determinant of the working properties of market processes. In speaking of the market as "the game of catallaxy" (Hayek 1976a: 115), the game of exchange, he wanted to emphasize that the competitive market process "proceeds, like all games, according to rules guiding the actions of individual participants" (ibid.: 71), and that the way the market game is played critically depends on the nature of these rules. He also made it clear that the legal–institutional framework within which markets operate is only rudimentarily described by the standard formula "private property and freedom of contract," and that the "relation between the character of the legal order and the functioning of the market system" (Hayek 1960: 229) is an issue that deserves careful study. To be sure, by contrast with the "choice of rules" emphasis of constitutional political economy, Hayek was rather skeptical about the promises of deliberate institutional design, putting much more trust in the discovery potential of evolutionary processes. How his evolutionary argument and the project of deliberate constitutional choice may be reconciled is one of the issues discussed in the present volume, in particular in Chapter 4.

That the rules and institutions that constitute a beneficially working market order cannot be expected to be self-generating and self-maintaining, but need the support of politics, has been the central tenet of the Freiburg School, founded in the 1930s by economist Walter Eucken and jurist Franz Böhm. It was their principal message that a functioning market order cannot be secured without an adequate *economic constitution*, a framework of rules and institutions that, ideally, allows for economic success to be had only through, as they called it, "*Leistungswettbewerb,*" i.e. competition in terms of better service to consumers. The creation and maintenance of such a framework was, they argued, a continuing political task, the task of *Ordnungspolitik*, a policy of institutional framing. While modern constitutional political economy has primarily focused on the issue of how the political process may be constrained by suitable rules to be responsive to citizens' interests, the principal focus of the Freiburg school has been on the institutional prerequisites for a market order that is responsive to consumer interests. To show how the two approaches can complement each other, and how they can be combined with a Hayekian evolutionary perspective, is one of the principal purposes of this book.

The articles included in this volume have been published over the past decade in dispersed places. They have been edited and, in part, slightly modified, but they are essentially reproduced in their original form. In the sequence in which they appear in this collection, the articles were originally published as follows:

Chapter 1: "Constitutionally constrained and safeguarded competition in markets and politics," originally published as "Constitutionally constrained and safeguarded competition in markets and politics with reference to a European constitution," *Journal des Economistes et des Etudes Humaines* 1993; IV: 3–27.

Chapter 2: "Markets and regulation: the contrast between free-market liberalism and constitutional liberalism," *Constitutional Political Economy* 1999; 10: 219–43.

Chapter 3: "The Freiburg school of law and economics: predecessor of constitutional economics," originally published as "Freiburg school of law and economics," in P. Newman (ed.), *The New Palgrave Dictionary of Economics and the Law*, Vol. 2, London: Macmillan, 1998; pp. 172–9. The version published here includes the endnotes, which were omitted from the *Palgrave* version.

Chapter 4: "Hayek's legacy and the future of liberal thought: Rational liberalism vs. evolutionary agnosticism," *Journal des Economistes et des Etudes Humaines* 1994; V: 451–81.

Chapter 5: "Hayek's theory of rules and the modern state," in S. Ratnapala and G.A. Moens (eds), *Jurisprudence of Liberty*, Sydney: Butterworth, 1996; pp. 47–66.

Chapter 6: "John R. Commons: institutional evolution through purposeful selection," originally published as "Institutional evolution through purposeful selection: the constitutional economics of John R. Commons," *Constitutional Political Economy* 1997; 8: 105–22.

Chapter 7: "The market as a creative process," *Economics and Philosophy* 1991; 7: 167–86.

Chapter 8: "A constitutional economics perspective on international trade," originally published as "A constitutional political economy perspective on international trade," *ORDO – Jahrbuch für die Ordnung von Wirtschaft und Gesellschaft* 1992; 43: 375–697.

The permission of the original publishers to reprint the above articles in the present volume is gratefully acknowledged.

This volume is dedicated with love and gratitude to my wife, Monika. For more than 30 years, she has been not only the center of my life but also the first reader of all my writing. Her suggestions and editorial support have been as essential to me in preparing the articles collected here as they have been to my earlier work.

1 Constitutionally constrained and safeguarded competition in markets and politics[1]

Introduction

The collapse of communism and the demise of socialist central planning have refocused attention on the merits of market principles. Yet, in spite of the apparent general increase in appreciation for markets, it is not quite as obvious how widely the more fundamental and more subtle lessons have been learned that the history of the socialist experiment has to offer. These more fundamental and subtle lessons have to do, in my view, with our understanding of the role of *competition* as an organizing principle in human social affairs. In what follows, I want to develop some thoughts on the functions that competition can serve in social organization, not only in markets but also in the realm of politics. More specifically, I want to discuss this question in a *constitutional* dimension, as an issue that pertains to the ground rules of a socioeconomic–political order. My argument falls into three main parts. In the first part, I shall review some of the familiar arguments on the role of competition in ordinary markets. The second part will be concerned with the role of competition as an organizing principle in politics. In the third and last part, I shall examine some implications for European constitutional concerns.

Competition and markets

If one were to argue to the members of a constitutional convention why it would be in their constituents' interests to adopt a constitution that emphasizes competition as an organizing principle, what reasons could one provide in support of such argument? There are, it seems to me, three main arguments related to three kinds of problems for which competition may provide a remedy; namely, as I shall label them, the *incentive* problem, the *power* problem, and the *knowledge* problem. I shall discuss these arguments, first, in the context in which they are most familiar, namely applied to competition in ordinary markets.

Adam Smith talked about the incentive problem when he noted, in one of his most often quoted statements, that it "is not from the benevolence of the butcher, the brewer, or the baker, that we expect our dinner, but from their regard to their own interest" (Smith 1981: 26f.). Of course, he was very clear about the fact that it is not the butcher's, the brewer's nor the baker's self-interest *per se* that assures us of their services, but, instead, the constraints that competition imposes on their behavior. It is the necessity to compete for customers that induces suppliers of goods and services to seek to find out, and to satisfy, consumer wants. Competition generates responsiveness to consumer interests, it places – as Franz Böhm, one of the major figures of German ordo-liberalism (Vanberg 1988; 1991), has put it – "the entrepreneur's pursuit of profit in the direct service of the consumer,"[2] or, stated more emphatically, "competition forms the moral back-bone of a free profit-based economy" (Böhm 1982: 110).

German ordo-liberals – such as Franz Böhm and his colleague at the University of Freiburg Walter Eucken – emphasized that, in addition to its role as an incentive mechanism, competition also works as a mechanism for limiting and dispersing power.[3] In Böhm's (1961: 42) words, "Competition is the most remarkable and ingenious instrument for reducing power known in history."[4] Competition means availability of alternative counterparts for trade, of alternative sources of supply, a condition that reduces the dependence of consumers on any particular supplier and, thereby, reduces the power that such dependence would provide to the latter.

The last of the three problems that I distinguished before, namely the knowledge problem, has been discussed, in particular, by Friedrich A. Hayek, who has stressed that what we may call the "economic problem of society" is in essence a problem of knowledge: "The problem of finding a method that not only best utilizes the knowledge dispersed among the individual members of society, but also best uses their abilities of discovering and exploring new ways of doing things" (Hayek 1979: 190).[5] Market competition constitutes an explorative learning process in which continuously new and potentially better solutions to a wide range of problems – from supplying bread or producing computer software to organizing large corporations – are tried out and put to test, under conditions that make for responsiveness to the interests of consumers, the ultimate judges of success and failure. Market competition is, in other words, a knowledge-creating process (Kerber 1991) or a "process of exploration" (Hayek 1978: 188); it is an open-ended evolutionary process that allows for, and provides incentives for, continuous and countless efforts to propose better solutions to problems than those that are currently available.[6] It is a process that facilitates adaptation in a world in which our knowledge and the problems we face change in ways that can never be fully anticipated, a process that, for these very reasons, by necessity "always leads into the unknown" (Hayek 1960: 40).[7]

Constitutionally constrained competition

So far, I have left unspecified what I mean by "competition." Competition, in the most general sense of a process in which different parties seek to obtain something that they all strive for but that not all can have, is, to be sure, a perennial phenomenon. As long as human wants exceed the means available for their satisfaction – and ever changing human desires prevent this discrepancy from ever disappearing – there will be competition for "scarce goods." This means that we cannot choose to live *without* competition. All we can do is to choose the *ways* in which competition is carried out.[8] And it is only in terms of the latter, not in the presence or absence of competition, that societies differ. In Hobbesian anarchy, "anything goes" is the order of the day, i.e. there are no effective constraints on the ways and means by which persons compete. What we call social order is made possible by effective limits being put on the strategies allowed in competition. Social order means, in other words, that competition is effectively *constrained by rules*. Societies can differ greatly in the nature of these rules, or, as we may call it, in their *competitive order* (*Wettbewerbsordnung*), and these differences can affect significantly their working characteristics. What distinguishes, in this sense, a socialist economy or a mercantilist system (Ekelund and Tollison 1982) from a market economy is not the absence of competition but the different nature of their respective competitive orders. To seek privileges (monopoly rights) from political authorities or to stand in waiting lines are no less methods to compete for scarce goods than is competition through the market-price mechanism. Yet, the working properties of economic systems that use these different methods of competition will, of course, differ significantly.

When Adam Smith described market competition as "the obvious and simple system of natural liberty," he did not mean to imply that competition is *per se* beneficial, irrespective of the ways and means by which it is carried out. Instead, he quite explicitly argued that competition will only work beneficially when carried out within the constraints of *appropriate rules*, within what he called the "laws of justice."[9] In his modern restatement of the principles of classical liberalism, Hayek has equally emphasized that, to operate beneficially, competition is to be "restrained by appropriate rules of law" (Hayek 1978: 125; 1988: 19), and he has explicitly noted that the fundamental principle of liberalism is misunderstood if it is interpreted "as absence of state activity rather then as a policy which ... uses the legal framework enforced by the state in order to make competition as effective and beneficial as possible" (Hayek 1948a: 110). To make only the most obvious point, we could compete with each other by means of fraud, threats, and coercion, but we would hardly consider such a competitive regime a desirable social order. Market competition is *constitutionally constrained competition*; competition within rules that serve to enhance its adaptive potential and its responsiveness to consumer interests, or, more briefly, by rules that secure the essential feature of market transactions, *voluntary* trade, and contracting.[10]

The German ordo-liberals Walter Eucken, Franz Böhm and others made it clear that the desirable working properties which the classical liberals had attributed to market competition could only be expected from what they called *Leistungswettbewerb*, competition according to rules which assure, as Wilhelm Röpke (1960: 31) worded it, "that the only road to business success is through the narrow gate of better performance in service of the consumer."[11] Also, they emphasized that to create and maintain an appropriate framework or

"*Ordnungsrahmen*" for *Leistungswettbewerb* is a genuine and indispensable political task, a task for *Ordnungspolitik* or *constitutional politics*. In fact, they saw a critical deficiency in some of the nineteenth century interpretations of classical liberal principles in their insufficient recognition of the role of government in maintaining a conducive legal–institutional framework for market competition.[12]

To be sure, what rules are *appropriate* for guiding competition in a desirable direction is a question that cannot be answered once and for all but that needs to be re-examined, at least in some of its aspects because relevant circumstances change. In this regard, we face, as Hayek (1960: 230) argues, a perennial "task of gradually amending our legal system to make it more conducive to the smooth working of competition." There is, he notes, "ample scope for experimentation and improvement within that permanent legal framework which makes it possible for a free society to operate most efficiently. We can probably at no point be certain that we have already found the best arrangements or institutions that will make the market economy work as beneficial as it could" (ibid.: 231).[13]

Constitutionally safeguarded competition

Beneficially working market competition needs not only appropriate constitutional constraints. A related, yet distinguishable, requirement is that a competitive order needs to be *safeguarded* against anti-competitive interests, interests that seek to escape competitive constraints through private arrangements or through political means. Their experience with the cartel problem in the German economy of their time had focused the German ordo-liberals' attention mainly on the first of these alternatives, i.e. the problem of private power. They emphasized that a functioning competitive order does not only require the government to refrain from directly inhibiting competition but also requires it "to ensure that the restricting of the market by private pressure groups does not take place" (Eucken 1982: 119). It has to prevent, the ordo-liberals argued, the freedom to contract which is "obviously central to the realization of a competitive system" being used as an instrument "to eliminate competition and to establish monopolistic positions" (ibid.: 123).[14] In this context, they pointed, in particular, to the problem of distortional indirect effects that may be caused by legislation in such areas as, for instance, trade policy or patent law.[15]

Although the German ordo-liberals were doubtlessly aware of the problem, they concerned themselves less with the issue of how the political process itself may be used to seek protection from competition in the form of subsidies, tax exemptions, tariffs, and import restrictions, as well as all kinds of regulations that create monopoly privileges of various sorts and degrees. To pursue this method for escaping competitive constraints means to lobby for protective legislation, like Frederik Bastiat's famous candle makers who lobbied for a building code disallowing windows in order to be protected from the sun's unfair competition. The use of the political "escape route" from competition has been extensively studied in modern public choice theory under the name of *rent-seeking*.[16] I shall concentrate my comments on this part of the issue of anti-competitive strategies.

It helps in understanding the problems that are involved here to employ the general distinction between two levels of choice, the constitutional and the sub-constitutional levels, or the choice among rules and the choice within rules. In analogy to this distinction, we can distinguish between two corresponding kinds of interests, namely *constitutional* interests and *sub-constitutional* or *action* interests. The first are our interests with regard to the constitutional regime or the rules under which we would like to live, interests that inform our choices at the constitutional level, e.g. when we vote on proposals for constitutional reform. The second are our interests with regard to the alternative strategy options that are available to us within the confines of a *given* constitutional–institutional framework, interests that inform our sub-constitutional choices in playing the game within given rules.

The *benefits from competition* that I have discussed before under the rubric of incentive, power, and knowledge problems would seem to suggest that it should be in everybody's *constitutional* interest to live in a competitive order and that, therefore, political support for a competitive framework should be easily forthcoming. Yet, this seems to be manifestly contradicted by the pervasiveness of anti-competitive, protectionist rules and regulations, i.e. of arrangements that serve to impede and restrict competition.[17] How can the economist's insight in the productivity of a competitive order and the reality of widespread anti-competitive practices be squared? At least part of the answer to this question can, as I want to suggest, be found in the distinction between *constitutional* and *action* interests.

If we had to choose to live either in a generally competitive system or in a system that is immobilized by pervasive anti-competitive regulations and protectionist rules, we would have good reasons to prefer the first environment because it promises to make for a wealthier society. Yet, this is not how the choice between competition and protectionism is typically presented to us. And for the choices that we really face, the presence of a *constitutional* preference for a generally competitive over a generally non-competitive environment does not at all mean that we would have no incentives to seek protection against competition for our own particular business or trade. The problem lies, of course, in the fact that there is an asymmetry of interests in the sense that our direct interest is in having others compete, not in us being subject to competitive constraints. In other words, competition is clearly desirable for those who are competed for; it is less desirable for those who have to compete. Or, as Hayek (1979a: 77) has noted:

> To those, with whom others compete, the fact that they have competitors is always a nuisance that prevents a quiet life; and such direct effects of

competition are always much more visible than the indirect benefits which we derive from it.[18]

If it were possible, we would like to have it both ways: to have our own business or trade protected from competitive pressure while enjoying the benefits that an otherwise competitive environment has to offer. And, conversely, we would certainly not want to be the only ones who have to compete, while all others on whose services we depend would be protected from competition.

Protectionist legislation is a discriminatory practice. It grants privileges to some, but not to others. Where such *differential treatment* or *discrimination* is practiced, where some may enjoy protection while others have to compete, we have a reason to wish to be among the former. By contrast, in a system that would not allow for any privileges, that would rule out such discriminatory treatment, and where, therefore, protectionist provisions could only be legislated as a *general principle*, granted either to each and every business or trade or to nobody at all, in such a system our preferences would be clearly different. Protection is only advantageous if one is the beneficiary of discriminatory treatment, not if it was practiced as a general rule. In other words, producer interests in protectionist privileges cannot be generalized, they are *not compatible* across the polity. A generalized protectionist system would be desirable for nobody. By contrast, what can be generalized and what is compatible across the polity are our interests as consumers. And what can be beneficially practiced as a general principle is a competitive order that serves these *consumer interests*.

This can be seen as the rationale behind the concept of consumer sovereignty, a rationale that Böhm appealed to when he noted that consumer interests are "the sole directly justifiable economic interests."[19] To be constrained by competition is not something that we like *per se*; it is, however, a price that we would most certainly be willing to pay if it were the entrance requirement to a system where everyone else is equally subject to the discipline of competition.

That our generalized consumer interests apparently have not prevailed is the result of the fact that, in the world "as it is," the political process has allowed for discriminatory treatment, thus inviting the whole set of problems that, as I mentioned before, public choice economists have discussed under the rubric of *rent-seeking* (Buchanan *et al.* 1980; Buchanan 1993).[20] In such a world, to seek protection is – in the terminology of game theory – the dominant choice in a prisoners' dilemma-type setting, resulting in an overall outcome that, in the end, makes all parties – the beneficiaries of existing protection included – worse off than they could be in an open, competitive environment (Ch. 8 in this volume). As long as discriminatory or privileged treatment can be obtained from governments and legislators, there will be rent-seeking or special interest lobbying, and in each case explanations will be readily produced for why, in the particular instance, the public interest was served by granting the privilege in question. It is difficult to see how this problem may be remedied in any way other than depriving legislators and governments of their *authority* and their *power* to discriminate. There are two principal means by which this can be brought about. Governments can be deprived from such *authority* through appropriate, explicit constitutional provisions. And they can be deprived from such *power* through the discipline of inter-governmental competition, an issue to which I shall return later.

Constitutional choice and political process

So far, I have discussed reasons why citizens of a polity may wish to rely on market competition as an organizing principle. I have discussed reasons why competition needs to be *constrained* by appropriate rules if it is to work to the general benefit of all parties involved. Also, I have argued why a competitive order needs constitutional *safeguards* against anti-competitive interests. In other words, I have provided reasons why competition may be a desirable organizing principle, and why it needs to be embedded in an appropriate constitutional framework or *Ordnungsrahmen*, the maintenance of which is a genuine political task.

To recognize the role of politics in creating and maintaining the institutional–constitutional framework within which markets operate means, of course, to raise another question, namely whether and, if so, under what conditions we may expect the political process to produce an "appropriate *Ordnungsrahmen*," a framework that suitably conditions and safeguards a competitive market order. The obvious starting point in examining this question is the fact that the political, rule-producing process itself operates under *rule constraints*, notably those that are specified in the "constitution" in the standard, narrower sense of the term. Yet, the political process is subject to *competitive constraints* as well, and its working properties will clearly depend upon the nature of both kinds of constraints. They determine, in particular, the extent to which the process can be expected to work to the benefit of its constituents, the citizens.

From a constitutional economics perspective, the issue at hand can be stated in terms of the following question: in drafting a constitution, what principles or devices might the citizens involved wish to include to make the political process more responsive to their, the citizens', interests? In other words, what constitutional provisions would promise to make the political process operate in ways that are desirable from the citizen's perspective? There are, to be sure, many elements of the Western constitutional tradition that are relevant in this context and that have been discussed in such contributions as Harold Berman's *Law and Revolution* (1983), Erik Jones's *The European Miracle* (1987), or Nathan Rosenberg's and Luther Birdzell's *How the West Grew Rich* (1986).[21] Staying within my chosen theme, I shall concentrate my comments on the role of *competition* in the realm of politics or, more precisely, on the role of *market-type* competition in politics.

When we speak of competition in politics, we can mean two different things, namely, on the one hand, competition *for* or *within* government and, on the other hand, competition *between* governments. Competition for government is competition for votes and competition between parties and candidates to be elected into political office. As competition within government, we can describe the system of checks and balances between different branches and levels of government. The rules of competition for and within government are a principal subject of constitutions in the standard sense. And it is through these rules that democratic systems of government seek to make office holders responsive to their constituents' interests. Competition between governments is competition for citizens – or, more generally, for resources – that governments want to attract to their jurisdiction (Sinn 1992).[22]

Competition between governments can be compared to ordinary market competition between firms,[23] even though, to be sure, an obvious major difference lies in the *territorial nature* of governments.[24] When a dissatisfied customer of an ordinary market firm decides to take his business elsewhere, this normally has little impact on other parts of his life. By contrast, when a dissatisfied citizen wants to "choose" a different government – not by marking a ballot, but by his individual and separate choice to get out from under the authority of a particular government[25] – he has to move physically from one jurisdiction to another, a transaction that can be very costly. Because such a choice typically involves significant costs, the conclusion is frequently drawn, prematurely in my view, that market-type competition cannot be of much relevance in the political realm.

It is certainly true that the costs of migrating between jurisdictions tend to be typically high compared with the costs of moving between alternative suppliers in ordinary markets. Yet, before any conclusions concerning the effectiveness of competition between governments are drawn, a number of things ought to be considered. First of all, relevant to market-type competition between governments is not only the migration of persons–taxpayers but also the migration of taxable resources, in particular capital. Migration costs are typically lower for resources than for persons, and the lower their migration costs are the more governments are under competitive constraints in their treatment of these resources. Financial capital has become enormously mobile in today's world, with predictable consequences for inter-governmental competition. Governments may be able to exploit capital that has been sunk in their jurisdiction, but they can do so only at the expense of their capability to attract financial investments in the future.[26]

Secondly, migration costs for persons–taxpayers can vary considerably. They vary, most obviously, with the size of jurisdictions. Moving between local communities is less costly than moving between states in a federation, and the latter is less costly than moving between nation-states.[27] Furthermore, they vary among citizens and, just as in ordinary markets, it is not necessary for all customers–citizens to respond to unsatisfactory performance to make competition effective. A sufficient number of "marginal citizens," i.e. of citizens for whom the choice between jurisdictions is associated with lower costs, can significantly increase the responsiveness of governments to citizens' interests, just like a sufficient number of "marginal customers" can make firms more responsive than they would be otherwise.

Third, and most importantly, migration costs are to some extent a function of conditions that are subject to constitutional choice, i.e. conditions that can be influenced by political decisions. If we know, for instance, that a decentralized, federal organization tends to reduce these costs, then choosing such a constitutional arrangement can be an instrument to increase the effectiveness of inter-governmental competition and, thus, the responsiveness of governments (Lowenberg and Yu 1992). To sum up, market-type competition between governments can be – and can be made to be – a more important mechanism than it may appear on first glance, an insight that hardly surprises anybody who still remembers the not-so-distant past when communist regimes made extraordinary efforts to keep their "subjects" from choosing for themselves, by migrating, a different government.

There are two notes that I want to add here to my previous comments on inter-governmental competition. First, in ordinary market competition, there is a "symmetry" between exit and entry in the sense that an alternative seller is readily available for whatever goods or services are provided by the firm from which one walks away. For polities, such symmetry does not necessarily exist;[28] yet the option to exit is, for obvious reason, not worth very much if one is not allowed entry into some other polity. If the right to exit is to work as an effective constraint on government, there have to be entry options available. Persons who want to adopt a constitutional framework that induces responsive governments should, therefore, have a constitutional interest in provisions that secure free exit and entry between polities, provisions that can be the subject of a federal constitution or some other contractual commitment among several polities.[29]

Second, to the extent that a federal government must be given authority and power to enforce the rules of inter-governmental competition, vis-à-vis the member-states, the problem of how such power can be effectively controlled and limited arises, of course, anew at the federal level. While intended to limit the power of the member-states by securing competition among them, the federal government may itself become, now on a larger scale, a source of the very same problems that it is supposed to remedy with regard to the former. At the federal level, these problems may even be magnified because with increasing size of the polity the effectiveness of both voice and exit tend to decrease. It is as a safeguard against unresponsive federal government that the collective analog to individual exit, namely *secession*, may be an essential ingredient of a constitution for an effectively *limited* federal government. As an instrument to induce responsive government, the right of sub-units to secede from inclusive polities would seem to be a natural complement to the individual's right to exit. This right should be of particular significance for groups that have traditionally strong ties to their living environment, be it for cultural, for ethnic, or for whatever reasons. To such groups, the option to walk away from an undesired government and to move into another jurisdiction may have little appeal. The presence of such ties – they are clearly a much more significant factor in Europe than, for instance, in the United States – obviously increases exit costs and, thereby, the degree to which a government can neglect the interests of those who have these preferences. The reduced effectiveness of exit can, in such cases, be compensated by the right of territorially defined sub-groups to exit from a given jurisdiction, either to join another polity or to constitute jurisdictions of their own. Switzerland provides an example for how such a device can work in a polity that is divided into many groups with their own cultural and ethnic identities. The rules for the Swiss confederation allow for parts of cantons to split off and to form a new canton, an option that seems to have helped to preempt or to solve conflicts that otherwise might have become much more troublesome.[30]

Competition between governments

Having introduced the notion of inter-governmental competition, I want to examine more closely the role it may play in the realm of politics. More specifically, I want to argue that *citizens* can benefit from such competition in essentially the same ways in which consumers can benefit from competition between firms in ordinary markets. In the political realm, just as in ordinary markets, competition can provide a remedy for the three types of problems that I discussed earlier: the *incentive* problem, the *power* problem, and the *knowledge* problem.

The relevance of inter-governmental competition for the incentive problem has already been pointed out in what I said before. I can, therefore, be brief here and just note that we would naturally expect governments that have to compete for citizens–taxpayers to be expected to be more responsive to their constituents' interests than governments that are not subject to the discipline of such competition. As Thomas Dye (1990a: 15) summarizes:

> Competition in the private marketplace forces sellers to become sensitive to preferences of consumers. Competition among governments forces public officials to become sensitive to the preferences of citizens. Lessened competition in the marketplace results in higher prices, reduced output, and greater inefficiency in production. Lessened competition among governments results in higher taxes, poorer performance and greater inefficiencies in the public sector.

The conclusion with regard to the *power* problem should likewise be obvious. The lower the costs at which a citizen can remove himself and/or his resources from any given jurisdiction, the less power the government of that jurisdiction will have over that person. The notion that the right and the capacity of individuals to move with their resources between jurisdictions impose effective constraints on the power of governments has, for obvious reasons, been an important theme in discussions on federalism in general, and on fiscal federalism in particular (Brennan and Buchanan 1980: 168ff.; Marlow 1992). In his 1939 article on "The economic conditions of interstate federalism," Hayek (1948b) noted that the free movement of men and the free movement of capital within a federation "limit to a great extent the scope of the economic policy of the individual states" (ibid.: 258) and that, as a consequence, "much of the interference with economic life to which we have become accustomed will be altogether impracticable under a federal organization" (ibid.: 265).

This is, perhaps, a good place to add a remark on the general issue of limiting the power of government, because the emphasis on this issue may not be entirely plausible to someone whose focus is on the government's capacity to carry out its intended functions. If we look at the relationship between citizens and government as a principal–agent relationship, we can certainly assume that the principals, the citizens, have an interest in a government that is powerful enough to carry out its assigned task. Yet, we can also assume that the principals–citizens will be concerned about the possibility that the power transferred to government may be used in ways that violate their interests, either in the form of direct misuse of power on the part of the agents or by other groups who use the political process for exploitative purposes, as an instrument of rent-seeking.[31] It is as a protection against such risks that constitutions are supposed to serve, and competition among governments is a provision that reinforces such protection.[32]

The third problem, the knowledge problem, has found lesser attention in discussions on the role of competition among governments than the other two, but it is no less important.[33] What has been said, in this regard, about the role of competition in markets can also be said about its role in the realm of politics.[34] Without the possibility of experimenting and exploration, and without competition between alternative potential solutions, we could not know what constitutional arrangements or political regimes are better equipped to serve the interests of constituents than others. To be sure, history provides us with rich evidence on what kinds of constitutional arrangements seem to have worked to the benefit of their respective constituents, and it provides us with, perhaps, even richer evidence on what has not worked. Yet, in a changing world and with changing knowledge, the need for exploration in institutional–constitutional matters has certainly not yet come to an end (Vanberg 1990; 1992).

It should be understood, of course, that experimenting and diversity in constitutional matters are not ends in themselves, just as experimenting and diversity are not *per se* an indication of good performance and responsiveness in ordinary markets. Competition can lead to a *de facto* dominance of particular kinds of problem solutions in markets, as a result of consumer choice. The absence of visible experimenting and diversity in such cases need not at all reflect a neglect of consumer interests. In the same sense, competition between governments may well produce a *de facto* "harmonization" of institutional–constitutional provisions in certain areas, as a consequence of citizens' revealed preferences; in such cases, the lack of experiments and diversity would not be a reason for alarm. Yet, such *ex post* "harmonization" that is produced by a competitive process is strictly to be distinguished from legislated *ex ante* harmonization. What is essential, in both contexts, is the *possibility* for experimenting and diversity, and the absence of monopoly privileges and regulatory provisions that rule out such experimenting and diversity (Donges *et al.* 1992).

It should also be understood that, when I speak of institutional–constitutional exploration, I mean *parallel* as opposed to *consecutive* experimenting. Experimenting in ordinary markets is, in this terminology, *parallel* experimenting in the sense that alternative solutions to problems are tried out simultaneously, providing market participants with the opportunity to, more or less directly, compare the attributes of relevant alternatives. Inter-governmental competition provides, in the political realm, a similar opportunity for parallel experimenting and diversity and allows citizens to compare, more or less directly, the working properties of alternative institutional–constitutional arrangements. Sometimes the notion of experimenting in the political realm is also meant in the sense of, what I call, *consecutive* experimenting. Under such a label, I classify the trying out of alternative institutional–constitutional arrangements over time, i.e. consecutive changes in the rules of the game that are adopted in a particular polity.[35] Even if carried out by a perfectly responsive government, consecutive experimenting cannot generate the information that would allow for a comparison among institutional–constitutional alternatives in the way that parallel experimenting does.

Competition between governments cannot only be said to help solve the same kinds of problems that market competition does; it is also subject to the same kind of qualifications as the latter. Its working properties depend, as much as the working properties of markets, on the presence of appropriate institutional–constitutional constraints. In both cases, what we mean by competition is *constitutionally constrained competition*. In markets, these constraints restrict the strategies that market participants may use in their competitive efforts. In the political realm, they restrict the strategies that governments are to use in their competition for citizens–taxpayers and their resources.[36] These rules may concern more obvious things such as the exclusion of certain inhibitions or barriers to the movement of persons and resources, as well as such matters as, for instance, the use of special subsidies or the granting of special privileges to attract business investments. And they may concern, more generally, problems of externalities between jurisdictions within a federation. For inter-governmental competition to work as an inducement for responsive government, the rules of the game ought to ensure *accountability* in the sense that the costs and benefits of policy choices of state and local governments are borne by the citizens–taxpayers in the respective jurisdiction. This principle implies that distortions of such accounting – as they are introduced, for instance, by federal transfer programs – undermine the very foundations on which the competition between jurisdictions rests.[37] It also implies, on the other hand, that *policy co-ordination* may be required in areas, such as environmental policies, in which positive externalities make policies profitable for more inclusive polities that would not be undertaken by smaller jurisdictions.

To provide an appropriate institutional–constitutional framework or *Ordnungsrahmen* for ordinary market competition is, as I stated earlier, a problem that has no simple and final solution in a world in which the problems that we face and our knowledge of how to deal with these problems constantly change. It requires the continuous efforts of an adequate constitutional politics or *Ordnungspolitik*. The same is true, and for the same reasons, with regard to the creation and maintenance of an appropriate institutional–constitutional framework or *Ordnungsrahmen* for inter-governmental competition. This too requires the continuous efforts of an adequate *federal Ordnungspolitik*.

Furthermore, a competitive order in the realm of politics is in need of *constitutional safeguards* against anti-competitive interests, no less so than the competitive order of the market. Politicians, like anybody else, do not like to be subject to competitive constraints, and they are not less tempted than others to seek relief from competitive pressure.[38] Competition in ordinary markets is there to benefit consumers, not to please businessmen; and competition between governments is there to benefit citizens, not to please politicians. Just as consumer interests are the only directly justifiable economic interests, so citizens' interests are the only directly justifiable interests in politics. The appropriate measuring rod for the desirability of the institutional–constitutional order of markets is its effectiveness in making suppliers responsive to consumer interests or, in other words, its effectiveness in enhancing consumer sovereignty. The appropriate measuring rod for the desirability of the institutional–constitutional order of politics is its effectiveness in making governments responsive to citizens or, in other words, its effectiveness in enhancing citizens sovereignty. Competition between firms and governments is desirable because it makes for responsiveness to consumers' and citizens' interests. And it is for the sake of consumers' and citizens' interests that competition needs constitutional safeguards in both arenas against the inclinations of those who would rather do without.

A European constitution: between centralist and competitive federalism

When I speak of a European constitution, I do so not in reference to a particular document but in a more general sense, referring to the set of ground rules that define the relations among, and the division of rights between, the citizens and the various levels of government in a united Europe. I want to contrast here two different paradigms that can be applied to this issue, paradigms that reflect fundamentally different concepts of what the creation of a federal Europe ought to be about, namely centralist federalism on the one side and competitive federalism on the other (Dye 1990a; Buchanan 1992). These two concepts are, to be sure, not meant to be descriptive of existing federal structures. They are, as I said, meant as paradigms, as principles that can be conceptually separated, even if empirically they can only be found in various kinds of mixtures. Nevertheless, their explicit conceptual separation is helpful for analytical purposes in providing a foil against which existing arrangements as well as constitutional proposals can be evaluated.

According to the centralist paradigm, to create a united federal Europe means to organize the polity "Europe" after the model of the nation-state; it means to form a federal government in the image of traditional national governments. The essence of such a process of integration would be to institute, at the federal European level, authorities that replace their respective counterparts at the national level. In other words, in forming the union, the national governments transfer part of their authority or sovereignty to a central European agency, such as, for instance, the transfer of monetary authority from national central banks to a European central bank. By contrast, according to the competitive paradigm, the principal subject of a European constitution would be the exchange of commitments among the member-nations, their joint commitment to rules that serve to constrain what the national governments are permitted to do in their dealings with each other, with third parties and, most importantly, in relation to their citizens and lower-level governments. Such joint commitments would constitute what I referred to earlier as a framework or *Ordnungsrahmen* for inter-governmental competition, a competitive order or *Wettbewerbsordnung* for governments.

By contrast to its centralist counterpart, competitive federalism means that, in forming the union, the national governments retain their authority in whatever area of politics is concerned, whether monetary or otherwise, but jointly submit to certain constraining rules that define the terms under which they can compete in the respective area of activity, rules that may need to be enforced by federal agencies, such as, in particular, a federal court. In the case of monetary politics, this could mean, for instance, that the national governments submit to a system of competing currencies, an arrangement under which they retain their monetary authority but submit to rules that impose on them the *discipline of competition*.

As I have already indicated, by drawing this distinction I do not want to suggest that a federation needs to be based either on the one or the other principle. The creation of a federal union will always include both components. My point, however, is that the *emphasis* can be more on one or the other principle, and that the nature of a federal union can be critically different, depending on where the overall weight lies. To be sure, under both principles the national governments will have to sacrifice part of their power. But this sacrifice means totally different things if the one rather than the other principle is applied. Under centralist federalism, authority is shifted from one political agency to another, from the national governments to a central government, increasing the degree of political centralization. Under competitive federalism, the power that national governments will have to sacrifice is not shifted to some other governmental authority but is, instead, dissipated in a competitive arrangement. It returns, in effect, to the ultimate sovereigns, the individual citizens whose choice options are increased compared with the previous national constitutional arrangement.

Although both principles, centralist and competitive federalism, mean a decrease in the power of national governments, the competitive variety does so to the benefit not of some other political authority but of the individual citizens.[39] This relates to another issue that I want to mention, if only briefly. The welfare gains that a competitive federalism promises have two principle sources: the creation of a larger market as a result of the removal of trade barriers between the member-nations, and the deregulation at the national level that is induced by inter-governmental competition. In this sense, one might say that competitive federalism provides a remedy for the protectionist and regulatory ballast that rent-seeking efforts have accumulated over time at the level of the nation-state, a ballast that considerably impedes economic activity. Yet, the creation of federal authorities may, of course, create new targets for rent-seeking at the federal level (Vaubel 1992), and, to the extent that this occurs, an emergence of protectionist or regulatory provisions at this level may be observed along with the deregulation that the federal unit induces at the national level. Whether such counteracting tendencies occur, and how quick the build-up of protectionist and regulatory provisions at the federal level may be, will depend, of course, on the authority that a federal government would command. The danger of a re-emergence of rent-seeking at the European level would clearly be less if the federal constitutional structure were closer to the competitive than to the centralist end of the spectrum.

The nation-state became the target for rent-seeking activities because it had, and has, the authority to legislate discriminatory treatment in the sense explained before: the authority to grant privileges through protection and regulation, to provide protection selectively. A reversal of this process by way of constitutional reform at the national level seems unlikely. Its reversal through inter-governmental competition in a European constitutional context may be the only realistic hope. Yet, if a European government is given the same authority, it will inevitably follow the same path as the nation-states, and any welfare gain that a European union may produce will be temporary only until the deregulation effects at the national level are offset by new regulations at the federal level. If the gains that a competitive federalism promises are to be secured permanently, a necessary requirement would seem to be to withhold from a European government the legislative authority that made the national governments the target of rent-seeking efforts.

The prospects of gains that a competitive federalism would have to offer to the citizens of Europe are considerable, while its demands on the scope and authority of a central federal government are relatively modest and, in any case, significantly less than what a centralist federalism would require. Although offering all the benefits of an open system, competitive federalism requires less of "national sovereignty" from member-countries to be transferred to central authorities, and it puts lesser demands on what the parties forming the federal union would have to agree upon, a fact that would make, among other things, the integration of new members such as the new democracies in middle and eastern Europe a much easier task. The essential authority that is required for a central government in a competitive federalism is the ability to enforce the constitutional commitments to the rules of a competitive order.

The fact that a competitive federalism puts lesser demands on what its members would have to agree upon is not a small advantage. What may have been lacking in the process by which European integration has been orchestrated so far is a sufficient appreciation of the essential differences between constitutional choice and ordinary politics, differences that concern, in particular, the much greater need for securing a broad consensus in the former than in the latter. Where the ground rules for the operation of a polity are to be chosen, and this is what the creation of a united Europe is ultimately about, broad agreement among the ultimate sovereigns, the citizens, is an essential prerequisite for stability and viability; a prerequisite that would seem to limit, at the same time, the constitutional framework to general principles that are genuinely agreeable.

2 Markets and regulation

The contrast between free-market
liberalism and constitutional
liberalism[1]

Introduction

In the New Palgrave's entry on "regulation and deregulation," the authors note, "Both theoretical and empirical research question the extent to which regulation can achieve the goals for which it has been promulgated" (Breyer and MacAvoy 1987: 129). The disillusioned view of the promises of regulatory policies expressed in this summary judgement has, by now, become widely accepted wisdom within the economics profession.[2] And public choice economists have long been arguing that regulation is the prime arena of rent-seeking politics; that it largely serves to provide privileges to concentrated interest groups at the expense of the public at large.

The purpose of this chapter is not to add to the discussion on the dismal record of regulatory politics. Its purpose is to inquire into some of the more fundamental conceptual and theoretical issues of the relation between markets and regulation. More specifically, confining my analysis to a classical liberal approach to the nature and the function of markets, I want to contrast two varieties of liberalism that, as I shall conjecture, systematically differ in their underlying view on "markets and regulation," even if they arrive at similar conclusions in most issues of practical economic policy. My thinking about this matter was stimulated by reading about an incident at the 1949 meeting of the Mont Pelerin Society (MPS), a society of classical liberals that F. A. Hayek had founded in 1947 at Mont Pelerin in Switzerland. In an article by Wilhelm Röpke, one of the MPS's founding members, in which he recounts his memories of Walter Eucken, also a member of the MPS and one of the founders of the Freiburg school of law and economics, Röpke reports that at the respective 1949 meeting (which took place in Seelisberg, Switzerland) an argument erupted between Ludwig von Mises and Walter Eucken. Röpke tells us not much about the encounter,[3] nor have I been able to find more detailed accounts in other sources.[4] It is apparent, though, from his report that Röpke considered the exchange between Eucken and von Mises to be symbolic of a conflict of opinion that, as he notes, repeatedly resurfaced within the Mont Pelerin Society, and it seems obvious to me that it must have been linked to the fact that the two persons, Eucken and von Mises, represented, with their respective works, distinctly different perspectives on the nature of the liberal market order, perspectives that revolve around different organizing concepts. In the case of von Mises, this is the notion of the *unhampered market*; in the case of Eucken, it is the notion of the market as a *constitutional order*. For the purpose of abbreviation, I contrast these perspectives as *free-market liberalism* and *constitutional liberalism*.

It seems to me that – without being necessarily associated with the names of their two early advocates – the two types of perspectives do continue to play an important role in classical liberal scholarship, and that the difference between them is of relevance for the issue of regulation, if not necessarily in the conclusions at which one ultimately arrives, but clearly so in the general logic of the arguments by which one arrives at these conclusions. In what follows, I want to examine more closely the ways in which the contrasting perspectives inform the general arguments that underlie liberal reasoning about the problems of regulation.

The "unhampered market" and the argument against regulation

At first glance, the Misesean concept of the "unhampered market economy" appears to provide a clear-cut and unambiguous criterion for deciding what counts, descriptively, as regulation as well as for answering the normative question of what is wrong with regulation.[5] If one can, as Israel Kirzner (1985) implies in his article on "The perils of regulation," clearly distinguish between "the hampered (that is, regulated) market economy" (ibid.: 122) and the unhampered, "unregulated market" (ibid.: 141), then any form of regulation must be viewed as an impediment to the smooth working of market processes.[6] On closer inspection, though, the issue quickly gets more complicated as soon as one acknowledges that regulation can hardly be said to be a well-defined, concise concept, but is, instead, a term that has taken on a rather broad and somewhat diffuse meaning. It has become a summary name for various kinds of policy measures that may exhibit certain common properties but that are clearly different in other regards.

There are, presumably, several dimensions along which the various policy measures that are commonly classified as regulations could be distinguished. Of particular importance in the present context is the contrast between, on one side, *regulation as intervention in market processes* and, on the other side, *regulation as framing of market processes*, in the sense of circumscribing the terms under which these market processes unfold. The difference that is of relevance here, and that can also be described as *regulation by commands* versus *regulation by rules*, is glossed over when the term regulation is equally applied to such things as "imposed price ceilings and floors," "mandated quality specifications" (Kirzner 1985: 139), "an impeded merger" (ibid.: 141) or "efforts of regulators to legislate prices at other than equilibrium levels" (ibid.: 143), as well as to provisions such as "child labor laws" (ibid.: 134) or regulations that concern "the side effects (such as environmental pollution, or spread of disease, or exposure of the young to pornography) generated by uncontrolled market activity" (ibid.: 139). Certainly, one may choose to use the term regulation in such an inclusive manner, but when it comes to diagnosing the detriments "of government regulation of the market process" (ibid.: 149) such undiscriminating use can be easily misleading.[7]

That clarity should require one to draw a clear distinction here, nobody has stressed more emphatically than F. A. Hayek. He points out, in particular, that confusion must result if the various kinds of regulations are equally described as government intervention. The term "interference" (or "intervention"), he insists, is properly applied only to specific orders, aimed at particular results (Hayek 1976a: 128), such as "decisions as to who is to be allowed to provide different services and commodities, at what prices or in what quantities" (Hayek 1960: 227). It is misapplied if it is used in reference to "all those general regulations of economic activity which can be laid down in the form of general rules specifying conditions which everybody who engages in a certain activity must satisfy" (ibid.: 224). It is apparent that von Mises, when he spoke of government interference and of regulated markets, was foremost thinking of regulation by command. He spoke of economic activities being "regulated, guided, and controlled by *authoritarian decrees and prohibitions*" (von Mises 1985: 76); in "fixing the prices of goods and services," he saw the "crucial acts of intervention" (ibid.), and he described the "hampered market economy" as one in which "government interferes with the operation of business by means of orders and prohibitions" (von Mises 1949: 714).[8] Accordingly, the arguments that von Mises advanced against government interference are arguments against regulation by command. It is essential for our purposes here to understand why such arguments cannot be simply extended to regulation by rules, and that, if a case against instances of the latter is to be made, it must be grounded on different kinds of arguments.

There is a straightforward argument for why interventions by regulatory commands "run counter to the very principle" (Hayek 1960: 222) of market co-ordination, and there is an equally straightforward argument for why attempts to improve market outcomes by such interventions are likely to make things worse. As Hayek (1976a: 115) has suggested, the best way to understand the operation of the market system is to think of it as a "wealth-creating game," the "game of catallaxy."[9] Within the rules that define the game, market participants are left free to use their resources in ways that they, based on specific knowledge, perceive to be most profitable. It is precisely because the knowledge that exists dispersed in people's heads can best be utilized in such a manner that the game of catallaxy can unfold its wealth-creating potential. Yet, as with any genuine game, one cannot have it both ways: One cannot play a game and, at the same time, seek to assure specific outcomes. The point of playing the game of catallaxy is to leave it to market participants to make their own choices within the rules of the game, with the consequence that the particular outcomes that emerge from their separate choices must remain indeterminate. It is inconsistent with the logic of such a game to seek to assure particular results by commanding the players how to play the game. Whether the game is worth playing can be properly judged only in terms of the desirability of its *pattern of outcomes*, not by looking at particular results and asking whether they might not be improved upon by discretionary intervention. We can certainly imagine instances in which such intervention may do some good. Yet, this is not the relevant issue. The relevant issue is whether by giving governments authority to intervene by discretionary commands we can realistically hope to arrive at more desirable overall patterns of outcomes than if governments are denied such authority.[10] Spelling out the reasons why this is not the case has been the essence of liberal teaching on the merits of the market order. These reasons have to do, in particular, with the knowledge problem that is the central theme of the von Mises–Hayek critique of central planning, a critique that can, indeed, be generalized to the issue of regulation by command.[11] And they have also to do with the fact that discretionary government interventions are susceptible to becoming instruments for granting privileged treatment to particular interests[12] and, thus, are bound to be plagued by the problems that modern public choice theory has discussed under the rubric of rent-seeking.

The above arguments are implied when Hayek (1960: 221) insists that "the method of specific orders and prohibitions" is ruled out as a matter of principle by the liberal concept of the market order, and that "direct control of prices by government is irreconcilable with a functioning free system" (ibid.: 227).[13] He also insists, however, that the same cannot be said about government regulation by rules.[14] He hastens to add that recognizing the need to distinguish in this regard between the two kinds of governmental measures does by no means imply that one need not worry about regulation by rules. On the contrary, he suspects that "many such measures will, of course, still be undesirable or even harmful" (ibid.: 222), and that we may often have good reasons for considering them "inexpedient, either because they will fail or because their costs will outweigh the advantages" (ibid.: 221). Yet, as he puts it, "so long as they are compatible with the rule of law, they cannot be rejected out of hand as government intervention but must be examined in each instance from the viewpoint of expediency" (ibid.).[15] In this context, he makes it unambiguously clear that he sees no merit in downplaying the difference between rejecting certain kinds of governmental measures as incompatible with the very principles of market co-ordination and faulting regulatory provisions on grounds of expediency:

> The habitual appeal to the principle of non-interference in the fight against all ill-considered or harmful measures has had the effect of blurring the fundamental distinction between the kinds of measures which are and those which are not compatible with a free system.
>
> (Ibid.)[16]

Admittedly, the distinction between regulation by specific orders and regulation by rules that is alluded to by Hayek and that I wanted to draw attention to in this section may not provide us with a perfectly sharp demarcation line in the sense that all conceivable instances of regulation can be unambiguously assigned to one side or the other. There may well exist "gray areas," and ambiguities may arise from the fact that, as a matter of linguistics, "specific orders" can be translated into suitably phrased "general rules." This should not distract, though, from the fact that, conceptually, the distinction is both meaningful and significant. Where governments regulate by command, they tell market participants how they are to play the game of catallaxy, and such *interference in the playing of the game* is in apparent conflict with the very purpose of the game. Where governments regulate by rules, they redefine the terms under which, or the framework within which, the game is played. Such *interference at the level of rules* may well be inexpedient in the sense of causing the game of catallaxy to exhibit less attractive working properties than would otherwise be the case. However, it cannot be said to be in principle contrary to the purpose of playing a game.

"Regulation by rules" and the market as a constitutional order

In what follows, I shall concern myself only with the issue of regulation by rules. As far as the issue of regulation by specific orders is concerned, the distinction between the "unhampered market approach" and the "constitutional approach" that is the central theme of my discussion is of no consequence. The differences that separate the two outlooks at the liberal order come to the surface, though, as soon as we seek to specify the systematic criteria on which a liberal critique of regulatory rules (as opposed to regulatory commands) can be based.

The formula of the unhampered market can surely not be meant to imply the notion of a market without any rules. That the market order is a rule-based order, and different from the "everything goes game" of pure anarchy, is certainly not controversial. The market simply cannot be described as the game of catallaxy without reference to the rules of the game. Although we can, of course, imagine (and consider desirable) a market without any interference by specific orders, we cannot imagine (and consider desirable) a market without any framework of rules and institutions.[17] If advocates of the concept of the unhampered market acknowledge the fact that there can be no market without framing rules, they cannot avoid specifying in substance which rules they consider to be constitutive of the unhampered, unregulated market in contrast to a hampered, regulated market.

Without explicitly using the term unhampered market, Kirzner (1994) specifies in a more recent contribution his own understanding of this concept in a manner that explicitly refers to "the institutions upon which markets must rest for their very existence" (ibid.: 107),[18] and that acknowledges the fact that the "function of the market ... can be defined only in the context of a given pattern of individual rights" (ibid.: 105), a context that, obviously, may vary among different societies. "Within such a context," Kirzner (ibid.: 105) notes, "it is the function of the market to promote mutual discovery, ... encouraging fullest exploitation *of all available opportunities* for mutually gainful exchange" (ibid.), where "available opportunities" is to be understood *relative to the "given rights system."*[19] In this understanding, it seems, for a market to be considered unhampered means that government does not interfere in the market discovery process as it unfolds *within the given rights framework*, it does not imply a judgement on the nature of that framework *itself*. And, in fact, in critique of standard market failure arguments, Kirzner explicitly stresses the need to distinguish sharply between the issue of the successful working of the market process within a given institutional framework, and the issue of the suitability of that very framework. As he describes his own view:

> If market outcomes, resulting from externalities, are deemed somehow unfortunate, this is seen immediately as attributable not to the failure of the market to co-ordinate with respect to the given rights system, but to the pattern of rights which the system has, rightly or wrongly, taken as its initial framework.
>
> (Ibid.: 108f.)

While this interpretation may give an unambiguous meaning to the notion of an unhampered market, it raises, of course, the question of how we are to escape the institutional relativism that appears to be implied if the "given rights system" were the unquestioned starting point of our inquiry into the functioning of the market process. Should we abstain from judging alternative frameworks, or, if not, what is the criterion that we may employ to pass judgement?[20]

The approach that I propose to call *constitutional liberalism* starts from the very premise that the market order, as defined by its institutional framework, is a matter of, and is subject to, (explicit or implicit) *constitutional choice*. It assumes that the working properties of market processes depend on the nature of the legal–institutional frameworks within which they take place, and that the issue of which rules are and which are not desirable elements of such frameworks ought to be judged as a *constitutional issue*, i.e. in terms of the relative desirability of relevant constitutional alternatives. In the same manner, the case for the market order in general, by contrast to centralized types of economic systems, is to be argued at the *constitutional level*, i.e. in terms of its desirability in comparison with economic constitutions of the central planning type.[21] This is the paradigmatic essence of the constitutional outlook at the liberal market order that Walter Eucken and the Freiburg school developed and that is implied in modern constitutional political economy, as founded on the work of James Buchanan.[22]

Different from a free-market liberalism that uses the concept of the unhampered market not only in the limited Kirznerian sense but as a standard against which the institutions that frame markets can themselves be judged, the constitutional approach does not claim to provide us with a universal criterion that allows for a straightforward and a priori answer to the question of which rules are to be recognized as constitutive of a desirable market order and which rules are to be rejected as hampering regulations. Instead, it requires us to take on the task of comparative analysis and evaluation of constitutional alternatives, a task that we should approach, of course, in light of our general theoretical knowledge and available empirical evidence but that we cannot circumvent by merely referring to the universal standard of an unhampered market. In fact, the body of research on the practice of regulation to which I referred in the introduction to this chapter provides important contributions to the very task of comparative institutional analysis and evaluation that the constitutional approach calls for. To the unhampered market approach, such research is of little systematic significance. It reaches its relevant conclusions beforehand.

If the concept of the free, unhampered market is claimed to provide the appropriate standard for judging, what could be its criterion for distinguishing between the rules of an unhampered market and regulatory rules that interfere with it? One obvious criterion may seem to be provided in the concept of private property. If "the institution of private property" (von Mises 1985: 30) can be said to provide the essential institutional foundation of a market economy,[23] we can conclude that private property rights define the constitutive rules of the game of catallaxy. Accordingly, interference with these rights seemingly provides an unambiguous criterion by which regulatory rules could be distinguished from the rules of the unhampered market, as well as a criterion on which they could be critically judged from a liberal perspective.[24] Yet, here again, the need for further specification becomes apparent as one examines the issue more closely.

When we speak of the role of property rights, two separable, though interconnected, issues are involved. The issue of *assigning* rights, i.e. the question of "who owns what?," and the issue of *defining* rights, i.e. the question of "what does it mean to own something?" In their rights-assigning role, property rights determine the allocation of entitlements, whereas in their rights-defining role they determine what the rules of the game are. In light of this distinction, it is not entirely unambiguous when regulations are said to "restrict the use of the property."[25] Regulations can restrict private property in the sense that they reassign property rights from private persons to the public or to the state. In doing this, regulations shift the dividing line between privately held rights and communal rights, as, for instance, in the case of regulations that require the owners of ocean-front property to allow for public access to the beach.

Yet, when regulations are said to restrict private property, this can also mean that they redefine property rights in the sense of changing the restrictions to which property holders are subject in using their assets. In doing this, regulations redefine the rules of the game for all property holders, i.e. they redefine what it means to own something, as, for instance, in the case of environmental regulation that sets certain general standards for permissible emission.[26]

To be sure, demarcating the two types of restrictions is not always an easy task and it may by no means be obvious exactly where the dividing line is to be drawn. Yet, these difficulties do not make the conceptual distinction meaningless. Nor should they make us overlook the fact that the kinds of arguments that one may advance against regulations which reassign property rights cannot be simply extended to regulations which redefine property rights, even though, of course, the latter are by no means immune to objections either. There are relevant differences between the two types of regulatory restrictions, and our interest in "providing a bulwark against excesses of government power" (Epstein 1985: 95) need not be best served by glossing over these differences.

The issues raised by regulations that shift the dividing line between the private and the public domain by "partial taking" of property from private holders appear to be the principal focus of Richard Epstein's critique of the regulatory state, when he charges that "there is no sharp dichotomy between government regulation ... and government ownership" (ibid.: XII), and when he comments on his notion of regulation as partial taking:

> Regulation takes certain elements from the owner's bundle of rights and transfers them to the state, where they again fall prey to the same difficulties that arose when central planning was defended on a grand scale.
>
> (Ibid.: XIIf.)

Even though such statements seem to be clearly concerned with the issue of reassigning rights from the private to the public domain, Epstein's apparent claim is that no sharp dividing line can be drawn between the taking of private property and general economic regulation. As he puts it: "All regulation, all taxes, and all modifications of liability rules are takings of private property prima facie compensable by the state" (ibid.: 95).[27]

Epstein's analysis is concerned with the issue of the legal status and the functional role of "the constitutional standard of just compensation" (Epstein 1986: 11). I need not question in the present context whether, with regard to this issue, he is right in insisting that there is a "tight, logical connection between taking private property and general economic regulation" (ibid.: 8). Yet, although the distinction, suggested above, between regulations that reassign and those that redefine property rights may be irrelevant for Epstein's purposes, it cannot be ignored when the task is to examine the logical foundations of the liberal critique of the regulatory state.

Regulations that shift the dividing line between privately held property rights and communal rights in favor of the latter clearly decrease the domain within which market forces can work and they are, accordingly, subject to the battery of liberal arguments that spell out the reasons why a system of private property rights promises to be superior, i.e. more attractive to all parties involved, to a system of communal rights. The logic of these arguments applies wherever property rights are transferred, in total or partially, from private holders to the state. To be sure, these arguments do not allow for the conclusion that communal ownership can never be preferable, in the sense noted, to private ownership. Yet, they point out why this can be expected to be true only under certain, limited circumstances. When the "rationality" of regulatory reassigning of rights from private holders to the state is concerned, the critical issue is whether communal control can be expected to be, overall, socially more beneficial than private control. And the central message of the liberal paradigm is, of course, that "taking well-defined rights away from individual owners, and placing them in a new common pool" (Epstein 1985: 203) will, as a rule, be a welfare-reducing rather than a welfare-improving recipe.[28]

Regulations that change the general rules of the game by redefining what it means to own something may well reduce the scope of permissible uses that private owners of assets may engage in, but they cannot be said, in the same sense as rights-reassigning regulations can, to decrease the domain of the market in favor of communal rights. Regulations of this sort respond, in Victor P. Goldberg's (1976a: 445) terms, "to such questions as: how should X's right to breathe clean air be protected from Y's productive activity which pollutes that air?" That is, their principal concern is with according to which rules the market game is to be played rather than with the issue of where the line between the private domain and the public domain is to be drawn. To be sure, there may often be difficulties in separating these two aspects, and what appear to be redefining regulations may often be instruments for transferring rights from private holders into common pools. Yet, the issue of whether it can be desirable to shift the line between privately held rights and communal rights in favor of the latter must surely be distinguished from the issue of whether it can be desirable to redefine the general restrictions to which the use of private property is subject.

The private property rights that constitute markets are inevitably "restricted" rights in the sense that they define socially sanctioned limits to what the owner of an asset is entitled to do, and which uses of his property are prohibited in order to protect the interests of other players in the game of catallaxy. In other words, the question of the desirability of regulation cannot be an issue of unrestricted versus restricted rights because a market based on literally unrestricted rights is unimaginable. It can only be an issue of which *kinds* of restrictions are overall more beneficial, i.e. that promise to make the game of catallaxy a more attractive game for all players involved. This issue can only be approached by comparing the observable and/or predictable working properties of alternative property rules.

There is no predefined, immutable standard for what the content of "well-*defined* private ownership" (Epstein 1986: 15) must be, nor does the formula of "the full bundle of rights" (ibid.: 8) inherent in "the original common law bundle" (ibid.: 14) seem to provide a substitute for such a standard. Property rights are socially defined,[29] and in a constantly changing world it is hard to deny the need "for adjusting legal relationships over time in an ongoing evolving social system" (Goldberg 1976b: 886).[30] The common-law process as well as the legislative process serve to bring about such adjustment.[31] Both processes may be analyzed and compared with regard to their general capacities to serve that function in the interest of all parties involved, contingent on the rules of the game to which they themselves are subject. And the specific modifications in rules that they produce may be analyzed in terms of their prospects of improving the game of catallaxy. Yet, it would clearly be misleading to suggest that the liberal paradigm can spare us the trouble of such comparative analysis by providing an immutable standard against which the "malleable" rights of common law and legislation could be directly judged as to their appropriateness.[32]

To argue that, for the reasons stated, rights-reassigning regulations must be distinguished from rights-redefining regulations is, of course, not at all the same as saying that the latter give no cause for concern from a liberal perspective. Legislative changes in the rules of the game, in particular, are subject to severe knowledge problems as well as to incentive problems that can easily cause well-intended initiatives to result in welfare-reducing rather than welfare-improving reforms.[33] The knowledge problems that Hayek has stressed must, therefore, be understood as a serious warning against light-hearted experimentation in these matters. And the incentive problems that have been amply discussed in the literature on rent-seeking must always be kept in mind as warning against the danger that the legislative process falls prey to the pressures of special interest groups who seek legislative privileges under the pretence of advocating generally beneficial rule changes.

As important as such warnings unquestionably are, they do not provide an argument against rule adjustments *per se*. Instead, they serve to remind us that the processes through which such rule changes take place should be properly constrained, such that the noted knowledge problems and incentive problems are sufficiently checked without losing the capability "for adjusting legal relationships over time in an ongoing evolving social system" (Goldberg 1976b: 886). The most important role that, in this regard, the *generality constraint* plays has been a central theme of the liberal paradigm throughout its entire history, i.e. the constraint imposed on legislation by the requirement to operate in terms of non-discriminatory general rules only.[34] Although he points to the fact that the generality constraint, even if it were in place, could not provide a perfect safeguard against discriminatory regulatory taking,[35] Epstein (1985: 195f.) explicitly acknowledges that the issue of generality may indeed mark a relevant difference between the two kinds of regulations that I have sought to separate here when he argues that:

> Many large-number takings are in the form of regulation, taxation, and modification of liability rules. In these instances, the problem of assessing the impact of the taking, no matter what its form, on each person can be divided into two inquiries. The first asks to what extent the government action limits the person's possession, use, or disposition of property and hence operates as a taking. The second asks to what extent the restrictions imposed by the general legislation upon the rights of others serve as compensation for the property taken. ... These benefits are more likely to take place under statutes of general application because a large number of

persons will be both benefited and burdened by the same rule. ... Each person whose property is taken by regulation receives implicit benefits from the parallel takings imposed upon others. ... The landowner who cannot erect a large sign is assured that his neighbor cannot put up a sign that will block his view.

As will be shown below, this Epsteinian outlook at general regulation comes quite close to the notion of *constitutional exchange* that is central to what I call *constitutional liberalism*.

Regulations and freedom of contract

At the root of the liberal preference for markets over communal arrangements is the concept of the market as an arena of voluntary choice and voluntary contract. The free society, Murray Rothbard (1970: 71) notes, is "a society based on voluntary action, entirely *unhampered* by violence or threat of violence"; in the free market, "individuals deal with one another only peacefully and never with violence" (ibid.: 765).[36] In fact, the ideal that voluntary agreements among individuals should be, to the largest extent possible, the principal method of social co-ordination can be said to be the essential normative premise of the liberal paradigm. This ideal is equally foundational to the two approaches of free-market liberalism and constitutional liberalism, the comparison of which is the theme of the present chapter. Where the two perspectives differ is in their more specific interpretations of this ideal, and, as I shall seek to substantiate in the remainder of this chapter, it is the constitutional perspective that provides the interpretation that appears to be more consistent with the inherent logic of the fundamental liberal ideal.

If one approaches the rationality-of-regulation issue in light of the notion of the market as an arena of *voluntary co-operation*,[37] it would seem natural to suppose that the principle of *freedom of contract* may provide the criterion for judging which general regulations are and which are not compatible with a liberal order. Accordingly, those regulations ought to be rejected that interfere with the process of voluntary contracts among market participants, i.e. regulations that prohibit transactions that market participants would otherwise voluntarily enter into. The obvious rationale behind such judgement would be that prohibiting voluntary transactions means to prevent the realization of mutual gains that the contracting parties expect to get, as indicated by their voluntary agreement. Accordingly, regulations that prohibit voluntary transaction between market participants could be said to be welfare decreasing and, in this sense, "irrational."

One question raised by the liberal ideal of voluntary co-operation concerns the role of coercion in providing the preconditions that must exist for the market to be viable as an arena of purely voluntary co-operation. To assure that, indeed, market participants use only non-violent or non-coercive means in their dealings with one another, the use of other means has to be effectively prevented, and ultimately this cannot be done by other than coercive means. This question can be answered by invoking the protective state as the agency that provides and secures the institutional framework within which the market can function as an arena of voluntary co-operation. Even though the state itself is a coercive apparatus, and as such in contrast to the liberal ideal of voluntarism, it is a necessary prerequisite for that liberal ideal to be realized at all.[38] The protective state can be said to be welfare enhancing as a facilitator of trade by creating conditions that enable people to realize gains from voluntary co-operation.

The critical issue concerns regulatory provisions that use the coercive power of the state beyond its necessary role as protective agent. In essence, the issue is whether regulations that reduce the scope for voluntary transactions, by prohibiting certain types of contracts, can ever be rational or beneficial in the sense of making all persons involved better off. From the perspective of a free-market liberalism, the answer to this question, it appears, must clearly be "no." The diagnosis that such regulations prohibit mutually beneficial voluntary transactions would seem to lead inevitably to the conclusion that they cannot be but welfare reducing.[39] The question that needs to be examined, however, is whether this conclusion necessarily follows from the fundamental liberal ideal of voluntary co-operation. From the perspective of a constitutional liberalism this is not so.

The constitutional approach insists that the questions of "what the specific content of the law of contract ought to be" (Hayek 1960: 229) and "what contracts should be enforceable" (Hayek 1948a: 113) are *constitutional* questions. They concern the rules of the game under which the game of catallaxy is to be played. What kinds of restrictions the "freedom of contract" should be subject to is a matter of *constitutional choice*, and which among potential alternative "regulations" are preferable is to be judged against the *constitutional interests* of the respective constituents, i.e. in terms of the constituents' preferences concerning the kind of constitutional order under which they want to live. It is a question that cannot be decided by looking only at whether the respective contracts provide mutual gains to the contracting parties. Instead, it has to be decided in terms of whether or not generally allowing for certain kinds of contracts makes the socioeconomic game more attractive to all participants than it would be if the respective contracts were prohibited.

Central to the constitutional approach is the explicit distinction between the *constitutional level*, at which the rules of the game are defined, and the *sub-constitutional level*, at which the players choose their strategies for playing the game within the limits set by the rules. The core notion is that individuals may exercise their freedom of contract at both levels, that they may seek gains from voluntary co-operation not only at the sub-constitutional level but also at the constitutional level. People may seek to realize "gains from voluntary co-operation" not only by engaging in mutually beneficial market transactions but also by jointly submitting to mutually beneficial constitutional constraints. While the free-market approach tends to limit its attention to the sub-constitutional level of voluntary contracting in the market arena, the constitutional approach accounts for the fact that people may choose to enter into *constitutional contracts*, the very purpose of which is to jointly restrict their freedom of contract at the sub-constitutional level, with the purpose of realizing mutual gains that they expect to flow from such mutually accepted restrictions. The very purpose of such contracts of joint commitment, or constitutional contracts, is to specify the terms – or the rules of the game – to which transactions on the sub-constitutional level are subject.

The distinction between the constitutional and the sub-constitutional level is, of course, not limited to the case where just two levels of contracting exist. It can be generalized to account for multi-level systems of contracting in which the distinction between constitutional and sub-constitutional contracts can be applied to any two adjacent levels, and in which the freedom of contract at any level may be subjected to mutually beneficial constraints that are the subject of a constitutional contract at the next higher level. Within such multi-level systems of contracting, people may exercise their freedom of contract at every level, and the question of whether contracts at any level are desirable or "rational" cannot be answered by looking only at whether they restrict the freedom of choice at a sub-constitutional level. Their "rationality" has to be assessed in terms of their overall consequences as constitutional constraints compared with relevant alternatives. Looked at in this manner, regulations that limit the freedom of contract at the level of market transactions can be interpreted as constitutional contracts, the rationality of which cannot be simply questioned because they prohibit voluntary transactions that otherwise would occur. Instead, their rationality must be judged in terms of whether or not they make for a "better" game, better in terms of the preferences of the relevant constituency, i.e. of the group of individuals on whose behalf the respective regulations are chosen. While to a free-market approach it is enough to show that regulations limit the freedom of contract in order to conclude that they are undesirable, a constitutional liberalism cannot reach such conclusion without considering the constitutional interests of the persons concerned.

I have noted above that a free-market liberalism and a constitutional liberalism differ in their respective interpretations of the liberal ideal of voluntary co-operation. In light of what has been said above, the critical difference between the two perspectives can be seen in the fact that the constitutional approach *generalizes* the concept of voluntary contract and voluntary co-operation so as to include constitutional contracts and, thus, to account systematically for the fact that people may seek to realize mutual gains by jointly submitting to constitutional constraints. By contrast, the free-market approach tends to focus on voluntary exchanges in the market as the principal vehicle of voluntary co-operation[40] and, accordingly, tends to view any restrictions on voluntary market exchange as welfare-reducing limitations of the freedom of contract. The constitutional approach, in other words, uses a more general concept of voluntary exchange than does the free-market approach. It includes within that category the kinds of mutually beneficial *constitutional exchanges* that are exemplified by the case of the landowners mentioned in the above quotation from Epstein. As it would seem arbitrary to limit the liberal ideal of voluntary co-operation to one level of contracting only, the constitutional interpretation of that ideal may be claimed to be more coherent than the free-market interpretation.

To say that the free-market approach concentrates only on exchange contracts and overlooks the role that constitutional contracts play in voluntary co-operation is, in fact, not entirely correct. Advocates of a free-market liberalism at least implicitly account for what may be called *private* constitutional contracts, i.e. mutually constraining contracts voluntarily entered into by market participants. They recognize the fact that, as Goldberg (1976a: 428) puts it, "Entering into a contract will generally entail placing restrictions on the contracting parties' future options. Freedom of contract is the freedom to impose restrictions on one's future behavior."[41] In other words, they acknowledge that "voluntary co-operation" may include, beyond ordinary market exchange transaction, the voluntary joint submission to restrictions on the parties' future freedom of contract, as they occur in various kinds of relational contracts that can be observed in the market.[42] What they fail to recognize is that internal consistency would seem to require a liberal approach to extend to public constitutional contracts the very same logic that it applies to private constitutional arrangements, i.e. that the "social contracts" that define the constitutions of political jurisdictions or polities should also be looked at as potential instruments by which people can realize mutual gains from voluntary co-operation.

To be sure, there are significant differences between private constitutional contracts concluded in a market context and public constitutional contracts. The very purpose of the institutional framework of the market is to insure *voluntariness* in contracting, and to the extent that this purpose is achieved we can suppose that the private constitutional contracts concluded in the market are based on voluntary agreement of the parties involved. The voluntary nature of public constitutional contracts is a much more uncertain matter, and the question of how, at this level, voluntariness may be secured, is by no means easy to answer. Yet, that these differences exist can hardly mean that we should not seek to provide, from within the liberal paradigm, a systematic account of public constitutional contracts, nor can it mean that, in approaching these types of contracts, we ought to employ different explanatory and normative principles from the ones that we apply to private constitutional contracts. To the extent that they can, in fact, be said to command voluntary agreement of the members of the relevant constituency, public constitutional contracts must be judged, from a liberal perspective, no less "efficient" than private constitutional contracts that are concluded in a market context.

An issue that can serve to illustrate the difference between a free-market and a constitutional outlook at regulations that restrict the freedom of contract is the case, mentioned in the above quotation from Hayek, of contracts "in restraint of trade." From the perspective of his notion of the unhampered market, Rothbard (1970) sees no reason why one should object to such contracts. "The whole concept of 'restricting production'," he argues, "is a fallacy when applied to the free market" (Rothbard 1970: 568). As he sees it, in the free market "consumers and producers adjust their actions in voluntary cooperation" (ibid.: 566), and that includes the freedom of producers to seek to maximize their income by "producing where their gains are at a maximum, through exchanges concluded voluntarily by producers and consumers alike" (ibid.: 571). Cartel agreements are, from his perspective, nothing but voluntary contracts among producers, equally legitimate as voluntary exchanges between producers and consumers. As he puts it:

> To regard a cartel as immoral or as hampering some sort of consumer sovereignty is therefore completely unwarranted. And this is true even in the seemingly "worst" case of a cartel that we may assume is founded solely for "restrictive" purposes.
>
> (Ibid.: 570)[43]

From a perspective that looks at the issue of contracts in restraint of trade only in terms of an unqualified principle of freedom of contract, it must indeed seem implausible to treat voluntary cartel agreements among producers differently from other voluntary agreements among market participants, and the appeal to the principle of consumer sovereignty may appear as an arbitrarily limited interpretation of the principle of "individual self-sovereignty" (Rothbard 1970: 560) that is constitutive of the free market and that covers individuals in their capacity as producers no less than consumers.[44] Accordingly, one might conclude, as Rothbard does, that a consistent interpretation of the ideal of self-sovereignty implies that the appropriate normative standard for judging the performance of the free market should not be the service to consumers alone, but the "principle of maximum service to consumers and producers alike" (ibid.: 657).

The issue appears in a quite different light as soon as one looks at it as a constitutional issue, i.e. when the prohibition or non-enforceability of contracts in restraint of trade is treated as a *constitutional constraint* on the freedom of contract and when consumer sovereignty is treated as a *constitutional ideal* for how the game of catallaxy should function. At the constitutional level, the relevant question is whether this game can be expected to be more attractive for all players involved if cartel agreements are generally prohibited, or at least not enforced, compared with how it would function in the absence of such a constraint. Whether this is in fact the case is, of course, a debatable issue. Yet, debating the issue of cartel agreements as a constitutional issue is an entirely different matter from discussing it in terms of whether or not the principle of freedom of contract *per se* allows for treating such contracts among producers differently from other voluntary contracts among market participants. That it can only adequately be discussed as a constitutional issue has been insisted upon by the founders of the Freiburg school, who argued that the freedom of contract on the sub-constitutional level cannot include the right of the players to abrogate the rules of the game that are established at the constitutional level.[45] Buchanan approaches the issue in essentially the same manner as from his constitutional economics perspective when he chastises "the libertarian blunder of extending the defense of the liberties of individuals to enter into ordinary voluntary exchanges to a defense of the liberties of individuals to enter into voluntary agreements in restraint of trade."[46] And, at least implicitly, authors such as Epstein[47] or Demsetz[48] seem, at places, to adopt similar views.

As a constitutional ideal, the principle of consumer sovereignty postulates that the rules of the game of catallaxy should be such that they ensure maximum responsiveness of producers to consumer interests. The rules of the game should be such that better service for consumers is, ideally, the only route to business success.[49] This ideal is, it would seem, what Adam Smith had in mind when he criticized the rules of the game of the mercantile system:

> Consumption is the sole end and purpose of all production; and the interest of the producer ought to be attended to only so far as it may be necessary for promoting that of the consumer. The maxim is so perfectly self-evident, that it would be absurd to attempt to prove it. But in the mercantile system, the interest of the consumer is almost constantly sacrificed to that of the producer.
>
> (Smith 1981: 660)

Smith's claim was clearly that the rules of the game of what he called the "obvious and simple system of natural liberty" (ibid.: 687) allowed for a more attractive game than a mercantilist economic constitution for all players involved and in all their capacities as consumers as well as producers.[50] It is apparent that William H. Hutt too, who is the target of Rothbard's critique,[51] had the constitutional dimension in mind when he used the concept of "consumer sovereignty"[52] to capture the Smithian ideal.[53] One can, of course, question whether the principle of consumer sovereignty is, in fact, a desirable constitutional ideal, in terms of the inclusive preferences of the respective constituents. Yet, as a constitutional matter, this issue has to be discussed in different terms from those used by a Rothbardian free-market approach. It is, of course, also open to debate what specific rules of the game ought to be recommended if consumer sovereignty is adopted as a constitutional ideal, and one may even question whether, as a matter of fact, this ideal would be served by prohibiting cartel agreements.[54] Yet, again, discussing these matters as constitutional issues requires us to go beyond the logic of the free-market approach.[55]

Constitutional liberalism: generalizing the concept of voluntary contract from the market level to the constitutional level

When Rothbard argues that the "sovereignty of the individual" rather than the sovereignty of the consumer must be considered to be the fundamental normative premise of the liberal paradigm, he is right. And, as noted before, there is no disagreement in this regard between his free-market approach and a constitutional approach.[56] He is wrong, however, when he concludes that, *therefore*, voluntary cartel agreements among producers cannot be considered illegitimate. He is wrong because he fails to appreciate the distinction between the constitutional and the sub-constitutional level. He ignores the fact that individuals may exercise their sovereignty at both levels, and that in exercising their sovereignty at the constitutional level they may voluntarily agree to impose constraints on their sovereign choices at the sub-constitutional level. Sovereign individuals may, in this sense, have good reasons to agree, at the constitutional level, to an economic constitution that seeks to implement the principle of consumer sovereignty, and, in fact, much of traditional liberal teaching is about why there are good reasons for people to enter into such a constitutional contract.

The failure to appreciate adequately the relevance of the distinction between the constitutional and sub-constitutional level is, I suppose, a general shortcoming of the free-market approach to the issue of regulation. The research program of the Freiburg school must be credited with having focused its attention on the constitutional dimension of the liberal paradigm, as well as for having made explicit that the liberal ideal of a free society is a *constitutional* ideal, that it has to be specified in constitutional terms, i.e. in terms of the specific rules of the game that it advocates, and that it has to be argued for in terms of its attractiveness as a constitutional regime. In advancing his proposals for the constitutional order of a free society, the liberal must ultimately appeal to people's constitutional interests, and his claim is, in the final analysis, that these interests are better served by such an order than by feasible alternative regimes.

In launching the research program of constitutional political economy, James M. Buchanan has, independently of the Freiburg school and with a somewhat different emphasis, in essence argued along similar lines. The particular significance of his contribution, though, must be seen in the special emphasis that he adds to the constitutional theme, namely his insistence that a consistent liberalism cannot confine its normative principles of individual freedom of choice and voluntary contract to the sub-constitutional level of market transactions but must extend them to the level of constitutional choice and constitutional contracting as well.[57] In other words, his emphasis is on the very simple but fundamental argument that the consistent liberal must allow individuals to be sovereign at the constitutional level no less than at the market level. It is Buchanan's singular merit to have generalized the liberal ideal of voluntary co-operation from market choices to constitutional choices, from exchange contracts to social contracts, and to have shown thereby how a free-market liberalism can be consistently generalized into a more inclusive constitutional liberalism.

The fundamental normative principle of the liberal paradigm, what Rothbard describes as "individual sovereignty" and what Buchanan calls "normative individualism," is an *internal* as well as a *procedural* standard. It is internal in the sense that its measuring rod for what is desirable or rational in social matters is, ultimately, to be found in the subjective preferences or interests of the individuals themselves who are involved in the respective social arrangement, by contrast to external standards of goodness that ignore what the actors themselves consider desirable. It is procedural in the sense that it does not judge social outcomes *per se* in terms of the attributes that they exhibit but in terms of the nature of the process by which they have been brought about. The question it asks is whether social outcomes can be reasonably said to have emerged from voluntary choices of the parties concerned, and it considers desirable whatever results from voluntary exchange or co-operation among individuals. This is the basic logic that the free-market approach applies to market transactions. The constitutional liberal only insists that the same logic be applied at the level of constitutional contracting. Accordingly, he concludes, that at this level too the liberal normative standard cannot be but internal and procedural. Its ultimate points of reference are the subjective constitutional preferences or interests of the persons concerned and their voluntary agreement to the constitutions under which they live.

The constitutional approach implies that we need to distinguish between the issue of voluntariness of agreements *within rules*, i.e. at the sub-constitutional level, and the voluntariness of agreements *on rules*, i.e. at the constitutional level. The voluntariness of market transactions is *voluntariness within the rules of the game* that define the constitution of the market. Whose *explicit* voluntary agreement is required for a transaction to count as a voluntary market exchange (or a voluntary private constitutional contract) depends on how the rules of the game of catallaxy are defined. If private property rights are defined so as to include a landowner's right to erect a large sign on his property, a voluntary contract between him and a construction company for erecting such a sign qualifies as a perfectly voluntary market exchange, even if his neighbor, whose view is blocked by the sign, is strongly opposed to such action and does not voluntarily agree to it at all.[58] If the rules of the game do not give a landowner the said right, his voluntary agreement with a construction company would not be sufficient to make the transaction a legitimate market exchange in the absence of his neighbor's explicit agreement to the transaction.

How the rules of the game should regulate such matters is, of course, linked with the externality issue. How property rights are defined decides, in effect, which of the ever present externalities of transactions third parties simply have to tolerate, and against which of such externalities they enjoy the protection of the law. Where this line is to be drawn is a matter of constitutional choice,[59] and this means that it is a matter of the constitutional interests of the persons involved and their voluntary agreement to the rules under which they want to live.[60] The consistent liberal cannot appeal to any a priori, external criteria for how the said line is to be drawn, criteria that would apply independently of what the members of the relevant constituencies themselves consider to be desirable. It is misleading to suggest that the liberal paradigm provides us with timeless, objective standards for which kinds of external effects constitute "molestation" and should, therefore, be considered incompatible with the "free market."[61] And it is misleading to suggest that the question is answered by saying that the externality problem is only a problem of "insufficient defense of private property against invasion" as the real issue is to define what counts as invasion.[62]

The free-market liberal may readily agree that the distinction between the issue of voluntariness in agreements within rules and the issue of voluntariness in agreements on rules applies to *private* constitutional contracts, such as contracts that govern employment relations or relations among the members in a partnership. The constitutional liberal insists that it must be extended to *public* constitutional contracts as well, and that it applies equally to the rules of the market itself.[63] What legitimizes the market as a constitutional order is, in the last resort, its voluntary acceptance as a constitutional order, and that legitimacy is not provided by the voluntary transactions that are carried out *within* the market order. That there is a distinction to be drawn here between sub-constitutional and constitutional agreements is overlooked by authors who, like Rothbard, suggest that, as each and every market exchange is a voluntary transaction, the market order itself can be said to be unanimously approved.[64] As much as the constitutional liberal agrees with the claim that the game of catallaxy provides benefits, and is attractive to all participants, he cannot agree that this claim is proven by the voluntariness of market transactions. The ultimate test for the attractiveness of the market order can only be its attractiveness and voluntary acceptance as a constitutional order. Even if this distinction may seem to border at sophistry, it is a distinction with important implications for how liberals argue their case for the market order to their fellow citizens. It implies that, ultimately, the liberal argument for the market order must appeal to individuals' constitutional interest and cannot bypass the individual's own judgement of what is desirable at the constitutional level. Ludwig von Mises (1985: 30) may have had this in mind when he said about the liberals: "If they considered the abolition of the institution of private property to be in the general interest, they would advocate that it be abolished."[65]

If we extend, as a constitutional liberalism requires, the fundamental normative principle of voluntary choice and voluntary contract to the constitutional level, the question arises of which meaning the concept of voluntariness can be given at that level. As noted, when we speak of voluntary market transactions, we do have a fairly clear understanding of what "voluntary" means. It is defined in terms of the rules that constitute the market as an arena of voluntary co-operation. To be sure, what voluntary choice and voluntary agreement in constitutional matters can mean is a much more complex issue. But the complexity of the issue can surely not be an acceptable excuse for ignoring it. In examining this issue, we have to inquire into the nature of the processes in which constitutional rules are generated and reformed, and we have to inquire into how these processes may themselves be subjected to rules such that voluntariness in constitutional choice can best be secured.

That the political processes in modern democracies, not to speak of other regimes, have grave deficiencies is widely acknowledged and has often been criticized from within the liberal paradigm. Where the liberal research agenda has remained comparatively underdeveloped is in regard to the *positive* question of how the political process might be structured so as to implement the principle of individual sovereignty at the constitutional level, accounting for the specific difficulties that the nature of things poses at that level.[66] Suggestions for how the political process might be reformed with that purpose in mind have been spelled out by Hayek in his work on constitutional reforms of modern democracy, and the general issue of such reforms is a major item on the research agenda of Buchanan's constitutional economics. His enterprise of developing a theoretical approach to "the state as a voluntary institution" has nothing to do with "Hegelian mysticism," as Rothbard charges,[67] but is an attempt to extend systematically and consistently the fundamental logic of the liberal paradigm from the level of market choices to the constitutional level.

Beyond options for reforming the political processes through which constitutional rules are collectively chosen by the members of jurisdictions, or by their representatives, the more effective means of enhancing and securing voluntariness in constitutional choice will be found in provisions that enable the individual to choose individually and separately among alternative constitutional regimes. As a conceptual benchmark, one may choose Robert Nozick's liberal utopia,[68] an imagined world where individuals are perfectly free to adopt within consenting groups any kind of constitutional order they like, and where everybody is perfectly free to move between the alternative constitutional orders that exist. Yet, the difficult pragmatic task begins when it comes to examining how, by what provision, and by what forms of political organization the options of individuals to choose freely for themselves among constitutional alternatives can be improved in the world in which we live. Important contributions to this issue have been made in such research areas as the theory of competitive federalism and in other areas,[69] but there remains much to be done. To take on this task could be an important part of our efforts in expanding the liberal paradigm.

3 The Freiburg school of law and economics

Predecessor of constitutional economics

Introduction

The school was founded in the 1930s at the University of Freiburg in Germany by economist Walter Eucken (1891–1950) and jurist Franz Böhm (1895–1977). They were joined by jurist Hans Großmann-Doerth (1894–1944), who was killed in World War II, causing his influence on the later development of the school to be less visible than that of the other two founders. Besides holding joint seminars on *law and economics* themes, the three undertook joint research efforts, as reflected in their founding in 1937 of a publication series titled *Ordnung der Wirtschaft* (The Order of the Economy).[1]

Also known under the name of *ordo-liberalism*, the ideas of the Freiburg school constituted a major part of the theoretical foundations on which the creation of the *social market economy* in post-World War II Germany was based. The school is often subsumed under the rubric of *German neo-liberalism*, which also includes such authors as Alfred Müller-Armack, Wilhelm Röpke, and Alexander Rüstow. Yet, although the two groups of authors shared important common ground, there also existed significant differences between them. In particular, the somewhat interventionist, outcome-oriented flavor of the concept of the *social market economy* was much more reflective of the thoughts of Müller-Armack, who invented the term, and of Röpke and Rüstow, than of the procedural and rule-oriented *ordo-liberalism* of the Freiburg school.

Outside of the German-speaking academic world, in particular in Anglo-American academia, the ideas of the Freiburg school have been given relatively little attention[2] as most of its research has been published only in German. On the suggestion of Friedrich A. Hayek, Terence W. Hutchison prepared an early English translation of Eucken's *Grundlagen der Nationalökonomie*, originally published in 1940, which appeared in 1950 as *The Foundations of Economics*. Yet, as the translator notes in his preface to the 1992 edition, the original translation aroused very little interest in Britain and the United States. More recently, the school's research program has attracted more attention, as a consequence of the growing recognition of the fact that it has much in common with such modern approaches in economics as, in particular, constitutional political economy and other subfields within the new institutional economics (Tumlir 1989: 126; Sally 1996: 250f.).[3]

Walter Eucken was born in 1891, the son of philosopher and Nobel Laureate (in literature) Rudolf Eucken. He took his doctorate in economics in 1914 at the University of Bonn, and, after military service from 1914 to 1918 in World War I, he completed his habilitation in 1921 at the University of Berlin where he taught as *Privatdozent* until 1925, the year he was appointed professor of economics at the University of Tübingen. In 1927, Eucken accepted a chair at the University of Freiburg, where he remained until his early death in 1950. Eucken was the only non-emigrant German who took part in the 1947 conference at Mont Pelerin in Switzerland that had been initiated by Hayek and that resulted in the founding of the Mont Pelerin Society. Hayek also arranged for Eucken's views on central planning to be published in *Economica* (Eucken 1948) and, together with Lionel Robbins, he invited Eucken to give a course of lectures at the London School of Economics and Political Science in 1950. During this visit, Eucken died in London. His lectures were posthumously published under the title *This Unsuccessful Age.*

Franz Böhm was born in 1895. After his military service in World War I, he earned law degrees at the University of Freiburg in 1922 and 1924. From 1925 to 1931, he worked at the cartel department of the ministry of economics (*Reichswirtschaftsministerium*) in Berlin. In 1931, he returned to Freiburg where he took his doctorate (1932) and his habilitation (1933), with Eucken and Großmann-Doerth on his committee. He taught at Freiburg as *Privatdozent* until 1936, when he was appointed professor of law at the University of Jena, a position from which he was dismissed in 1938 because of critical comments he had made on the National Socialist regime's treatment of Jews. Shortly after the war, Böhm was appointed professor of law at the University of Freiburg, and in 1946 at the University of Frankfurt. Yet, the center of his activities shifted into politics. He served from 1948 as an advisor to West Germany's department of economics, was a member (for the Christian Democratic Union) from 1953 to 1965 of the Bundestag, and was one of the principal drafters of West Germany's anti-cartel legislation (the final result of which he considered, however, as too much "watered down" by concessions to special interests). Böhm died in 1977.

The "second generation" of the Freiburg school includes: Friedrich A. Lutz, an assistant of Eucken; Paul Hensel; Hans Otto Lenel; and Ernst-Joachim Mestmäcker, a disciple of Franz Böhm. The yearbook *ORDO*, founded by Eucken and Böhm in 1948, has been, and continues to be, one of the principal outlets for publications in the tradition of the Freiburg research program. Freiburg university's "Fakultät für Rechts- und Staatswissenschaften," including law as well as economics, provided a conducive framework for the combination of legal and economic perspective that is characteristic of the Freiburg school and of the ordo-liberal tradition. As Böhm later said in retrospect, the founders of the school were united in their common concern for the question of the constitutional foundations of a free economy and society. In the first volume (Böhm 1937) of their jointly edited publication series *Ordnung der Wirtschaft*, the three editors included a co-authored programmatic introduction entitled

"Our task" (Böhm *et al.* 1989), in which they emphasized their opposition to the, then still influential, heritage of Gustav von Schmoller's *historical school* and to the unprincipled relativism that, in their view, this heritage had brought about in German jurisprudence and political economy. By contrast, they stated as their guiding principle that the "treatment of all practical politico-legal and politico-economic questions must be keyed to the idea of the economic constitution" (ibid.: 23), a task for which, they said, the collaboration of law and economics "is clearly essential" (ibid.: 25).

Eucken developed his own work as an explicit alternative to Schmoller's program and its continuing influence on economic thought and economic policy in Germany.[4] Under Schmoller's leadership, he censured, German economists had given up theoretical analysis and had lost the capability of looking at specific issues of economic policy within the context of the broader issue of the economic constitution as a whole (Eucken 1938: 79).[5] With his *"Staatliche Strukturwandlungen und die Krise des Kapitalismus"* (Eucken 1932) and with his two major works, the *Grundlagen der Nationalökonomie* [Eucken 1989a (1939)] and the *Grundsätze der Wirtschaftspolitik* [Eucken 1990 (1952)], Eucken wanted to provide an alternative to the historical school's atheoretical approach to economic analysis as well as to its unprincipled discretionary approach to economic policy.[6] His aim was to develop a systematically integrated approach to the theoretical study and the political shaping of a constitutional social–economic–political order, or, to use the German terminology, a systematic approach to *Ordnungstheorie* and *Ordnungspolitik*.

Economic order and constitutional choice

As the term *Ordnung* (order) is *the* central concept in the research program of the Freiburg school, it is important to note that, in the context of that program, it is related to the concept of the *economic constitution*, in the sense of the *rules of the game*, upon which economies or economic systems are based (Eucken 1989a: 240; 1992: 314).[7] Eucken and Böhm as well as their followers used it as an analytical concept that is meant to emphasize the systematic relation between the rules of the game, the economic constitution, and the order or patterns of economic activities that result under different kinds of rules or economic constitutions. It is definitely not meant to imply any of the conservative or authoritarian connotations that the word *"Ordnung"* – or the English term *order* – may have had, or do have, in other uses.[8]

Economic order (Wirtschaftsordnung) means the typical structure and systematic patterns of economic activities, or the regularities of the economic process, that characterize particular economies, in the sense in which one may speak of, for instance, of the "Athenian economic order at the age of Pericles, or the economic order of the Flemish towns around 1270" (Eucken 1989a: 234; 1992: 308).[9] As Eucken (1989a: 50; 1992: 80) insists, all economic activities take place within some economic order and can be adequately understood only in the context of the respective order.[10] As he put it, the research-guiding question must be: "What are the rules of the game?" (Eucken 1992: 81). Economic orders, this is the main message, must be understood in terms of the underlying *economic constitutions*, by which is primarily meant the formal legal–institutional framework, but which is also meant to include informal conventions and traditions that govern economic activities in the respective communities (Eucken 1990: 377).[11] According to Eucken (1990: 21), the large variety of specific economic orders that have existed in the past and exist in the present can be understood as varied compositions of two basic principles, namely, on the one side, the decentralized *co-ordination* of economic activities within a framework of general rules of the game and, on the other side, the principle of *sub-ordination* within a centralized, administrative system (Eucken 1989a: 79; 1992: 118).[12] One of the major themes of the ordo-liberal school was the contrast between a centrally planned economy, such as the German war economy or the socialist economies, and the exchange or market economy (*Verkehrswirtschaft*). They developed a critique of central planning (*Zentralverwaltungswirtschaft*) with arguments very similar to those advanced by von Mises and Hayek (Eucken 1942; 1990: 361ff.).[13]

Factual economic orders may, of course, be more or less efficient or desirable (Eucken 1989a: 238f.; 1992: 313f.), and the founders of the Freiburg school emphasized that the principal means by which economic policy can seek to improve on them is by improving the rules of the game, i.e. by implementing appropriate economic constitutions (Eucken 1990: 378). What motivated their work was an interest in applying theoretical insights from law and economics to the practical problem "of understanding and fashioning the legal instruments for an economic constitution" (Böhm *et al.* 1989: 24),[14] a concern that they saw as part of the broader project of inquiring into the constitutional foundations of a functioning and humane socioeconomic–political order.[15] As a name for what can count as such an order, Eucken adopted the Latin word *ordo*, a term with apparent natural law connotations, which can, however, be separated from such connotations and be interpreted in the straightforward sense of an order that is desirable for the human beings who live in it (Vanberg 1997).[16] Eucken and Böhm emphasized that their interest was not in developing a research program as a purely academic enterprise but in seeking answers to the practical question of how a desirable economic order may be created and maintained, a question that they approached as a problem of *constitutional choice*, i.e. as a question of how a desirable economic order can be generated by creating an appropriate economic constitution.[17] The joint efforts of law and economics were to them an indispensable prerequisite for what they called "*Wirtschaftsverfassungspolitik*" (constitutional economic policy),[18] a policy that seeks to improve the resulting economic order in an *indirect* manner by reforming the rules of the game in contrast to an economic policy that seeks to improve outcomes directly by way of specific interventions into the economic process.[19] The general aim that, in their view, such constitutional economic policy had to pursue was to create conditions under which economic actors in seeking to further their own interest also promote the common interest (Eucken 1938:

80).[20] In other terms, they considered it the task of *Wirtschaftsverfassungspolitik* to *create* conditions under which the "invisible hand" that Adam Smith had described could be expected to do its work.[21]

Against historicist notions of an unalterable course of societal evolution, whether in their Marxian or other versions, Eucken and Böhm emphasized that the socioeconomic orders in which people find themselves are to a significant extent subject to collective, political choice (Böhm 1960: 164). They acknowledged that all empirical societies and economies are to a considerable extent the product of evolutionary forces and not the creation of a master plan (Eucken 1989a: 51, 53; 1992: 82), and that, in particular, the market order has not been invented or implemented by deliberate design but has gradually evolved over millennia.[22] Yet, they insisted that, nevertheless, economic orders are subject to human design, and that they can be improved upon by deliberate reform.[23] As Eucken (1992: 314) said about the problem of achieving a functioning and humane economic order,

> The problem will not solve itself simply by our letting economic systems grow up spontaneously. The history of the last century has shown this plainly enough. The economic system has to be consciously shaped. The detailed problems of economic policy, trade policy, credit, monopoly, or tax policy, or of company or bankruptcy law, are part of the great problem of how the whole economy, national and international, and its rules, are to be shaped.

It is in this sense that the Freiburg ordo-liberals spoke of an *economic constitution* as the inclusive decision of a community about how its economic life is to be ordered.[24] And they took care to point out that an effective constitutional economic policy has to pay attention to the complex ways in which the various elements of the legal–institutional framework may interact (Eucken 1942: 42f.). As the founders of the school put it, it is essential to understand that such areas of law as "bankruptcy law, ... the law of obligations, real estate law, family law, labor law, administrative law, and all other parts of the law" (Böhm *et al.* 1989: 24) together constitute the economic constitution, and that between them systematic interdependencies may exist that *Ordnungspolitik* has to pay attention to.[25]

In the sense noted, the research program of the Freiburg school can be said to comprise a *theoretical paradigm* as well as a *policy paradigm*. The theoretical paradigm is based on the premise that an adequate analysis and explanation of economic phenomena has to account for the nature of the constitutional framework, or the rules of the game, under which they occur. The policy paradigm is based on the premise that economic policy should seek to improve the framework of rules, the economic constitution, such that a well-functioning and desirable economic order results, rather than seeking to bring about desired outcomes directly by specific interventions into the resulting economic order. *Ordnungstheorie* is the name for the explanatory part of the Freiburg research program, the enterprise of systematically studying the working properties of alternative institutional–constitutional arrangements, and the complex interdependencies between various components (company law, patent law, tax laws, labor law, etc.) of a nation's economic constitution. *Ordnungspolitik* is the name for its policy paradigm, for an integrated approach to the various components of the legal–institutional framework in which a market economy is embedded.[26] In terms of Hayek's (1969) useful distinction between the *order of rules* and the *order of actions* that results under the rules, the explanatory paradigm of the Freiburg school can be said to focus on the question of how differences and changes in the order of rules result in differences or changes in the emerging order of actions, whereas the policy paradigm can be said to focus on the question of how the resulting economic order or order of actions can be improved by suitable reforms in the economic constitution or the order of rules.

Ordo-liberalism versus *laissez-faire* liberalism

While the founders of the Freiburg school placed themselves firmly in the tradition of classical liberalism, they emphasized, in contrast to some varieties of liberalism, that a free-market order is not simply what one would find if and where government is absent, that it is not a natural event but a political–cultural product, based on a constitutional order, that requires careful "cultivation" for its maintenance and proper functioning.[27] In this regard, they found it necessary to distance themselves from a *laissez-faire liberalism*[28] that failed to appreciate the essential positive role that government has to play in creating and maintaining an appropriate framework of rules and institutions that allows market competition to work effectively.[29] They took care to distinguish between the spontaneous working of markets, provided an appropriate legal–institutional framework is in place, and the issue of how the framework itself comes about. In other words, they clearly distinguished between the *sub-constitutional* issue of how market competition works within given rules and the *constitutional* issue of how the rules that make market competition work are themselves established and enforced.

That the founders of the Freiburg school accused some of their nineteenth century liberal predecessors of an unjustified "confidence in the spontaneous emergence of the natural order" (Eucken 1989b: 38)[30] does not mean that they did not fully share the classical liberals' confidence in the self-regulating properties of market processes. It only means that they saw no justification for extending such confidence to what they called the *Ordnungsrahmen*, i.e. the legal–institutional framework. An appropriate *Ordnungsrahmen* for market competition can, so they argued, not be assumed to be self-generating, to evolve naturally and spontaneously.[31]

According to the Freiburg ordo-liberals, the essence of the *market economy* or a *free economic constitution* (Böhm 1937: 67) is that it should be an order of *free competition* in which all economic players meet as legal equals, and in which voluntary exchange and voluntary contract are the only means by which economic activities are co-ordinated.[32] They knew of course that the principles of equality and voluntariness are nowhere perfectly realized, and they pointed out that any criticism of the "market economy" must distinguish between the issue of how well or imperfectly particular institutional realizations work that we observe and the issue of what kind of legal–institutional framework might make for a well-functioning market order (Böhm 1937: 67, 72, 124). They regarded these principles as normative standards against which existing economic orders and potential reforms can be judged, and as a reference criterion that can provide guidance to efforts in constitutional reform.[33] They saw a major historical step toward the realization of an economic order that meets these criteria in the liberal movements of the late eighteenth century and early nineteenth century (Eucken 1982: 124; 1990: 276) that marked the transition from the feudal society to what Böhm (1980: 105ff.; 1989: 46ff.) called the *Privatrechtsgesellschaft* (private law society) or *Zivilrechtsgesellschaft* (civil law society).[34] The driving force of these movements was the idea of transforming the feudal "multi-tier society into a private law society consisting of equally free people with equal rights" (Böhm 1980: 140; 1989: 54), "the idea that in society everyone should have the same rights and status, namely the status of a person under private law" (Böhm 1980: 107; 1989: 46). Its foremost goal was to eliminate inequalities in the law, the most objectionable of which were seen in "the feudal sovereign rights ... and the trade and industrial privileges" (Böhm 1980: 141; 1989: 56).[35]

> The exchange agreement and its fulfillment is the characteristic mode of cooperation between independent traders with equal rights. In this respect, therefore, the private law system is very decisively involved in controlling free-market processes.
>
> (Böhm 1980: 121; 1989: 53)

In other words, the emergence of the market economy can be seen as a by-product of the transition from the feudal order to the order of civil law, a transition that meant the abolition of feudal privileges and a multitude of restrictions on economic activities, creating an economic arena in which individuals are free to trade and to compete as legal equals. Böhm and Eucken insisted, though, that creating and maintaining a well-functioning competitive market order requires more than replacing feudal privileges and restrictions by free trade and freedom of contract. It requires, they claimed, an economic constitution that in its entirety is tuned to upholding competition in the face of anti-competitive interests, and a policy that aims at creating and maintaining such an economic constitution they considered to be something quite different from *laissez-faire*.[36]

The ordo-liberals' critique of *laissez-faire* was probably more motivated by their concern to fend off stereotype misrepresentations of the classical liberal doctrine than by their wish to provide a balanced account of nineteenth century liberal doctrine. It should therefore be assigned lesser weight than the positive part of their message, i.e. their argument that an appropriate economic constitution is a prerequisite of a well-functioning market economy. They conceded that the policy of *laissez-faire* did not aim at a *"staatsfreie Wirtschaft"* (Eucken 1990: 26), an economy without the state, but realized the importance of property rights, contract law, corporation law, patent law, etc. They censured, however, that it failed to recognize the monitoring of the economic order at large as a political task but, instead, assumed that a suitable economic order would spontaneously evolve within the framework of the law.[37] By contrast, the founders of the Freiburg school took care to point out that there is not simply *"the* free market" that emerges wherever and whenever property rights are enforced, and where free trade and freedom of contract are realized. They emphasized that markets can work quite differently and that it depends on the nature of the entire framework of the rules of the game whether market competition exhibits desirable working properties. The free-market economy, this was their principal message, is more than a free play of economic forces, it is a constitutional regime with particular rules of the game, and its proper functioning depends on the nature and the effective enforcement of these rules. And they considered it of the utmost importance to recognize that opting for a market economy is a matter of *positive constitutional choice*; that it means to adopt a particular economic constitution that must be upheld against adverse interests if market competition is to work to the common benefit of all players involved.

The whole logic of the Freiburg research program rests on the distinction between the *constitutional level* at which political choices regarding a society's economic constitution are made, and the *sub-constitutional level* at which private choices within the constitutionally determined rules of the game are made. As the ordo-liberals put it: "The economic constitution must be understood as a general political decision as to how the economic life of the nation is to be structured." (Böhm *et al.* 1989: 24).

The free-market order is seen as "a political and constitutional–legal order" (Böhm 1937: 18),[38] as an order that is adopted by explicit constitutional choice, not an order that would be self-creating and self-maintaining in the absence of a political–constitutional will to sustain it. As a constitutional order, it is subject to political–constitutional choice, even though the very nature of the market as a constitutional regime is that it provides for an arena in which private voluntary transactions can be carried out protected from government interference. Eucken and Böhm were quite clear about the fact that "the power to establish generally binding norms is essentially a political power" (Böhm 1980: 125; 1989: 55), and that the decision in favor of the market as an arena of private, voluntary co-ordination is, in itself, a political choice. In this sense, they recognized that there is a logical priority of the political–constitutional choice *of* a market order in relation to sub-constitutional choices made *within* that order.

Central to the Freiburg approach is the notion that the choice of the rules of the game is one that is made on behalf of the entire constituency of a jurisdiction, and that individual "players" or members of a jurisdiction cannot be allowed to abrogate or renegotiate the rules at the sub-constitutional level by way of private contracting (Böhm 1960: 39–44, 67). As Eucken (1982: 120; 1990: 267) argued:

> Keeping markets open helps to promote a country's economy. Hence, private pressure groups cannot be given the right to eradicate this. That right forms part of the regulative policy (Ordnungspolitik) and it must not be left to private persons.[39]

This is the issue that the ordo-liberals had in mind when they insisted that the *freedom of contract*, which is of obvious importance for a competitive market economy, cannot be allowed to serve as an instrument "to eliminate competition and to establish monopolistic positions" (Eucken 1982: 123; 1990: 275) and must not be permitted to be "used for the purpose of entering into contracts which restrict or eliminate the freedom of contract" (Eucken 1982: 125; 1990: 278).[40] They insisted, in other words, that it is incompatible with the notion of playing according to rules if the players retained the right unilaterally to change the rules by separate agreements among sub-coalitions, and that it is, in particular, incompatible with the constitutional decision for a competitive economy to allow economic agents to dispense themselves, through private contracting, from the constraints that the rules of the game of competition are meant to impose on them (Böhm 1960: 27–30; 1980: 233–36, 238, 256f., 260f.).[41] This is Böhm's main argument why cartel agreements are in principle incompatible with a competitive economic constitution, and why he considered the decision of the highest German court, in 1897, to grant the protection of the law to cartel agreements a fundamental judicial mistake (Böhm 1937: 150ff.; Eucken 1989a: 55).[42] And this is why they did not see any reason to believe that the *"selbstgeschaffene Recht der Wirtschaft,"* the "self-produced law of the business community" [Großmann-Doerth 1933; Böhm *et al.* 1989 (1937: X); Eucken 1989a: 56],[43] can be trusted generally to serve the common interest rather than serving producer interests at the expense of consumer interests.[44] As Eucken (1989a: 32) noted:

> It must be asked whether the rules and regulations made by economic power groups to control activity among themselves in fact are tending to take the place of statute law. How far has such "self-made" law transformed the legal order? The question is of great importance in the modern industrialized world.

Competitive economic constitution and private power

Böhm was concerned with *The Problem of Private Power* (the title of a 1928 publication of his) and the threat that it poses to the viability of a competitive order, a concern that he shared with Eucken.[45] Expressly agreeing with the classical economists of the *Scottish School*, he emphasized in *Wettbewerb und Monopolkampf* (Böhm 1933) that consumer interests are "the sole directly justifiable economic interests" (Böhm 1982: 107) and that the essential function of competition is "to place the entrepreneur's pursuit of profit in the direct service of the consumer" (ibid.: 109). Referring to Adam Smith's view that the impulse of human selfishness loses its "anti-social aspects under the impact of competition," Böhm described competition as "the moral backbone of a free profit-based economy," invoking the basic theme that runs through his entire work: the notion that, as he phrased it in later writings (Böhm 1960: 22), "competition is by no means only an incentive-mechanism but, first of all, an instrument for the deprivation of power (Entmachtungsinstrument), ... the most magnificent and most ingenious instrument of deprivation of power in history."

The Freiburg ordo-liberals made it clear that the desirable working properties that the classical liberals attributed to market competition cannot be expected from any unqualified competitive process *per se*, but only from what they called *Leistungswettbewerb*, "achievement" or "performance competition," i.e. competition in terms of better service to consumers (Eucken 1990: 43),[46] as opposed to *Behinderungswettbewerb*, "prevention competition," i.e. competition by means that are directed at preventing competition from other producers rather than improving one's own performance (Böhm 1937: 107, 123–27, 153; 1960: 29, 32; Eucken 1938: 81; 1990: 329, 358f.).[47] Creating and maintaining an appropriate framework of "rules of the game of *Leistungswettbewerb*" (Eucken 1942: 38) is, in their view, a genuine and indispensable political task, a task for *Wirtschaftsverfassungspolitik* or *Ordnungspolitik* (Eucken 1990: 266f.).[48] This task they likened to the activities of a gardener who does not construct things, like an engineer, but provides for conditions that are conducive to the natural growth of what is considered desirable while holding back the growth of what is not desired. As Böhm (1980: 200) put it, to maintain a well-functioning market economy requires a continuous nursing and gardening, similar to creating and maintaining a highly cultivated park.[49]

Ordnungspolitik in the Freiburg sense is foremost *competition policy*; a policy that aims at securing a competitive process with desirable working properties, one that works to the benefit of consumer interests. Yet, while Eucken and Böhm were fairly clear about the general aim that they wanted competition policy to pursue, namely to realize to the largest extent possible *consumer sovereignty*, some ambiguity arose in their more specific recommendations for how such policy should proceed. They introduced, in addition to the criterion of *Leistungswettbewerb* (performance competition), another criterion that should guide competition policy, namely "complete competition" (*vollständige Konkurrenz*),[50] a criterion that does not appear to be quite compatible with the first nor does it seem to be compatible with the procedural logic of the Freiburg paradigm. The concept of *Leistungswettbewerb* clearly points in the direction of a rule-oriented competition policy that would seek to specify rules of the game that define which kinds of competitive strategies should be, or should not be, permitted because they can be predicted to work, or not to work, to the benefit of the consumer.[51] To be sure, there may be considerable scope for disagreement on where the dividing line between permissible and prohibited strategies should be drawn, and the *Leistungswettbewerb* criterion is not immune against being misused in support of anti-competitive interests.[52] Yet, it clearly constitutes a *procedural* criterion that is in line with the logic of *Ordnungspolitik*, or constitutional policy, and that can be rationally discussed as to the appropriateness of its particular applications.[53] By contrast, the criterion of "complete competition" (*vollständige Konkurrenz*) is *outcome oriented* in the sense that it looks at the resulting market structure, identifying as desirable a situation where there are on both sides of the market numerous economic players without any market power (Böhm 1937: 105f.; 1960: 62f.; Eucken 1990: 202; 1992: 270).[54]

The problem with the concept of 'complete' or perfect competition is, of course, that it is in contrast to the procedural thrust of *Ordnungspolitik* and that it may lead to policy recommendations that conflict with the concept of *Leistungswettbewerb* (Eucken 1990: 375f.).[55] Since the latter's focus is on the nature of the procedures by which outcomes are generated rather than on the outcomes as such, it would have to allow for market structures that deviate from complete competition as long as they are the result of *Leistungswettbewerb*, while the former criterion would recommend against such structures even if they are solely the result of *Leistungswettbewerb*. That the views that Eucken and Böhm voiced on competition policy are in need of clarification has often been noted, and these views have been further developed within the Freiburg school,[56] just as the theoretical outlooks at competition have changed considerably over the past 50 years in the rest of the economics profession.[57] These issues, important as they are, should be considered, however, of secondary importance relative to the general notion that the ordo-liberals sought to advance, namely that an appropriate competitive order – one that exhibits desirable working properties – is not a self-generating and self-maintaining gift of nature but something that needs to be actively pursued and cultivated. There is clearly scope for arguments on what may be the most suitable kind of *Ordnungspolitik* to serve that purpose, and one may well disagree with some of what the founders of the Freiburg school had to say on this issue, while still agreeing with their principal argument that *market competition* is not just any kind of competition but one that requires appropriate rules of the game.[58]

To what extent "private economic power" poses, indeed, a threat to a properly working competitive market order (Eucken 1990: 359) is an issue that many of today's economists, even among those working in the Freiburg tradition, would judge somewhat differently, sharing less of the concerns that moved Eucken and Böhm and seeing the roots of anti-competitive contrivances more in the political than in the private arena. If, as Böhm (1960: 32) argues, the essence of economic power lies in the ability of inferior suppliers to prevent customers from accessing more attractive alternatives,[59] the question arises of how such power may be obtained within a properly enforced order of private law and in the absence of legal privileges.[60] Indeed, Eucken and Böhm were not blind to the fact that many of the problems which they discussed under the rubric of "private economic power" are indirect consequences of misguided government interventions or of defects in the existing legal–institutional framework. As Eucken (1989: 33) noted:

> The formation of monopolies can be encouraged by the state itself through, for example, its patent policy, trade policy, tax policy, *et cetera*. This has happened often in recent times. The state first encourages the formation of private economic power and then becomes partially dependent on it.[61]

Whatever the contemporary relevance of what the founders of the Freiburg school thought about the need to defend a competitive economic constitution against threats from private power, what is clearly still most relevant, and much in line with modern political economy, is what they had to say about a problem that they described as *"refeudalisation"* (Böhm 1980: 258) and that in contemporary economics is discussed as the problem of *rent-seeking* (Streit 1992: 690f.).[62] As noted above, the ordo-liberals saw the essential feature of the competitive market order in the fact that it is a privilege-free, non-discriminating constitutional order within which economic actors meet as legal equals. The transition from the privilege-based feudal order to the civil law society that had marked, in their view, the major historical step toward the realization of such an order had been motivated by the liberal principle that "the state should on no account be allowed to confer privileges" (Böhm 1980: 141; 1989: 57). Accordingly, they regarded the granting of special privileges to particular groups as a violation of the very principles on which a competitive market order is built, as a violation of the fundamental constitutional commitment that is entailed in opting for the market order and the privilege-free civil law society (Böhm 1980: 164).[63] Privilege-seeking and privilege-granting is, as they emphasized, in essence a movement back to the kind of discriminatory order of privileges that had been characteristic of the feudal society (Eucken 1990: 329). In no lesser clarity than modern public choice discussions on the problem of rent-seeking, the Freiburg ordo-liberals described the fatal political dynamics that result where governments and legislators are empowered to grant privileges and where, in consequence, special interest groups work the political process in order to obtain such privileges. As Böhm (1980: 166; 1989: 66) phrased it, the government

> ... is constantly faced with a considerable temptation to meet the

contradictory demands of many pressure groups. ... The fact that this tendency is, as it were, in the nature of things makes it a weakness of the system which must be taken seriously.[64]

In search of a political constitution

What the ordo-liberals made clear with their *constitutional approach* to market competition was that the competitive order must be considered a *public good*, and that – as in all public good cases – it is important to distinguish clearly between a person's interest in enjoying the benefits of a public good and that person's interest in contributing to its production. Applied to the *competitive order* as a public good, it is important to distinguish between, on the one side, the issue of whether it is desirable for a person to live within a competitive market environment and, on the other side, the issue of whether it is in that person's interest to comply with the rules that constitute a competitive market order.[65] That legislator and government act in accordance with their "constitutionally determined mandate ... to create, preserve and manage that regulative framework which guarantees the functioning of the free market," Böhm (1980: 158; 1989: 63f.) notes, "is desired not only for itself, it is also in the interest of all citizens of the state that the government adheres strictly to this mandate." Such common interest does not prevent, however, that "it is possible for any participant and for any group of participants to obtain benefits by violating the rules, ... at the expense of other participants or groups of participants" (Böhm 1980: 158; 1989: 64), be it by direct rule violations such as the forming of cartels, be it by lobbying for special privileges. The latter strategy is, as Böhm (1980: 158f.; 1989: 64) pointed out, particularly attractive because

> ... in this case, the individual does not expose himself to the odium of cheating but demands are made of the legislator or the government to elevate cheating to a legislative or governmental programme ... Protective duties, tax privileges, direct subsidies, price supports, initial support for establishing monopoly or "orderly markets" can be demanded. ... It is the state itself which is to be enjoined to override the rules of the prevailing order in favor of one group and at the expense of other groups of citizens.[66]

Even if they did not use the term public good, nor the concepts of game theory, the ordo-liberals clearly recognized that the *game of competition* represents a prisoners' dilemma, in the sense that although all players are better off living under a competitive regime, compared with potential alternative regimes, everybody has an interest in being exempted from the constraints that competition imposes. Yet, if all successfully seek protection from competition for themselves, they will end up in a through-and-through protectionist regime[67] that is desirable for nobody, and that nobody would choose over the competitive alternative if the choice were between the two. It is in order to escape from that dilemma[68] that all can benefit from committing to a competitive economic constitution, if that commitment is made credible by the presence of a government that effectively enforces the rules of the game of competition. And it is a violation of such commitment, a violation of the rules of the game, if players seek to escape the discipline of competition through private contrivances or by the means of politics (Böhm 1937: 126). This is the logic behind the ordo-liberals' diagnosis that the competitive market order is not self-generating and self-maintaining but needs the assistance of *Ordnungspolitik*.[69] In today's language, one might say that to them a major and principal task of *Ordnungspolitik* is to allow the economic players to escape from prisoners' dilemmas.

In assigning to the state the task of acting as "guardian of the competitive order," as "*Hüter der Wettbewerbsordnung*" (Eucken 1990: 327), the Freiburg ordo-liberals found themselves facing a fundamental dilemma. The logic of their argument implied that the solution to the problem of guarding the competitive order had to come from an agency, the government, that they recognized, at the same time, to be a major source of the defects that it was supposed to cure. They did certainly not suppose that, under the existing political structure, government could be expected to do what is in the common interest, and they explicitly criticized the illusionary belief that government can be trusted to act as a benign and omniscient agent of the common good.[70] Yet, they also insisted that the existing political order should not be taken as an unalterable fate, but should be regarded as something that can be and must be reformed[71] in the awareness that the real problem is, in the political realm no less than in the economy, to establish a framework that induces ordinary, self-interested people to do, in pursuit of their own interest, what is in the common interest.[72] In other words, they recognized, much in line with modern constitutional economics, that the solution to the problem of rent-seeking must ultimately be found in the political constitution.[73] They saw that, before the state can be trusted to be a reliable guardian of the competitive economic constitution, the constitutional order of the state, or the rules of the game of politics, is in need of reform.[74] And they were aware, of course, of the fact that such reform can, again, only be achieved through the political process, and that therefore there can be no guarantees that a solution to the twofold constitutional problem will be achieved. But to them this was not an acceptable excuse for not making an effort to address this problem.[75]

That the noted dilemma exists is not the fault of the Freiburg research program; it lies in the nature of things. And it speaks to the intellectual honesty of the founders of this program that they did not pretend to be able to offer an easy answer. A phrase that they used, and that has often been misunderstood, is the argument that a "strong state" is needed to fend off interest group pressures. This was clearly not meant as an argument in favor of an authoritarian state with large discretionary power. To the contrary, the Freiburg ordo-liberals expressly noted that it is the modern growth of the state's apparatus and activities that have made it "a plaything in the hands of interest groups" (Böhm

1980: 258; Eucken 1990: 326).[76] The formula "strong state" was meant by them as a shorthand for a state that is properly constrained by a political constitution such that government cannot serve as a promising target of special interest rent-seeking.[77] What such a constitution was to entail, i.e. how constitutional safeguards may be installed that effectively prevent the dynamics of privilege-seeking and privilege-granting, they did not discuss in detail. But they would have certainly subscribed to the general recommendation that the authority and the power must be taken away from governments and legislators to discriminate among citizens by granting privileges.[78]

Eucken, in particular, emphasized the importance of extending the logic of *Ordnungspolitik* from the realm of the economic constitution to that of the political constitution. He explicitly stated that, just as *Ordnungspolitik* is needed in order to establish and to maintain an appropriate economic constitution, *Ordnungspolitik* is also needed at the level of politics in order to establish and to maintain an appropriate political constitution.[79] His early death prevented Eucken from working out his thoughts on the notion of *Ordnungspolitik* for the political realm. But the paradigm that he and Böhm have launched clearly invites such an extension of its logic from the market arena to the political arena, and it remains a task to be pursued by those who carry on the Freiburg tradition.

4   Hayek's legacy and the future of liberal thought

Rational liberalism versus evolutionary agnosticism[1]

Introduction

Friedrich A. Hayek's work represents, without doubt, the most comprehensive and influential contribution to what has been described as the modern "rebirth of classical liberalism" (Gray 1982).[2] His legacy will, therefore, surely be of decisive influence on the future development of classical liberal thought.

The question that I want to raise, and seek to answer, in this chapter concerns Hayek's liberal legacy. What is his lasting contribution to our understanding of a classical liberal approach to political economy? More specifically, I want to examine what his work implies for the role of rational institutional design and constructive reform within a liberal political agenda. This issue is less trivial than might appear on first glance. Certainly, Hayek's general critique of socialism will be an indisputable, principal component of his legacy. Yet, as one looks beyond the critical part to the positive political implications of his work, his message seems not as indisputable. In fact, with regard to the issue of what role his liberal program assigns to deliberate institutional reform, Hayek's work appears to contain a fundamental tension, in the sense that support can be found for two critically different messages, messages that I want to contrast as *rational liberalism* and *evolutionary agnosticism*. By rational liberalism I mean the message implied in those parts of Hayek's writings that provide rational arguments in favor of the liberal order, arguments that spell out reasons why such an order can be considered superior to alternative arrangements, and what can be done to establish and maintain it. By contrast, the label evolutionary agnosticism is meant to describe a certain tenor in Hayek's thoughts on cultural evolution which seems to suggest that any efforts in deliberate institutional reform and construction must ultimately be futile as we cannot but bow to an evolutionary process that decides what will survive, irrespective of what we may consider to be desirable or beneficial.

What I refer to as rational liberalism is visible, for instance, when Hayek says about his *The Constitution of Liberty* that its "emphasis is on the positive task of improving our institutions" (Hayek 1960: 5), and when he adds that, in order to "produce desirable and workable results," such efforts need to be "guided by some general conception of the social order desired, some coherent image of the kind of world in which the people want to live" (ibid.: 114).[3] In contrast, what I call evolutionary agnosticism is illustrated by statements such as the following quote from *The Fatal Conceit*, in which, in reference to his theory of cultural evolution, Hayek notes (1988: 27),

> I have no intention to commit what is often called the genetic or naturalistic fallacy. I do not claim that the results of group selection of traditions are necessarily "good" – any more than I claim that other things that have long survived in the course of evolution, such as cockroaches, have moral value.

That such a tension exists in Hayek's work is, of course, not a new discovery, but has been pointed out by a number of other authors before. Chandran Kukathas, for instance, notes in his study on *Hayek and Modern Liberalism* that Hayek's "thought is governed by two incompatible philosophical attitudes" (Kukathas 1990: 206), a "rationalist advocacy of liberal reforms" and an "anti-rationalist critique of all social reconstruction" (ibid.: 215).[4] And Norman Barry (1994: 160) similarly notes that the "critical rationalism" in Hayek's writings appears incompatible with "a certain kind of fatalism, that we must wait for evolution to pronounce its verdict."[5]

My interest here is not in stating one more time that Hayek's work suffers, indeed, from the noted discrepancy. Instead, my intention is to show that this tension or discrepancy can be reconciled in a manner that, although requiring a reinterpretation or reconstruction of some of Hayek's arguments, is truthful to the principal thrust of his overall approach. The source of the problem that I want to address lies, in my view, in certain ambiguities in Hayek's theory of cultural evolution; therefore, a critical review of his arguments on this subject will form a major part of my suggested reconciliation. The fact that Hayek's rational liberalism is mainly expressed in some of his earlier writings, while the evolutionary theme has become increasingly prominent in his later writings, may lead – and has led – students of his work to believe that the evolutionary argument represents the more mature version of Hayek's liberalism, and that it replaces or overrides his earlier, more constructive outlook at the liberal agenda. Such interpretation is, unfortunately in my view, reinforced by the prominent role that *The Fatal Conceit* (Hayek 1988) plays in some debates on Hayek's thought. As his last major publication and lead volume of his *Collected Works*, it has gained disproportional attention and is widely regarded as the definite and authoritative summary of his ideas. Yet it is, among Hayek's writings, also the book in which his rational liberalism is least visible, whereas the evolutionary message is not only most dominant but also most biased toward what I describe as evolutionary agnosticism.

My contention in this chapter is that a one-sided focus on Hayek's evolutionary theme must result in a distorted picture of his system of thought. To be sure, apart from its agnostic biases, his evolutionary argument constitutes a major and essential part of his overall approach. Yet, as I want to argue, it is only in conjunction with, and not as an alternative to, his rational liberalism, that Hayek's evolutionism makes good sense. To the extent that it is defendable, the evolutionary argument is compatible with the rational, constructive component of his liberalism. And to the extent that it is not compatible with the latter, the evolutionary argument turns out to be problematic. Both components can and should be understood as mutually compatible and complementary perspectives.

In a sense, then, this chapter can be characterized as an effort to protect Hayek's legacy from being unduly overshadowed by the message that seems to come out of *The Fatal Conceit*. If one looks for the liberal theme in Hayek's work, *The Fatal Conceit* can only provide a very limited, and potentially biased picture. Like some other of Hayek's later writings, it adds an important dimension to his liberal paradigm with its evolutionary outlook. But, considered only by itself and apart from the rationalist dimension of Hayek's liberalism, it is bound to be misleading.

The chapter is organized as follows: as a corrective to an evolutionary bias in the reception of Hayek's works, the next section will document, in some detail, Hayek's early rational liberalism. The following three sections examine Hayek's evolutionary approach and argue that a reinterpretation or reconstruction of some of his arguments is necessary in order to make his message coherent. The sixth section examines Hayek's conception of the market process as a model for a properly understood evolutionary argument. The seventh section explains in what sense the evolutionary outlook can be said to supplement Hayek's rational liberalism; and the eighth section shows in what sense, on the other hand, the rational component is a necessary complement to Hayek's evolutionism, if the latter is to fit consistently into his classical liberal program. Finally, there is a conclusion to the chapter.

Hayek on the "positive tasks of liberal legislation"

Classical liberalism clearly had a reformist thrust, and with his efforts to provide a modern restatement of the philosophy of classical liberalism Hayek aimed, no less than the classical founders, at portraying the fundamental principles of a desirable social order and at identifying provisions that are required to establish and maintain such an order.[6] And we can assume that he included himself when in *The Trend of Economic Thinking*, his 1932 inaugural lecture at the London School of Economics (reprinted in Hayek 1991: 17–34), he noted:

> It is probably true that economic analysis has never been the product of detached intellectual curiosity about the why of social phenomena, but of an intense urge to reconstruct a world which gives rise to profound dissatisfaction.
>
> (Ibid.: 1991: 19)

If there was a difference between Hayek and other reform-minded economists, it was not about the ultimate goal "to build a juster society" (ibid.: 40) itself, but about the ways in which we can hope effectively to promote this goal.

It has been said of Adam Smith and other eighteenth-century founders of classical liberalism that they were largely engaged in what may be described as the "science of legislation," i.e. in a systematic effort to examine the workings of the ground rules of social order and to identify possibilities for their improvement.[7] It is clearly as a continuation of such a liberal science of legislation that Hayek understood his own enterprise. And his efforts at revitalizing this classical concept were not only aimed at strengthening liberal intellectual forces in a predominantly non-liberal environment, they were also meant as a corrective to tendencies in the liberal tradition itself that, in Hayek's judgement, had come to distract from the genuine spirit of the original message.[8]

Distancing himself from the *laissez-faire* image of liberalism that, rightly or wrongly, had been attributed to some of its nineteenth-century advocates, Hayek sought to draw attention to the positive role that government has to play in providing and maintaining a framework of rules and institutions that allows a liberal order to flourish. As he noted about the study of this issue:

> Neither the much abused and much understood phrase of "laissez faire" nor the still older formula of "the protection of life, liberty, and property" are of much help. In fact, in so far as both tend to suggest that we can just leave things as they are, they may be worse than no answer; they certainly do not tell us what are and what are not desirable or necessary fields of government activity.
>
> (Hayek 1948: 17)

And, in the same spirit, Hayek argued in *The Road to Serfdom* [1976b (1944): 17]:

> There is nothing in the basic principles of liberalism to make it a stationary creed; there are no hard-and-fast rules fixed once and for all. The fundamental principle that in the ordering of our affairs we should make as much use as possible of the spontaneous forces of society, and resort as little as possible to coercion, is capable of an infinite variety of applications. There is, in particular, all the difference between deliberately creating a system within which competition will work as beneficially as possible and passively accepting institutions as they are. Probably nothing has done so much harm to the liberal cause as the wooden insistence of some liberals on certain rough rules of thumb, above all the principle of laissez faire.[9]

In his 1939 pamphlet "Freedom and the economic system"[10] as well as in *The Road to Serfdom*, Hayek took particular care to point out that his criticism of "modern planners" was not about "whether we ought to choose intelligently between the various possible organizations of society,"[11] but about the ways in which we can reasonably hope to improve the order of society by planning and rational construction. There is, he argues, an important distinction between two kinds of "social planning," namely the "distinction between the construction of a rational system of law, under the rule of which people are free to follow their preferences, and a system of specific orders and prohibitions" (Hayek 1939: 9). Although liberalism denies that the latter kind of social planning, the "*central* direction and organization of all our activities according to some consciously constructed 'blueprint'" [Hayek 1976b (1944): 35], can be a suitable tool for social improvement, it is not only compatible with the former type of planning. Rather, in Hayek's understanding, such planning has to be considered the principal means by which we can hope to improve our social condition.[12] And Hayek, in fact, notes as a shortcoming of the liberal tradition that it has paid insufficient attention to this issue and that the "task of creating a rational framework of law has by no means been carried through consistently by the early liberals" (Hayek 1939: 11). He even suspects that the neglect "of this kind of planning ... has tended to throw the whole liberal doctrine into discredit" (ibid.).

The paper on "'Free' enterprise and competitive order" that Hayek presented in 1947 at the initial meeting of what was later to become the Mont Pelerin Society (published in 1948) was clearly intended to correct for this deficiency and to stress the role that the classical liberal doctrine, in his view, ought to assign to the positive task of improving the "legal framework" (Hayek 1948a: 110). It was, he notes there, "probably the most fatal tactical mistake of many nineteenth-century liberals to have given the impression that the abandonment of all harmful or unnecessary state activity was the consummation of all political wisdom" (ibid.: 109). And he suggests that it is more adequate to interpret "the fundamental principle of liberalism" not as absence of state activity but "as a policy which deliberately adopts competition, the market, and prices as its ordering principle and uses the legal framework enforced by the state in order to make competition as effective and beneficial as possible" (ibid.: 110). What was required, in Hayek's view, for an advancement of liberalism, was a renewed concern for the "[p]ositive tasks of liberal legislation" (1978: 145), a concern that he found lacking in nineteenth-century liberal doctrine, but which he recognised in some more recent 'neo-liberal' approaches that explicitly address the issue of what the positive content of the legal framework must be in order "to make the market mechanism operate satisfactorily" (ibid.: 146).[13] Though Hayek does not specify which 'neo-liberal' approaches he has in mind, his description certainly fits German ordo-liberals of the so-called Freiburg school, like Walter Eucken and Franz Böhm.[14] It clearly corresponds to their understanding of the role of 'liberal legislation' when Hayek (1976b [1944]: 18) notes that the "attitude of the liberal toward society is like that of the gardener" who seeks to create favorable conditions for natural growth.[15]

What the ordo-liberals discussed under the rubrik of *Ordnungspolitik* is of the same spirit as what Hayek had to say about "a policy for a competitive order" (1948a: 112). Stressing the "task of creating a suitable framework for the beneficial working of competition," Hayek (1976b [1944]: 39) notes: "In no system that could be rationally defended would the state just do nothing. An effective competitive system needs an intellegently designed and continuously adjusted legal framework as much as any other." Hayek clearly does not expect a beneficial competitive order to simply establish and maintain itself. His liberalism, like that of the German ordo-liberals, includes an essential role for legislation and deliberate institutional design. In his words: "The liberal argument is in favor of making the best possible use of the forces of competition as a means of co-ordinating human efforts, not an argument for leaving things just as they are. ... It does not deny, but even emphasises, that, in order that competition should work beneficially, a careful thought-out legal framework is required and that neither the existing nor the past legal rules are free from grave defects" (1976b [1944]: 36).[16] And Hayek notes on this issue: "I myself have no doubt that legislation has important tasks to perform in this field" (1948a: 114).

Hayek's evolutionism

The theoretical context in which Hayek places his evolutionary argument is familiar, and a brief summary may suffice in the present context.[17] Speaking of the "twin ideas of spontaneous order and evolution," he wants to emphasize the close connection between his evolutionary argument and his concept of spontaneous order. A spontaneous social order results from the interplay of actors who pursue their own interests within the confines of certain general rules of conduct. The general nature of the resulting order will critically depend on the nature of the general rules that govern the actors' behavior. In Hayek's terminology, the nature of the *order of rules* will determine the character of the resulting *order of actions*. Not just any order of rules will result in an order of actions with desirable properties. For a beneficial order to emerge, "suitable" or "appropriate" rules are required (Hayek 1969: 180). This raises, of course, the question of how we may hope to find such rules, and it is in this context that Hayek advances his theory of cultural evolution, i.e. the notion of a spontaneous evolutionary process in which alternative rules are experimented with and in which, through trial and error, experience about which kinds of rules work well and which do not is accumulated.

Associated with Hayek's argument on the "twin ideas of spontaneous order and evolution" is his critique of what he calls "constructivist rationalism," an attitude of intellectual hubris that, he argues, by far overestimates what rational planning can achieve in matters of social organization. Corresponding to the twin ideas, this critique comes in two parts. The spontaneous order argument is critical of a central planning mentality which presumes that it is "in our power to build a desirable society by simply putting together the particular elements that by themselves appear desirable" (Hayek 1973: 56). The fundamental flaw of this mentality is, in Hayek's account, that it fails to appreciate the *role of rules* and that it fails to see how much we have to rely on general rules as co-ordinating devices if we want to utilize the knowledge that exists dispersed in the mind of individual persons and to benefit from the explorative and innovative potential of a spontaneous process. The evolutionary argument, on the other hand, is critical of a certain "conception of the formation of social institutions" (ibid.: 5), a conception which, while recognizing the role of rules, assumes that all rules and social institutions "are, and ought to be, the product of deliberate design" (ibid.). This mentality, Hayek argues, fails to see that most of our "useful" social rules and institutions are not deliberate creations, but a largely unintended outcome of slow evolutionary growth, and that we need to rely on evolutionary forces for further improvements in our received institutional frameworks.

Hayek's theory of cultural evolution is not a tightly reasoned, well-integrated body of arguments, but, instead, a more loosely connected set of general ideas and conjectures that have invited a number of criticisms.[18] My exclusive interest in the present context is whether it has implications that would contradict Hayek's rational liberalism as described in the previous section. Rather than going through the various particular statements that Hayek has made on this subject, I want to approach this issue by asking what kinds of claims his theory of cultural evolution would have to make in order to contradict his rational liberalism, and what kinds of claims it could make without doing so.

A number of arguments that Hayek advances under the evolutionary rubric are, quite obviously, not at all in discord with his emphasis on the positive tasks of liberal legislation. This is, in particular, true for those parts of his argument that make essentially a *historical claim* about the genesis of existing rules, as, for instance, when he argues that

> ... most of the rules which do govern existing society are not the result of our deliberate making {but} ... the product of a process of evolution in the course of which much more experience and knowledge has been precipitated in them than any one person can fully know.
>
> (Hayek 1967: 92)

This historical claim, and similar ones that can be found in Hayek's contribution to this subject, may well be, and probably are, correct. Yet, whether they are true or not, they do not tell us what role we should assign to deliberate institutional design and rational reform. There is a clear difference between the factual issue of whether beneficial institutions did in fact – or can, in principle – come about without foresight, and the political issue of whether, and to what extent, we should employ rational institutional analysis and deliberate reform in our efforts to improve our social condition. That good things came, and may come, about without foresight does surely not imply that we should proceed without foresight, whether in institutional or in other matters.

If a conflict is seen to exist between Hayek's rational liberalism and his evolutionary argument, it is because the latter is understood to imply the claim that there is a spontaneous evolutionary process operating at the level of rules and institutions which tends to promote beneficial results, and that it can only be detrimental to interfere in this process by deliberate institutional construction. There would clearly be a conflict if Hayek's claim were, indeed, that we should rely on cultural evolution to promote desirable rules, and that we can trust its spontaneous forces to provide a better guide to institutional improvement than our deliberate efforts in rational design and constructive reform.

Such a claim may seem quite clearly implied when Hayek talks about cultural evolution as "a competitive process in which success decides" (Hayek 1988: 73), a process "guided not by reason but by success" (Hayek 1979a: 166), or when he suggests that evolutionary competition leads to "the survival of the successful" (Hayek 1960: 57), "to the prevalence of the more effective institutions" (Hayek 1979a: 154), and to "successful adaptations of society that are constantly improved" (Hayek 1960: 34). Yet, do such statements indeed tell us that, instead of seeking deliberately to design and reform the institutional framework within which we live, we ought to let evolution work its own way? Hayek's evolutionary argument can have such implication only if it makes two kinds of claims: namely, first, the *factual claim* that cultural evolution will tend to select in favor of institutions with certain characteristics, and, second, the *normative claim* that institutions with these kinds of characteristics are beneficial. More briefly, Hayek's argument would have to have *empirical* and *normative* content. It would need to have empirical content in the sense that it tells us what kinds of rules and institutions can be expected to prevail in evolutionary competition. And it would need to have normative content in the sense that it would tell us why the kinds of rules and institutions that tend to survive in evolutionary competition are desirable.

On the empirical content of Hayek's evolutionism

If Hayek's evolutionary argument had no empirical content, i.e. if it did not say which kinds of rules evolution tends to favor, we could, for obvious reasons, not conclude that those which survive are desirable. If, on the other hand, Hayek's theory did say something about the likely attributes of surviving institutions, but had no normative content, i.e. if it would provide no argument why institutions with such attributes are desirable, we would have no reason to conclude that we ought to relinquish efforts in institutional design and, instead, leave our fate to the workings of evolutionary forces. What needs to be examined, then, is the question of what empirical and normative content Hayek's theory can be said actually to contain.

The language of evolutionary theory can easily be deceptive about the actual content of particular statements. For instance, when Hayek speaks of "the prevalence of the more effective institutions in a process of competition" (Hayek 1979a: 154f.), one may be inclined to interpret this as a contentful claim about the workings of the evolutionary process. Yet, if "effective" just means the capacity to survive in a process of competition, the statement is without empirical content. It says that institutions with the better capacity to prevail do so in competition. Yet, as long as "effective" is not defined independently of survival, we are not told what properties prevailing institutions, as opposed to those that do not prevail, are likely to have.

The notion of the survival of the successful is, obviously, no more than a tautology if success is not defined independently of survival. It can be given empirical content only if other attributes of successful institutions are identified that are conceptually independent of survival, yet are claimed *de facto* to promote survival. Such attributes can, however, not be identified as long as the nature of the evolutionary process remains unspecified. Put differently, they cannot be identified as long as we do not know the kinds of constraints under which the relevant process occurs. For instance, if we know that a tennis tournament is carried out under standard rules, we can predict that the "better" players will tend to "survive," where "better" may be defined in terms of criteria that are independent of survival in the respective tournament, such as, for example, their endurance, accuracy in serving, or speed. Such prediction need, of course, not be perfect because players' momentary dispositions as well as random factors may affect the outcome. Yet, the "standard rules" would define constraints that allow us to form expectations about what kinds of attributes are likely to make a player successful. If, however, we had no knowledge at all about the rules of the tournament and what kinds of strategies players may use (e.g. whether wrestling down or poisoning the opponent would be allowed), we would be unable to predict the attributes that surviving players are likely to exhibit.

Elsewhere (Vanberg 1994a), I have suggested the distinction between *conditional* and *unconditional* evolutionary claims or conjectures to help to clarify what is at issue here. Unconditional claims are statements about "evolution *per se*," statements that leave totally unspecified the kinds of constraints under which the evolutionary process occurs. Such claims provide no information that would allow one to say anything substantive about what it is that can be expected to survive. In such context, the notion of the survival of the successful remains inevitably tautological. Conditional claims, by contrast, are statements about the workings of an evolutionary process under particular constraints. To the extent that the constraints under which evolutionary competition occurs are specified, we can conceptually distinguish between success and survival, turning the notion of the survival of the successful into an empirically contentful conjecture.

If the Hayekian argument is to be more than a tautological exercise, it must be interpreted, or reconstructed, as a conditional conjecture. That is, it must be understood as an argument about what kinds of rules or institutions we can expect to survive if the evolutionary process is subject to specified constraints. Such understanding requires us, as indicated, to some extent to *reconstruct* his argument because his theory of cultural evolution is not very explicit about the kinds of constraints that he seems to presuppose in some of his conjectures on the working properties of evolutionary competition. Indeed, some of Hayek's remarks on the subject sound as if he explicitly wanted to make an unconditional claim.[19] Yet, as I shall argue below (see pp. 67ff.), one can find important clues as to what a Hayekian conditional evolutionary argument should look like in his arguments on market competition.

A digression may be appropriate, at this point, into an argument that has played a somewhat dubious role in some of Hayek's last writings, namely the argument that, in cultural evolution, the success of institutions is measured in terms of population size and that evolved "rules were shaped mainly by their suitability for increasing our number" (Hayek 1988: 134).[20] While this argument may appear to add empirical content to his theory, what Hayek has to say on the "close connection between population size and the presence of, and benefit of, certain evolved practices, institutions, and forms of human interaction" (ibid.: 120) is quite ambiguous and questionable.[21]

If Hayek wanted literally to claim that population size is the principal measuring rod for the "success" of institutions, considering such examples as China or India would surely suggest that this is a somewhat dubious claim. And if his argument were only that, without a population that practices them, institutions could not survive, this would be a correct, but rather trivial, claim. Rather, it seems that only two claims are defendable in his argument on the population issue. First, that the *potential* to support large populations varies with the wealth-creating capacity of institutions. And, second, that, with *market institutions*, an increase in population size tends to increase wealth, through its effects on the size of the market and the division of labor.[22] Although these are, without doubt, sound arguments, they hardly support the claim that we ought to look at population size in order to identify successful institutions.

It is almost tautologically true that wealthier societies have the capacity to support larger populations.[23] And it is plausible to assume that their wealth-creating potential generally increases their survival capacity.[24] But this does not mean that wealthier societies do, in fact, have larger populations than poorer societies, or that wealth-creating institutions survive *because* they support larger populations. Even though there is very good evidence that societies with market institutions tend to be wealthier than those that rely on other institutional arrangements,[25] it is not at all the case that market societies stand out in terms of population size. And while Hayek is probably right when he claims that, of today's world population, "most live only because of the market order" (Hayek 1988: 133),[26] it is not from their historical record in supporting large populations that we, or Hayek, conclude that market institutions are "superior." It is our, and Hayek's, confidence in their wealth-creating potential that lets us believe in their *capacity* to support large numbers.[27]

In summary, then, Hayek's comments on the population issue do not support the assumption that, in cultural evolution, population size is the mark of successful institutions (and there can be no unconditional evolutionary argument that would support such an assumption, except in the already noted tautological sense that it is only through people practicing them that institutions can survive). What his comments really imply is that market institutions have a superior wealth-creating potential and, therefore, the capacity to support larger populations. But this claim does not need really to come out of Hayek's evolutionary theory. It is a rational argument in comparative institutional analysis, an argument that is, to be sure, supported by ample historical evidence.

On the normative content of Hayek's evolutionism

In the previous section, my concern was with the issue of the empirical content of Hayek's evolutionism. I want to turn now to a discussion of its normative content. Here, again, the language of evolutionary theory can be deceptive. Because of our common usage of the term, we tend to attribute normative significance to the notion of "success" and are, therefore, inclined to read into the phrase of the "survival of the successful" a normative claim. Yet, in evolutionary theory, the term success does, *per se*, not carry any normative meaning. Success simply means survival. For the notion of the survival of the successful to have normative content, the claim would have to be made that what survives in evolutionary competition is *desirable* in terms of some normative criterion. The question that needs to be examined is, therefore, whether Hayek makes such a normative claim about the results of cultural evolution, and which is his criterion of "desirability."[28]

Some of Hayek's comments on the evolutionary theme sound as if he has no intention to make any claim of this kind, as if all he wants is to present a purely naturalistic argument. And any normative intention seems to be equally ruled out when he argues that "demands for justice are simply inappropriate to a naturalistic evolutionary process – inappropriate not just to what has happened in the past, but to what is going on at present. ... *Evolution cannot be just*" (Hayek 1988: 74, emphasis in the original).

If this were so, the issue that this chapter seeks to discuss would, of course, disappear. If no claim were made that cultural evolution tends to generate "beneficial" institutions, Hayek's argument would have no implications for the issue of what role we should assign to rational institutional construction, and what role we should allow evolutionary forces to play. A purely naturalistic theory may tell us what we *can* or *cannot* do. It does not tell us what we *ought* to do. It could be in conflict with Hayek's rational liberalism only if it were to imply that the "positive tasks of liberal legislation" that he speaks of could not possibly be carried out successfully, and that human design can do nothing against the dictates of evolution. If the claim were that the forces of cultural evolution render any effort in deliberate institutional reform futile, there could, for obvious reasons, be no meaningful role for liberal legislation. Some of Hayek's comments in *The Fatal Conceit* seem, indeed, to imply such an argument. For instance, when he notes that "[w]e may not like the fact that our rules were shaped mainly by their suitability for increasing our numbers, but we have little choice in the matter now (if we ever did)" (Hayek 1988: 134), and when he adds: "in any case, our desires and wishes are largely irrelevant" (ibid.). And it seems also implied when he argues that "the main 'purpose' to which man's ... traditions are adapted is to produce other human beings" (ibid.: 133), and concludes:

> There is no real point in asking whether those of his actions which do so contribute are really "good," particularly if thus it is intended to inquire

whether we *like* the results. For, as we have seen, we have never been able to choose our morals.

(Ibid.)

Nevertheless, whatever such statements may mean, Hayek provides very little, if any, sustainable argument for the alleged futility of human efforts in institutional construction.[29] Moreover, such a claim would, indeed, be very much in contrast to the whole thrust of his work.[30]

Whatever may be said about the naturalistic part of Hayek's thoughts on cultural evolution, his writings on the subject offer plenty of evidence, explicit as well as implicit, that he *does* want to attach a normative claim to his evolutionary argument. And this is, in any case, how his argument is widely understood. A normative claim seems apparent, for instance, when he speaks of cultural evolution as a process in which "rules become increasingly better adjusted to generate order" (Hayek 1988: 20), or as a process that leads "to the prevalence of the more effective institutions" (Hayek 1979a: 154) and to "successful adaptations of society that are constantly improved" (Hayek 1960: 34).[31] The question, therefore, remains: if he does suggest that cultural evolution tends to promote "beneficial" (Hayek 1988: 136) institutions, what is the normative criterion that he employs?[32]

Although Hayek cannot be said to be unambiguous in this matter, the principal candidate, I submit, is a criterion that not only appears again and again throughout his work, but that is also most consistent with the classical liberal foundations of his philosophy, namely the notion that institutions are beneficial if, and to the extent that, they serve the interests of the persons living with them, i.e. make them "better off."[33] In other words, I claim that it is the benefits that result to their individual *constituents* that make rules and institutions beneficial in Hayek's account. If one wants to use a label, one can characterize this standard as *normative individualism* (Buchanan 1991c).

The classical liberalism of David Hume and Adam Smith embodied, as Hayek notes, a "conception of a desirable order" (Hayek 1967: 160). Hayek's own restatement of their liberal principles shares their concern, as well as their individualist understanding of what constitutes a "desirable" social order. This is apparent, for instance, when he describes the latter as "the kind of world in which people want to live" (Hayek 1960: 114), or when he speaks of the "endeavor to make society good in the sense that we shall like to live in it" (Hayek 1973: 33).[34] The same criterion of desirability is implied when he defines the "conception of the common welfare or the common good of a free society" as an abstract order which provides "the best chance for any member selected at random successfully to use his knowledge for his purposes" (Hayek 1967: 163).[35] And it is quite explicitly stated when Hayek suggests that:

> ... we should regard as the most desirable order of society one which we would choose if we knew that our initial position in it would be decided purely by chance (such as the fact of our being born into a particular family).
> (Hayek 1976a: 132)

At this point, a digression may be appropriate concerning some of Hayek's comments on the nature of the liberal order that may seem to be in conflict with the normative individualism that, as I claim, informs his work. If the Hayekian, liberal standard is, indeed, individualist in the sense described, and if the liberal order is claimed to be desirable, then, by implication, it must be claimed to be desirable to its individual constituents. This, again, would imply that a liberal order can be recommended to its actual or prospective constituents on *rational grounds*, in terms of their own interests. In fact, the ultimate test for the validity of the liberal claim would seem to be that the actual or prospective constituents can be convinced of the preferability of such an order over feasible alternatives. Yet, in Hayek's work, we find surprisingly little of such optimism about the rational defendability of a liberal order. On the contrary, it sometimes appears as if, in his understanding, the liberal order has arisen, and must be defended *against human wants and desires*. He argues, for instance, against "hedonistic theories of ethics" (Hayek 1988: 69), that "happiness" is an irrelevant consideration in assessing the suitability of rules (ibid.). He declares: "Man has been civilized very much against his wishes" (Hayek 1979a: 168).[36] Or he speaks of man facing "the bitter necessity of submitting to rules he does not like" (Hayek 1988: 76).[37] Such statements may seem to conflict with Hayek's presumed normative individualism and to indicate that he wants to invoke some other, non-individualist, criterion. Yet, I do not think that such conclusions need to be drawn at all. Instead, I want to suggest that these statements can be made consistent with an individualist account, if they are read in the light of a distinction between different kinds of human interests, namely between *action interests* and *constitutional interests* (Vanberg 1994b, Ch. 4). Although this distinction is not Hayek's, it can be used to clarify his argument.

There is a difference between the question of whether we like to respect rules of property and the question of whether we like to live in a society in which property rights are respected. A thief, by his actions, clearly indicates that he does not want to respect property. But, if he were made to choose between a society where property rights are enforced and one where no property rights are respected whatsoever, we can rest assured that he will opt for the first because it is bound to be the wealthier society. It is in this sense that we can distinguish between our *action interests*, i.e. our preferences over alternative courses of action that are open to us under given constraints, and our *constitutional* or *rule interests*, i.e. our preferences over alternative rule regimes under which we may come to live. When Hayek speaks of man facing the "bitter necessity of submitting to rules he does not like," it makes a big difference whether this is read as an argument about action interests or constitutional interests. It is certainly true for many of the rules that constitute a liberal order that we may "not like them" in the sense that we dislike the constraints they impose on us, and that we would prefer if we, personally, were not bound by them. But this does not mean at all that we would not have a constitutional interest in them, and that we could not be convinced that living in an order where they are enforced is much more attractive to us than living in one without them. In this sense, we can interpret the above quotes as arguments about rules which "man does not like" in terms of his action interests, but which still can be shown to be in his constitutional interests. That this may, indeed, be what Hayek has, at least implicitly, in mind, can be inferred, for instance, when he talks about moral rules that "do not directly serve the satisfaction of individual desires, but are required to assist the functioning of an order" (Hayek 1978: 17), or when he notes:

> The rules we are discussing are those that are not so much useful to the individuals who observe them, as those that (if they are *generally* observed) make all members of the group more effective, because they give them opportunities to act within a social *order*.
>
> (Ibid.: 7)

We can agree with Hayek's argument on the tensions between human inclinations and the rule requirements of a liberal order and still maintain that such an order can be rationally defended in terms of constituents' interests.[38] When Hayek talks about man's dislike for the rules of a liberal order, he surely does not want to suggest that we should assess the desirability of such an order in terms other than human wants. It can only mean that its desirability ought to be assessed not in terms of "the apparent pleasantness of its immediately visible effects" (Hayek 1988: 7), but in terms of those human wants that provide the relevant and appropriate standard for the evaluation of alternative social institutional regimes, namely persons' constitutional interests. Rationally to advocate a liberal order to a person means to convince the person that this order will further his or her interest better than feasible alternatives. Such an argument, by its very nature, appeals to persons' constitutional interests, to their preferences over alternative institutional regimes.[39] The desirability of rules in these terms is not tested by their immediate appeal to us or by our willingness to adopt them unilaterally, independent of what the others do, but in our willingness to enter into mutual commitments to follow them, provided others do so as well; commitments that, in order to be credible, will typically require adequate enforcement.

Returning to the main theme of this section, if Hayek's criterion for the desirability of rules and institutions is, in fact, their desirability to their constituents, i.e. to the persons living with them, what would this imply for his evolutionary argument? To the extent that he, indeed, wants to assert that the evolutionary process selects in favor of beneficial or desirable institutions, his claim would, quite obviously, have to be that cultural evolution favors institutions that are desirable to the persons involved. Note that the *normative* component of his argument lies only in the claim that the desirability to their constituents is the relevant criterion for judging the "goodness" of institutions. The normative issue is concerned with which criterion we should apply. The claim that cultural evolution selects in favor of rules and institutions that are desirable to their constituents is, as such, not a normative but a *factual* claim. It implies the conjecture that the evolutionary process will favor institutions with attributes that their constituents find desirable, a conjecture that can, quite obviously, be correct or false. In the generality in which this claim is stated, it seems to be false; and we can certainly suppose that Hayek would not have agreed that this is what he meant. But, if he does not mean to say that evolutionary competition universally produces desirable results, is there a modified, or qualified, claim about the workings of cultural evolution that we can infer from his argument?

The answer to this question lies, in my view, in the distinction that I introduced earlier between conditional and unconditional evolutionary claims. In what way this distinction can help to clarify the problems in Hayek's evolutionary argument can be very clearly seen if we look at his theory of the market process from this perspective. I shall, therefore, apply the distinction first to his view of the market, before returning to his evolutionary theory.

Markets: competition within constraints

According to Hayek, "the fundamental principle of liberalism" lies in "a policy which deliberately adopts competition, the market, and prices as its ordering principles" (Hayek 1948a: 110). Apart from what he has to say on the socialist calculation issue, Hayek's main argument in favor of market competition is its role as a discovery process. Markets, he reasons, do not only allow for the utilization of knowledge fragmented and dispersed among innumerous individuals. They also promote the growth of problem-solving knowledge by providing an arena for trying out and competitively comparing tentative alternative solutions for a wide range of problems. Since we cannot know in advance what goods and services consumers will value most, nor how these goods and services can be produced most efficiently, we have good reasons, Hayek argues, to rely on markets as arenas in which the independent and competitive efforts of many result in a process of constant exploration and learning. Or, more generally, as we can never know in advance what the best solutions to our problems may be, we should make sure that the possibility as well as the incentives exist to try out new ways of doing things that may prove to be superior to existing practices.[40]

When Hayek suggests that the described features of market arrangements are desirable, he clearly means that they are desirable to the persons involved, in the sense that they "secure for any random member ... a better chance over a wide range of opportunities available to all than any rival system could offer" (Hayek 1988: 85). The competitive market process is claimed to be efficient in the sense that it serves the interests of the participants in the market nexus. Yet this claim is not an unconditional claim. It is not made for competition *per se*, irrespective of its terms, and not for any kind of "spontaneous" process, no matter what its particular nature. There are many different kinds of competition and of spontaneous processes conceivable, and Hayek's claim as to the efficiency of markets is, by no means, an unqualified claim that would include all of them. No less than those before him in the classical liberal tradition, he is quite explicit about the fact that, in order to have the noted desirable properties, market competition has to be constrained by *appropriate* "rules of the game," by a legal framework that guides the competitive efforts of market participants into socially productive directions.[41]

In fact, what liberals such as Hayek mean by *market competition* is *constitutionally constrained* competition, competition within rules that assure its beneficial working. As he points out, it has been commonly taken for granted in the liberal tradition that "a functioning market presupposes not only the prevention of violence and fraud but the protection of certain rights, such as property, and the enforcement of contracts" (Hayek 1948: 110f.).[42] Moreover, he sees this whole issue as a continuing challenge, as a problem that we cannot hope to solve once and for all but that requires us to monitor constantly the ways in which the existing "order of rules" affects the properties of the resulting "order of actions" under constantly changing circumstances and in the light of our constantly changing knowledge. As noted earlier, if he has any quarrels with his liberal predecessors, it is because, in his view, they did not always pay sufficient attention to the issues that arise *beyond* an acceptance of the general "principles of private property and freedom of contract" (ibid.: 111), namely to determine what, under given circumstances, the most appropriate *form* of the rules of property and contract may be.[43]

When Hayek advocates competitive markets as desirable social arrangements, it is quite obvious that he intends to make, in terms of the above distinction, a *conditional* rather than an *unconditional* claim about the workings of the competitive process. He views the market process as an explorative evolutionary process that occurs within a constraining framework of rules, and the beneficial working of the process is seen contingent on the nature of this framework. A logical conclusion which follows from such understanding is that, to the extent to which we can determine what conditions or rule constraints are favorable to the beneficial working of market competition, we may seek to create or establish such conditions.[44] In this sense, the concept of the market process as a spontaneous, evolutionary process and the notion of deliberate institutional design are not only compatible with each other. Rather, the liberal understanding of the institutional *requirements* for a well-working market implies that there is a role for what the German ordo-liberals called *Ordnungspolitik*, a policy aimed at providing and maintaining a suitable legal framework for a well-functioning market order. If, and to the extent that, an appropriate framework of rules cannot be expected to spring up "naturally," and to be maintained as well as continuously adjusted by spontaneous forces alone, deliberate efforts in institutional design and legislative reform are essential ingredients to a viable liberal order.

The ordo-liberals distinguished clearly between the spontaneous *internal* workings of the market and the question of how the institutional framework that conditions the market's operation is created and maintained. One of their central claims was that we cannot expect that the market will out of itself, through its own operation, generate and maintain a framework of rules that assures its beneficial working. The task of providing such a framework was, in their view, unavoidably a political task. Although Hayek's evolutionary argument occasionally sounds as if he believes in the spontaneous, endogenous generation of the rules within which markets operate,[45] such sporadic evidence is far outweighed by numerous arguments, for example those documented above (see pp. 55ff.), which clearly state the important role that he assigns to deliberate institutional reform, to "a policy which ... uses the legal framework enforced by the state in order to make competition as effective and beneficial as possible" (Hayek 1948a: 110).[46]

Understood as a *conditional* argument, Hayek's evolutionary account tells us that, on the one hand, we need to rely on competitive evolutionary processes as discovery procedures because we cannot know in advance what the best solutions to our problems may be, and that, on the other hand, we need to constrain evolutionary competition by a framework of appropriate rules in order to make it responsive to the interests of the persons involved. To the extent that the creation of such a framework requires deliberate legislative action, institutional design is not opposed to the role of spontaneous forces, but is a prerequisite for their beneficial working.

There is a second sense in which the market example shows that *design* and *evolutionary competition* are compatible and complementary notions. This aspect is quite obvious (and, therefore, rarely discussed explicitly) in the case of market processes, but it is far less obvious and more significant in the case of cultural evolution. A brief look at the market version of the argument can help to recognize more clearly its relevance for the discussion on cultural evolution. As noted earlier, from a Hayekian evolutionary perspective, the market can be viewed as an arena in which alternative solutions to a wide range of problems compete within the confines of certain rules of the game. The spontaneous nature of the competitive market process is dependent on the *nature* of these rules. But it is not necessary that these rules are themselves of spontaneous origin. They may well, as Hayek points out, be deliberately designed. This concerns the, previously noted, first sense in which *design* can be compatible with *spontaneous evolution*. The second sense in which such compatibility exists concerns the simple fact that the *inputs* into the competitive market process may well be *designed*, and this fact does not invalidate in the least the spontaneous, evolutionary nature of the overall process. The solutions to problems that are entered into the competition typically are, to a larger or lesser extent, the product of explicit rational planning. Cars and video-recorders are, of course, designed products. And the same is, to a large extent, true for the solutions to social–institutional problems that compete in markets, such as the organizational structure of business firms.

What is essential for an evolutionary process is *not* that its competing inputs are undesigned, nor that its constraining rules are of spontaneous origin. What is essential is that the framing rules are of a kind that allows for, and maintains, a competitive process with desirable characteristics, "desirable," that is, for the persons involved. A principal feature of a well-functioning competitive order is, in Hayek's account, its openness to the entry of alternative, and potentially superior, solutions to problems. Such a competitive order, he argues,

> ... does not presuppose what economic theory calls "perfect competition" but only that there are no obstacles to the entry into each trade and that the market functions adequately in spreading information about opportunities.
>
> (Hayek 1967: 174)[47]

And – with an eye to what he considers a misguided concern of some "neoliberals" with the issue of market power – he notes specifically on the monopoly issue that "it is not monopoly but only the prevention of competition" (Hayek 1979a: 83) which constitutes the real problem. Monopolies may, Hayek argues, "even be a desirable result of competition" (ibid.: 73) as long as they maintain their position "solely by serving their customers better than anyone else, and not by preventing those who think they could do still better from trying to do so" (ibid.).

Cultural evolution and designed inputs

My principal conjecture in this chapter is that Hayek's theory of cultural evolution, in order to be a meaningful and consistent part of his liberal philosophy, must be interpreted in light of his argument on market competition. That is to say, it must be read not as an argument about institutional competition *per se*, in whatever terms it might occur, but as a *conditional* claim about the workings of evolutionary competition within certain constraints, within a framework of appropriate rules. If interpreted in this fashion, Hayek's argument on cultural evolution is just as compatible with the notion of deliberate design as is his argument on market competition. It allows for the institutional inputs into the evolutionary process to be designed. And it requires deliberate efforts in creating and maintaining a framework of rules that serves to make the evolutionary process work in favor of beneficial institutions, i.e. institutions that are desirable to their constituents. The first issue will be discussed in the this section, and the second will be discussed in the following section.[48]

Deliberate institutional reforms are an essential part of the experimental *input* into the evolutionary process. Although part of this input may indeed, as Hayek (1960: 32) suggests, consist of "undesigned novelties that constantly emerge in the process of adaptation," *designed* novelties surely play an important part as well. There is no contradiction between the notion of deliberate institutional design and the notion of a competitive evolutionary process, just as there is no contradiction between the notion of deliberate organized production and the notion of a spontaneous market process in which such deliberate production experiments compete. What is essential for the overall process to be of an evolutionary nature is that the experimental inputs are subject to competitive selection in an environment that is open for the entry of new challengers.

Similar to his view on market competition, Hayek's view on cultural evolution is based on the argument that in the realm of rules, no less than in other areas of problem-solving efforts, we need to rely on competition as a *discovery procedure* (Hayek 1978: 149; 1979a: 67ff.). And his argument against "constructivist rationalism" in the realm of rules and institutions is not meant as an objection against institutional design *per se*, but against excessive claims that ignore the limits of our knowledge and reason. It is an argument against the "pretence of knowledge" that underlies proposals for a total redesign of our social order,[49] and it is an argument against exclusive privileges and monopolistic power in institutional matters. Or, stated positively, it is an argument for piecemeal and corrigible reforms, for reforms that are carried out in awareness of the fallibility of our efforts. And it is an argument for competitive arrangements in which alternative conjectural solutions can be compared, and established practices can be challenged by new institutional "conjectures," whether these are deliberately designed or emerge unintendedly. "The relevant distinction" is, as Hayek (1960: 37) puts it,

> ... between conditions, on the one hand, in which alternative ways based on different views or practices may be tried and conditions, on the other, in which one agency has the exclusive right and the power to prevent others from trying.

Hayek's argument in favor of utilizing the explorative potential of competitive evolutionary settings cannot sensibly be meant as an argument against the use of rational analysis and of reason in matters of institutional reform, and he explicitly states that it is not:

> None of these conclusions are arguments against the use of reason, but only arguments against such uses as require any exclusive and coercive powers of government; not arguments against experimentation, but arguments against all exclusive, monopolistic power to experiment in a particular field – power which brooks no alternative and which lays a claim to the possession of superior wisdom – and against the consequent preclusion of solutions better than the ones to which those in power have committed themselves.
>
> (Hayek 1960: 70)[50]

In contrast to the constructivist rationalism that he rejects, Hayek suggests that his own approach may be properly characterized as "evolutionary rationalism" (Hayek 1973: 5). And it is apparent that with this label he wants to describe an attitude that combines the notion of rational institutional reform with the willingness to have one's designs exposed to an environment in which they can be challenged by alternative, and potentially superior, constructions.

He does not advocate, as he puts it, "an abdication of reason" (Hayek 1960: 69), but an awareness of its conjectural nature and its use within a framework in which it is subject to the discipline of an experimental and competitive process.

To advocate the utilization of competitive evolutionary processes as a critical check on our institutional constructions is not the same as to claim that we could get along without any rational institutional design. Such a claim would be analogous to advocating a competitive automobile market and saying that this market could function without the design work of engineers and production planners. Furthermore, the argument for the utilization of evolutionary competition *is itself a rational argument*. It is the argument that a proper insight into the limits of our knowledge and reason should lead us, *on rational grounds*, to stay away from exclusive, monopolistic solutions and to opt, instead, in favor of competitive frameworks. We should use our reason and knowledge in attempting to improve the order of rules under which we live. But we should take into account and prepare for the fact that our designs are fallible, that they may turn out to be failures or inferior to potential alternatives.[51]

It is in the above sense that Hayek sees liberalism based "on an insight into the limits of the powers of human reason" (Hayek 1967: 161), and that he speaks of "that intellectual humility which is the essence of the true liberalism that regards with reverence those spontaneous social forces through which the individual creates things greater than he knows" (Hayek 1992: 244). What is meant is surely not that liberalism would advise against the use of human reason in matters of social organization but, instead, that liberalism argues *on rational grounds* why the recognition of the limits of reason should lead us to favor certain kinds of institutional arrangements. In other words, it provides a rational argument about the appropriate conclusions that, with regard to the problem of social reform, we should draw from the insight into the limits of reason.

The principal conclusion that Hayek suggests to us is that in no area of human problem-solving efforts, neither in those that we entrust to ordinary markets nor in those which we seek to solve through the political process, can we know in advance what the "best solution" may be, and that, therefore, we ought to rely on competitive, explorative processes wherever possible.

Evolution within constraints: the role of *Ordnungspolitik*

A sensible interpretation of Hayek's theory of cultural evolution must be to view it as a conditional claim about evolutionary competition. If read as an unconditional claim about cultural evolution *per se*, Hayek's evolutionary argument makes little sense, and it would be inconsistent with the liberal thrust of his work. Yet, although it needs clearly to be understood as a conditional claim, Hayek has made very little effort to state explicitly what the relevant characteristics of a beneficial process of cultural evolution are, i.e. of a process that selects in favor of rules which are desirable to the persons in the relevant constituency. This means that we have to reconstruct his notion of a properly constrained process from his writings. And, as noted above, we can gain important suggestions on this issue from his arguments on market processes. Just as his argument on market competition is a conditional argument, namely that competition works beneficially provided it is constrained by appropriate rules, his argument on cultural evolution as a process of competitive selection among rules and institutions needs to be qualified in similar ways.

That Hayek has in mind a process with particular characteristics rather than just any kind of process when he attributes desirable working properties to cultural evolution is implied when he talks about "coercive interference in the process of cultural evolution" (Hayek 1988: 20), when he notes that the "evolution of rules was far from unhindered" (ibid.), or when he deplores that, for instance in the case of monetary institutions, "selective processes are interfered with" (Hayek 1988: 103), and that "selection by evolution is prevented by government monopolies that make competitive experimentation impossible" (ibid.). Such comments clearly imply that, as a standard of reference, Hayek has a "proper" evolutionary process in mind. And the general attributes of this process can be inferred from his argument on the workings of market competition. Like the latter, the competitive process of cultural evolution can be said to require a framework of appropriate rules if it is to work to the benefit of the persons involved. As noted earlier, competition can conceivably be carried out with all kinds of strategies and on all kinds of terms, including warfare and genocide. And we surely cannot expect that the terms of competition leave unaffected what kinds of institutions are likely to survive. It is only for a properly constrained competitive process that we can predict working attributes which qualify as desirable if measured against liberal standards, namely as desirable to the persons involved.

Consistency requires that all the arguments made above about Hayek's conception of a beneficially working market process be extended to his notion of cultural evolution if both theories are to be considered as parts of a coherent liberal philosophy. This includes, in particular, what has been said about the role of liberal legislation or *Ordnungspolitik*. If, and to the extent that, the rule constraints that serve to make the process of evolutionary competition work beneficially can be identified, efforts to create and maintain such constraints become a principal task of liberal reform. In a sense, with Hayek's theory of cultural evolution, the argument on the prerequisites for beneficially working markets is shifted one level upwards. At both levels, i.e. at the level of ordinary market competition and at the level of institutional competition, the concern of liberal legislation or *Ordnungspolitik* lies in creating and maintaining a framework of rules within which a dynamic, evolutionary process of experimentation and exploration can take place that advances human interests. We can assume that it is this kind of institutional politics that Hayek has in mind when he speaks of "liberal constitutionalism" (Hayek 1969: 199), and when he talks of the task to provide "a beneficial framework for the free growth of society" (Hayek 1979a: 152), the task to "create the conditions in which society can gradually evolve improved formations" (ibid.: 14).[52]

Hayek has been quite explicit about the role of liberal legislation or *Ordnungspolitik* with regard to the market process.[53] Yet, just as he has not been very explicit about the relevant constraints that are required for a beneficially working process of cultural evolution, he has been conspicuously silent about the role of *Ordnungspolitik* at this level. A principal reason for this seems to me to lie in Hayek's failure to take into account the difference between two kinds of "design approaches," a difference that he clearly recognizes in his discussion on market processes. There, he emphasizes the distinction between *Ordnungspolitik* (without using this term, though) and *interventionism*, i.e. between a policy that seeks to provide a beneficial framework of rules within which market processes can unfold and a policy that seeks to bring about particular outcomes by intervening in the market process by specific measures.[54] While Hayek objects to the second type of policy on the grounds that it runs counter to the very working properties of markets, he expressly states that the first is not only compatible with market principles but is the main instrument by which we can seek to make markets work better.[55] Logic requires that the same distinction between types of policies be made with regard to the process of institutional competition that Hayek's theory of cultural evolution is concerned with. Here, too, we need to distinguish between, on the one hand, a policy that seeks to constrain the process of cultural evolution by a framework of rules, and, on the other, a policy that intervenes into the evolutionary process with specific measures in order to secure particular, predetermined outcomes. The first type of policy, an *Ordnungspolitik for cultural evolution*, is both compatible with an evolutionary process and a principal instrument for conditioning its general working properties. The second, by contrast, clearly falls under the same verdict that Hayek pronounces on interventionist policies in ordinary markets. Just as we cannot, at the same time, enjoy the benefits of the explorative potential of market processes *and* assure specific, predetermined results, we cannot benefit from the discovery procedure of cultural evolution and, at the same time, seek to direct the evolutionary process toward particular, predetermined outcomes.

That at the level of cultural evolution just as at the level of ordinary market processes we need to distinguish between legitimate *Ordnungspolitik* and objectionable interventionism, is an insight that can clearly be reconstructed from Hayek's argument, but that he has not explicitly recognized. To the contrary, his comments on the issue sound as if he considers any effort to guide the process to fall under the verdict of interventionism. Referring to what he describes as the "morally blind results" of cultural evolution, he argues, for instance:

> Understandable aversion to such morally blind results, results inseparable from any process of trial-and-error, leads men to want to achieve a contradiction in terms: namely, to wrest control of evolution – i.e. of the procedure of trial-and-error – and to shape it to their present wishes.
>
> (Hayek 1988: 74)

Such comments seem to ignore the critical difference between seeking to condition the general nature of a trial-and-error process by means of a framework of rules of the game and seeking to direct such a process toward predetermined outcomes. To seek "to wrest control of evolution" in the second sense is, indeed, clearly incompatible with the open-ended nature of an evolutionary process, and on such efforts Hayek may rightly comment that "evolution cannot be guided by and often will not produce what men demand" (ibid.)

Hayek is certainly right when he notes that to "confine evolution to what we can foresee would be to stop progress" (Hayek 1979a: 169), but when he points out that we can "create conditions favorable to it" (ibid.) he implicitly acknowledges that there is a legitimate role for *Ordnungspolitik* at the level of cultural evolution, in much the same way in which it plays a role at the level of ordinary markets. And Hayek is equally right when he says that "to pretend to know the desirable direction of progress seems to me to be the extreme of hubris" (ibid.), but, again, this does not mean at all that we could not seek to use appropriate constraining rules to shape the general working properties of the evolutionary process in a desirable manner.

To use criteria for judging what kinds of institutions are desirable, and to determine the characteristics of evolutionary processes that are likely to select in favor of such institutions, is something totally different from claiming to be able to determine in advance which particular results the process will generate. As I have sought to show above, Hayek's work clearly implies a criterion for evaluating institutions, namely the individualist standard that institutions should be considered desirable if, and to the extent that, they are judged so by their individual constituents. And his argument on the institutional prerequisites for beneficially working markets clearly suggests that an analogous argument can be made for cultural evolution as a process of institutional competition. Here, too, we can seek to determine, and then to establish, the rule constraints that promise to guide the evolutionary process into selecting in favor of rules and institutions that are desirable to the persons involved (Vanberg 1994a; Vanberg and Kerber 1994).

Conclusion

Once the (necessarily) conditional nature of Hayek's arguments on market competition and on cultural evolution is fully appreciated, the systematic connection between his evolutionary emphasis and his emphasis on the positive tasks of liberal legislation can be understood. We need, this is his argument, to rely on evolutionary competitive processes as discovery procedures because we cannot know in advance what the best solutions to our problems may be (nor can we know in advance what new problems we may face tomorrow). On the other hand, in order to make evolutionary competitive processes operate responsively to the interests of the individuals involved, we need to impose appropriate rule constraints. And as we cannot know in advance what the most appropriate constraints may be, we need to rely, on the level of rules as well, on competition as a discovery procedure.

This integrated concept of cultural evolution and liberal legislation suggests a liberal perspective that appreciates Hayek's evolutionary argument without adopting the agnostic attitude that is characteristic of some of the contemporary reception of Hayekian evolutionism. And it suggests a liberal perspective that emphasizes the positive task of liberal legislation in establishing an appropriate institutional framework for market competition and cultural evolution, without taking on the rationalist arrogance that is the target of Hayek's critique of rational constructivism. It suggests a liberal perspective that sees a role for deliberate legislation in constraining evolution, and in designing institutions that are subjected to the forces of evolutionary competition. And it sees a role for evolution in assisting and testing our efforts in deliberate institutional design.

5 Hayek's theory of rules and the modern state

Introduction

Hayek has a highly skeptical view of the modern state, if by "modern state" we mean the kinds of government that are usually subsumed under the rubric *Western democracies*. The "particular set of institutions which today prevails in all Western democracies" (Hayek 1979a: 1), he tells us in his study on *Law, Legislation and Liberty*, "produces an aggregate of measures that not only is not wanted by anybody, but that could not as a whole be approved by any rational mind because it is inherently contradictory" (ibid.: 6). There are, Hayek claims, "certain deeply entrenched defects of construction of the generally accepted type of 'democratic' government" (ibid.: xiii) that "lead us away from the ideals it was intended to serve," that let us drift "towards a system which nobody wanted" (Hayek 1973: 3). And it is his diagnosis of these defects that made him, as he notes, "think through alternative arrangements" (Hayek 1979a: xiii) and led him to come up with "a proposal of basic alteration of the structure of democratic government" (ibid.), "a suggestion for a radical departure from established tradition" (Hayek 1973: 4).

Hayek's critique of Western democratic institutions and his proposals for reform – as detailed, in particular, in the chapter on "A model constitution" in volume III of *Law, Legislation and Liberty* (Hayek 1979a: 105–27) – are well known. What is, however, less well understood is how they fit into his overall approach. In fact, a number of commentators have pointed to the discrepancy that they see between, on the one side, the rationalist flavor of his argument on the reform of democratic institutions and, on the other side, his critique of what he calls *constructivist rationalism* (or *rationalist constructivism*), a critique that plays such a fundamental role in his system of thought. While the thrust of this critique is to warn us against jeopardizing the implicit wisdom of traditional institutions by rationalist reconstruction, it seems as if Hayek ignores his own warnings when, with regard to the institutions of Western democracies, he calls "for a radical departure from established tradition" (Hayek 1973: 4), for "institutional invention" (ibid.: 3) and "constitutional design" (ibid.: 4).

My purpose in this chapter is to show how the two components of his work, despite their seeming inconsistency, can be understood in a manner that constitutes a coherent argument. More specifically, I want to argue that Hayek's critique of the institutions of Western democracies, and his suggestions for their reform, are consistent with, and systematically connected with, core assumptions of his work, in particular the *theory of rules* that informs his critique of constructivist rationalism.

Constructivist rationalism and the role of rules

Closer inspection shows that Hayek's critique of constructivist rationalism is directed against two distinguishable notions which I propose to call *constructivist rationalism I* and *constructivist rationalism II*.

The critique of constructivist rationalism I is central to Hayek's rejection of the notion of central planning, i.e. his rejection of the "claim that man can achieve a desirable order of society by concretely arranging all its parts in full knowledge of all the relevant facts" (Hayek 1967: 88). Such a claim, Hayek argues, "ignores the limitations that are set to the powers of reason" (ibid.), it implies "a colossal presumption concerning our intellectual powers" (ibid.: 90). Not only is it, according to Hayek, impossible for a single person to co-ordinate "his activities successfully through a full explicit evaluation of the consequences of all possible alternatives of action, and in full knowledge of all possible circumstances" (ibid.). It is *a fortiori* impossible to co-ordinate innumerable individual actions in such manner. It is impossible for anyone to take "conscious account of all the particular facts which enter into the order of society" (Hayek 1973: 13f.), "on which the overall order of the activities in a Great Society is based" (Hayek 1976a: 8). The limits of our knowledge and reason make it necessary for us, Hayek asserts, to *rely on rules* in our personal affairs and even more so in the social realm. The rationalist–constructivist claim "that conscious reason ought to determine every particular action" (Hayek 1973: 29) ignores the need for rules. It fails to see that the "whole rationale of the phenomenon of rule-guided action" (Hayek 1976a: 20), the fact that "makes rules necessary," lies in our "inescapable ignorance of most of the particular circumstances which determine the effects of our actions" (ibid.).[1]

Hayek's critique of what I classify here as constructivist rationalism I is, in summary, directed against the claim that we can create a desirable social order by discretionary planning and particular commands, by centrally directing the "activities of all ... according to a single plan laid down by a central authority" (Hayek 1967: 82). The alternative view that he advocates emphasizes the notion "of a self-generating or spontaneous order in social affairs" (ibid.: 162), a notion that was espoused by Adam Smith and other authors in the classical liberal tradition.[2] It is the notion of an order that is not the product of deliberate design, but, instead, emerges as an unintended outcome from the mutual adjustments of individuals who are left free to pursue their own purposes, based on their own knowledge, within the constraints of a framework of general rules of conduct; rules that typically specify what they may not do, instead of telling them what they have to do. Hayek's familiar argument in favor of such spontaneously formed order is that it makes possible the utilization of far more knowledge than a deliberately arranged and centrally planned order could ever do.[3] To be sure, Hayek acknowledges that deliberate organization and central direction can be an efficient principle of co-ordination for limited purposes, such as the co-ordination within firms, or in organizations more generally. What he disputes is that it can be successfully extended to an entire economy or society. In Hayek's view, this is simply not feasible and, if tried, can only result in an undesirable order.[4]

Because it is based on general rules, the nature of a spontaneous order depends on the nature of these rules. There is, as Hayek puts it, a systematic connection between the *order of rules* and the *order of actions* that results from these rules,[5] a connection that is illustrated, for instance, by the manner in which the resulting pattern of actions in a game of sports is dependent on the rules of the game. The freedom of individual choice within a framework of general rules allows, as noted before, for the utilization of more knowledge in a rule-based spontaneous order, and it accounts for the potential superiority of spontaneous over centrally planned orders. Yet, this does not *per se* assure that the resulting order of actions is "desirable" from the perspective of the persons involved. Whether this is the case or not will depend on the *nature of the rules*.[6] For a desirable or beneficial order to result, rules are required that are suitable or appropriate to that task; a fact that, as Hayek notes, the classical liberal advocates of the spontaneous market order were well aware of,[7] that, however, some of their later successors in the liberal tradition did not always sufficiently appreciate.[8]

This raises, of course, the issue of how we can expect suitable and appropriate rules to come about, and how we can hope to achieve improvements in these rules.[9] It is with regard to this issue that the part of Hayek's critique of constructivist rationalism becomes relevant that targets what I propose to call constructivist rationalism II. Hayek's critique of constructivist rationalism in the realm of rules is not an outright rejection of the idea of rational institutional design, it is a rejection of the presumptuous rationalist claim "that it is both possible and desirable to reconstruct all grown institutions in accordance with a preconceived plan" (Hayek 1967: 161). It is a critique of a mind set that ignores the extent to which, in our efforts to improve our rules and institutions, we need to rely on experience that has been made in the past and that has been transmitted to us in our cultural traditions (ibid.: 88).[10]

Not only does Hayek not deny the role of deliberate institutional reform but he explicitly argues that such efforts are our principal means to improve our social condition. His critique of constructivist rationalism I implies that it is impossible for us to create a desirable social order by deliberate arrangement, and that it is, for the same reasons, also impossible to improve the order of society by specific interventions. As we need, in his account, to rely on rules as co-ordinating devices in order to achieve a desirable social order, we need to rely on *improvements in these rules* in order to improve the order of actions. The principal means for improving our social condition is, therefore, to *improve the rules of the game*.[11] In fact, he notes that his rejection of central planning is not about "whether we ought to choose intelligently between the various possible organizations of society" (Hayek 1978: 234), and he explicitly contrasts the kind of "central planning" which he rejects, with what he calls the "liberal plan," the deliberate reform of the framework of rules and institutions.[12] Hayek insists, though, that such efforts in institutional reform can only aim at "piecemeal change" (Hayek 1960: 114), rather than at an effort in total reconstruction.[13] As Hayek puts it, "although we must always strive to improve our institutions, we can never aim to remake them as a whole" (ibid.: 63). Furthermore, our efforts in deliberate reform ought to be carried out in the awareness of the fallibility of our design, in the recognition that the process of institutional change can only be an experimental process of trial and error.[14]

It is in the context of his criticism of constructivist rationalism II that Hayek introduces the notion of "cultural evolution," by which he primarily means the decentralized process where, *within* a society or polity, different individuals or groups of persons experiment with alternative practices and where from these competing practices the ones that are perceived as more advantageous become more widely adopted whereas others are abandoned as less successful. Interpreted in this sense, cultural evolution is in contrast to legislation, the latter being a mechanism for *deliberate* rule change through the political process of collective choice.[15] Note, however, that, as indicated above, Hayek's criticism of constructivist rationalism II is not an argument against legislation *per se*, even if its general thrust certainly favors the decentralized evolutionary process in which, for instance, customs and traditions develop or which is, in some sense, exemplified by the common law process. Yet, Hayek explicitly acknowledges that such spontaneous evolution may not work for all kinds of rules on which the order of society is based,[16] nor can it be expected to work beneficially under all circumstances.[17] And he points to the special role of the rules of law "which, because we can deliberately alter them, become the chief instrument whereby we can affect the resulting order" (Hayek 1973: 45).[18] There is, as he argues, "ample scope for experimentation and improvement within that permanent legal framework which makes it possible for a free society to operate most efficiently," and he adds: "We can probably at no point be certain that we have already found the best arrangements or institutions" (Hayek 1960: 231).

Notwithstanding his emphasis on the spontaneous evolution of rules and institutions, Hayek expressly recognizes the role of legislation, of deliberate institutional reform through political, collective choice. Both cultural evolution and legislation have their place in his understanding of how the institutional–constitutional framework of society changes over time. For the purposes of this chapter, I can set aside the issues raised by Hayek's notion of cultural evolution,[19] and concentrate exclusively on his view of the role of legislation. In what follows, I shall examine Hayek's understanding of legislation as part of the political process, and his understanding of the relation between the institutional framework of politics, in particular the institutional framework of Western democracies, and the working properties of the legislative process.

The rules of government and the order of politics

As noted earlier, the social order that we call "society" is, in Hayek's account, necessarily a spontaneous order. It comprises, however, many organizations, one of which is the special organization called "state," which Hayek defines as "the organization of the people of a territory under a single government" (Hayek 1979a: 140).[20]

Hayek sees the principal task of government in creating and maintaining a suitable framework of rules within which individuals, separately and in groups, can successfully pursue their purposes. This task includes, as its most essential part, the enforcement of the "body of abstract rules which are required to secure the formation of the spontaneous overall order" (Hayek 1964: 10),[21] as well as the task of improving and further developing the framework of rules as circumstances change.[22] Hayek sees a secondary task of governments in what he calls their "service functions," i.e. the rendering of "other services which the spontaneous order cannot produce adequately" (Hayek 1978: 111).[23] How well government performs its functions will depend on how it is organized, or, in other words, on its organizational structure. It is in the context of this issue that Hayek's critique of prevailing forms of Western democracy and his proposals for reform have to be evaluated.

In Hayek's distinction between "two kinds of social order" (1964; 1973: 36 ff.), he contrasts, in first approximation, *spontaneous order* and *organization* as *rule*-based and *command*-based orders. A spontaneous social order results from the mutual adaptation of separate individual choices made within a framework of general rules of conduct. In an organization-type order, by contrast, a central authority gives instructions or commands to participating actors. As Hayek points out, however, an organization beyond even a minimal level of complexity cannot entirely operate on specific commands, but has also to use rules as co-ordinating devices.[24] In this sense, organizations are also "rule-based" orders, although, as Hayek explains, there are "important differences between the kinds of rules which the two kinds of order require" (Hayek 1973: 48). By contrast to the *general rules of conduct* on which spontaneous orders are based, organizational rules are "rules for the performance of assigned tasks," they are "different for the different members of the organization according to the different roles which have been assigned to them" (ibid.: 49). Insofar as organizations are themselves based on rules, we can, with regard to them too, speak of the connection between the *order of rules* and the *order of actions*, in a sense similar to what was said above about spontaneous orders even though the nature of the rules, and the nature of the connection between rules and the resulting order, are critically different in the two cases. In the case of spontaneous orders, the general rules of conduct are the principal co-ordinating devices. Within the general constraints that they define, individuals are left free to pursue their own purposes in ways that they see fit. Within organizations, not only are the relevant rules different in nature. Individuals are also placed within a hierarchy of authority; and a principal instrument of co-ordination is the specific commands issued within that hierarchy.

What is true for organizations in general is also true for the special organization that we call government, namely that "beyond its simplest and most primitive forms, [it] also cannot be conducted exclusively by *ad hoc* commands of the ruler" (Hayek 1973: 124), but "will require distinct rules of its own which determine its structure, aims, and functions" (ibid.).[25] The rules which "determine the organization of government" (Hayek 1976a: 31) make up what we can call, in a broad sense, the *constitution* of a state. More specifically, the rules that are commonly subsumed under this label can themselves be divided into two categories, namely into *constituting* and *limiting* rules of government. The constituting rules are organizational rules in the strict sense (Hayek 1973: 134), i.e. they are "chiefly concerned with the organization of government and the allocation of the different powers to the various parts of this organization" (Hayek 1979a: 37). Or, in other words, they define the procedures that allow the multitude of persons who make up a polity to engage in organized collective action. They constitute government in the sense of enabling it to operate as an organized unit.[26] The limiting rules, by contrast, are more like "rules of conduct" in the sense that they define general constraints on what the organization "government" or its agents may do, similar to the way in which the general rules of conduct on which the spontaneous order of society is based define limits on what individuals are allowed to do in their private capacities.[27] In fact, what we mean by "government under the law" is a government that is subject to the specific limits defined for it in the constitution, as well as to the (applicable) general rules of conduct that constrain its citizens (Hayek 1979a: 123).[28]

What has been said earlier about the connection between the order of rules and the order of actions can be applied, with the above qualifications, to the connection between the *constitutional order of rules* and the *order of political actions* that emerges under these rules.[29] To be sure, what the political process generates will critically depend on what particular policies are chosen within the constraints that the constitutional rules define. Yet, the nature of these rules will affect the general nature of the political order that results, similar to the ways in which the general rules of conduct affect the general nature of the spontaneous order of actions that emerges from these rules. As the suitability of the latter rules is, in Hayek's account, to be judged in terms of the quality of the spontaneous order that they help to form, the suitability of the rules of politics is to be judged in terms of the quality of the overall political order, or the pattern of political outcomes, that they generate. The rules of politics determine the general working properties of the political process. Although political outcomes can surely be "improved" by the selection of "better" politicians and the choice of "better" policies, the overall order of politics will critically depend on the order of constitutional rules, and it is through an improvement in these rules that we can hope to achieve a systematic improvement in the order of politics similar to the sense in which it was said above that an improvement in its framework of rules is the principal means of improving the spontaneous order of society.[30]

It is in the context of this notion of the interrelation between the order of constitutional rules and the order of politics that Hayek's critique of the prevailing form of Western democracy and his proposals for constitutional reform have to be seen. As he emphasizes, the deficiencies that he sees in this form of government are "not due to a failure of the principle of democracy as such" (Hayek 1979a: 98), but result from the "particular set of institutions" (ibid.: 1) that have been adopted. In his view, it is because of its particular institutional structure that the democratic process tends to "produce aggregate results that few people have either wanted or foreseen" (ibid.).[31] And it is only through a correction of the defects in the constitutional framework that he sees a prospect for systematic improvement in the resulting pattern of political outcomes.

The constitutional defects of majoritarian democracy

As noted earlier, for Hayek the principal task of government lies in maintaining an "appropriate" framework of rules, i.e. a framework that allows for a spontaneous order of society with desirable characteristics, a task that includes the effective enforcement of existing rules as well as their adaptation and improvement over time. The principle measuring rod by which, from Hayek's perspective, the performance of government should, therefore, be evaluated is its capacity to fulfill this task, and it is in this regard that Hayek finds fault with "the particular set of institutions which today prevails in all Western democracies, and in which a majority of a representative body lays down the law and directs government" (Hayek 1979a: 1).

Hayek's critique of the "present structure of democratic government" is focused on what he considers its principal defect, namely the "fact that we have charged the representative assemblies with two altogether different tasks" (ibid.: 22): on the one side, "the articulation and approval of general rules of conduct" and, on the other side, "the direction of the measures of government concerning particular matters" (ibid.). When he speaks of the "deeply entrenched defects of construction of the generally accepted type of 'democratic' government" (ibid.: xiii), Hayek has in mind the combination of these two different functions within the same body, called "legislature," a combination because of which "the task of stating rules of just conduct and the task of directing particular activities of government to specific ends would come to be hopelessly confounded" (ibid.: 105). This has, in Hayek's account, lead to a situation in which

> … we have not only forgotten that government is different from legislation but have come to think that an instruction to government to take particular actions is the normal content of an act of law-giving.
>
> (Ibid.: 22)[32]

The most serious consequence that, in Hayek's view, resulted from the misconstruction that he identifies is that it critically undermines the capacity of the democratic legislature to go about its principal assignment, namely to deal with "the grave and difficult questions of the improvement of the legal framework, or of the framework of rules within which the struggle of divergent interests ought to be conducted" (ibid.: 27). It has had the effect, he argues, that the legislative role became subservient to the administrative role,

> ... that the very structure and organization of the representative assemblies has been determined by the needs of their governmental tasks but is unfavourable to wise rule-making.
>
> (Ibid.: 22)[33]

The main reason for this is that, although rules should be chosen for their long-term effects, the temptation for a governmental assembly that has legislative powers is too great to define the rules according to its current administrative expediencies, in particular the rules that are to impose constraints on what it may do.[34] As Hayek (1979a: 26) puts it:

> An assembly whose chief task is to decide what particular things should be done, and which in a parliamentary democracy supervises its executive committee (called government) in the carrying out of a general program of action approved by it, has no inducement or interest to tie itself by general rules.

We cannot, he argues, trust such an assembly to be fit to define the rules that are to bind its own choices, no more than we would expect an individual person to be fit to make practical choices and, at the same time, to choose the moral rules that that person is supposed to obey in making these choices.[35] As Hayek charges, such an arrangement means in effect that there are no effective limits on the power of the democratic legislature, it means "the unlimited power of the democratically elected assembly" (ibid.: 20).[36]

While he emphasizes that it "is not democracy or representative government as such, but the particular institutions, chosen by us" (ibid.: 11) that are to blame for the problems which he identifies, Hayek sees a systematic connection between the rise of the ideal of democracy and the lessened appreciation for the role of constitutional limits on governmental power. Constitutionalism, i.e. the ideal of limited government, long preceded, as Hayek notes, the rise of democracy. As he points out, efforts to limit the power of government extended over centuries, and they were "the great aim of the founders of constitutional government in the seventeenth and eighteenth century" (Hayek 1973: 128). Yet, with the "victory of the democratic ideal" (Hayek 1979a: 101), the concern for constitutional limits on government seemed to have faded away, fueled, presumably, by the implicit assumption that such limits are expendable where government is under democratic control, an assumption that Hayek characterizes as a "tragic illusion."[37]

The belief that a democratic control of government "would adequately replace the traditional limitations" (ibid.: 3), or that the "democratic control of the exercise of power provided a sufficient safeguard against its excessive growth" (ibid.: 128), is, in Hayek's eyes, an illusion because it fails to appreciate that the "ideal of a democratic control of government and that of the limitation of government by law" (ibid.: 26) are different ideals, ideals that are compatible and that can complement each other but that cannot be substituted for each other. Whereas the latter, liberalism, is concerned with the functions of government and particularly with the extent and limitations of its power, the former, democracy, "is concerned with the question of who is to direct government" (Hayek 1978: 143).[38] Another factor that, according to Hayek, further contributed to the rise of *unlimited democracy* is an erroneous concept of "popular sovereignty," which confused the (correct) notion that, in a democracy, the people are the ultimate sovereign and, as such, are not subject to any other power with the (erroneous) notion that their power should not be subject to any limitations. As Hayek (1979a: 33) puts it, the error with this concept of popular sovereignty

> lies not in the belief that whatever power there is should be in the hands of the people, and that their wishes will have to be expressed by majority decisions, but in the belief that this ultimate source of power must be unlimited.

Because of the absence of effective limitations on the authority of democratic legislatures, Western democracy means, in effect, unlimited democracy,[39] a fact that, as Hayek argues, has, in particular, two interrelated detrimental consequences. First of all, an unlimited legislature, not prevented from decreeing discriminatory measures, cannot avoid acting in an "unprincipled manner" (Hayek 1978: 157). Lacking the guidance that only the genuine commitment to general principles can provide, it will tend to generate an aggregate of incoherent and contradictory outcomes that leaves almost everybody unsatisfied.[40] Second, and seemingly paradoxically, the very fact of its *unlimited power* makes democratic government in the end a very weak government because "a government with unlimited powers will be forced to secure the continued support of a majority, to use its unlimited powers in the service of special interests – such groups as particular trades, the inhabitants of particular regions, etc." (ibid.: 107).[41] The "domination of government by coalitions of organized interests" is, as Hayek (1979a: 15) suggests, an "inescapable result of a system in which government has unlimited powers to take whatever measures are required to satisfy the wishes of those on whose support it relies."[42]

Invoking a theme that modern public choice theory discusses under the rubric of *rent-seeking* (Buchanan *et al.* 1980), Hayek (1979a: 138) argues that the presence of an "omnipotent and omnicompetent single democratic assembly" necessarily invites rent-seeking by special interests, i.e. efforts to secure privileges of some sort. In consequence, "an ever larger part of human activity is diverted from production into political efforts" (ibid.), seeking wealth not by providing services for others in the marketplace but, instead, through redistribution via the political mechanism. And, at the same time, the "arbitrariness and partiality" (ibid.: 3) that the discriminatory granting of special benefits implies undermines the fundamental working principles of the spontaneous order of society and the market.[43]

Like public choice theorists, Hayek insists that the deficiencies of such political regime have their principal roots in a defective institutional structure, i.e. in the rules of the game, not in personality defects of the politicians who operate under these rules. Given the rules as they are, Hayek notes "even a statesman wholly devoted to the common interest of all the citizens will be under the constant necessity of satisfying special interests" (1978: 108).[44] A systematic cure can, therefore, not be expected from appeals to politicians to resist more steadfastly the pressures from special interests, it can only come from a reform of the institutional structure itself.[45]

Constitutional reform

As Hayek is eager to stress, the malfunctioning of the common form of modern democratic government is, in his view, "not due to a failure of the principle of democracy as such but to our having tried it the wrong way" (Hayek 1979a: 98), and he declares: "It is because I am anxious to rescue the true ideal ... that I am trying to find out the mistake we made and how we can prevent the bad consequences of the democratic procedure we have observed" (ibid.).

According to Hayek, our Western "predominant model of liberal democratic institutions" (Hayek 1973: 2) is derived from the "conception of a limiting constitution" (ibid.: 1) that had grown up in England, and that inspired, in particular, the framers of the American Constitution. Although acknowledging the achievements of "the American experiment in constitutionalism," Hayek (1960: 191) suggests that its method of limiting government through the separation of powers must, from today's perspective, be regarded as a failure in the sense that it did not achieve, in the long run, what it was meant to accomplish, namely "to provide institutional safeguards of individual freedom" (Hayek 1973: 1).[46] That the Western model of constitutionally limited democratic government worked fairly well in its original setting over a significant period of time must, in Hayek's assessment, be attributed to "unwritten traditions and beliefs, which ... had for a long time restrained the abuse of the majority power" (Hayek 1979a: 108). Yet, with the erosion of these informal constraints, and with the "export" of the Western model into different cultural environments, it became, as he suggests, apparent that the formal constitutional framework in and by itself does not provide a sufficient safeguard against a continuous expansion of the power of democratic government.[47]

Hayek's conclusion from the above diagnosis is that a new attempt needs to be made at solving "the problem in which the founders of liberal constitutionalism failed" (Hayek 1973: 4). What, in his view, is needed is a genuine revival of the constitutionalist ideal "that the power of all authorities exercising governmental functions ought to be limited by long run rules which nobody has the power to alter or abrogate in the service of particular ends" (Hayek 1979a: 129). We need, as he puts it, to ask what the "founders of liberal constitutionalism would do today if, pursuing the aims they did, they could command all the experience we have gained in the meantime" (Hayek 1973: 1f.).[48] Understanding why the means that they suggested failed, we need to come up with "new institutional invention" (ibid.: 2) and new "constitutional design" (ibid.: 4), we need to *replace* the tottering structure by some better edifice" (Hayek 1979a: 152). If this sounds like a project in "rational construction," this is because it is in the nature of things. As Hayek notes, "(g)overnment is necessarily the product of *intellectual design*" (Hayek 1979a: 152), and the rules of the organization of government, i.e. constitutional rules, have always been a matter of deliberate design (Hayek 1973: 90, 124).[49] Whatever some of his arguments on *cultural evolution* may suggest with regard to general rules of conduct (Vanberg 1986; 1994a), as far as the constitutional rules of government are concerned Hayek clearly does not assume that we can wait for an "invisible hand" to generate a beneficial constitutional order for us.

Since Hayek sees the principal defect of the existing forms of democratic government in their insufficient separation of the rule-making authority from the administrative power, his suggestions for constitutional reform focus, of course, on the issue of how a more effective division between these two functions might be achieved. The core element of his proposal for "A model constitution" (Hayek 1979a: 105ff.) is the idea of an arrangement "which would secure a real separation of powers between two distinct representative bodies whereby law-making in the narrow sense as well as government proper would be conducted democratically, but by different and mutually independent agencies" (ibid.: 107). And in a refined "constitutional model" that takes account of the difference in nature between, on the one side, the general rules of conduct upon which the spontaneous order of society is based and, on the other side, the constitutional rules on which the organization of government rests, Hayek has proposed:

> a three-tiered system of representative bodies ... of which one would be concerned with the semi-permanent framework of the constitution, ... another with the continuous task of gradual improvement of the general rules of just conduct, and a third with the current conduct of government, that is, the administration of the resources entrusted to it.
>
> (ibid.: 38)[50]

Much of the discussion on Hayek's reform proposal has concentrated on the details of his particular suggestions for how the institutional separation between the legislative and administrative representative bodies might be implemented. It is not only because of space limitations that I do not enter this debate here. More importantly, it seems to me that the details of Hayek's proposal can easily distract from his principal argument, the validity of which is completely independent of the soundness of the specifics of his reform ideas. The essentials of his exposition lie in his general diagnosis of the systematic defects of the standard model of democratic government, and his general argument that a remedy can only be found in a genuine revival of the ideal of constitutionally limited government. Hayek's principal argument is his call for an institutional arrangement that effectively insulates the rule-making authority from the short-term demands of day-to-day government, and for effective constraints that subject governmental authority to the discipline of general principles.[51] Whether these aims can best be achieved with the particular institutional reforms that Hayek himself has suggested, or whether one could imagine more effective alternative structures, is a question of second order. If his principal arguments should find acceptance, the search for appropriate institutional reforms should not be the most difficult part of the task. Should his basic argument be rejected, there would be no point in discussing the particulars of his reform proposal.

Conclusion

The purpose of this chapter has been to show how Hayek's critique of the institutional structure of Western democracy, and his venture in constitutional design and institutional invention, can be systematically related to his arguments on the role of rules that are at the core of his political philosophy. His rational and constructive approach to the issue of constitutional reform in our democratic institutions is not, as one might perhaps suspect, an alien and *ad hoc* addendum to the main thrust of his work which is imbued by his critique of what he calls rational constructivism. It is, instead, a logical extension of his general argument on the interrelation between the order of rules and the order of actions, and his understanding of how we may hope to improve our social condition by improving the rules of the game.

A principal task of politics is, in Hayek's account, to enforce and to develop further a suitable framework of rules within which a beneficial order of society can form itself. Whether, and to what extent, the political process is suitable for this task will depend, again, on the rules under which this process itself operates. It is, primarily, in these terms that Hayek finds the institutional structure of the prevailing form of democratic government wanting. And his proposals for institutional reform aim, primarily, at making the institutional framework more conducive to that task.

More generally, Hayek's argument is that the same principle that applies to the spontaneous order of society and the market also applies to the realm of politics; that our principal means to improve the order that emerges in either realm is through our efforts to improve the framework of rules.

6   John R. Commons

Institutional evolution through purposeful selection

Introduction

With the *Legal Foundations of Capitalism* (1924), John R. Commons established himself as one of the leading members of the group of American economists who called themselves institutionalists and whose more prominent figures, apart from Commons himself, included foremost Thorstein Veblen and William C. Mitchell.[1] What united these authors was their critical distance from the predominantly neo-classical school of thought in economics, whose deficiencies they saw, in particular, in an inadequate behavioral model and in the disregard of the role of institutions in economic life. Apart from this uniting skepticism toward orthodox economics, the American institutionalists shared only limited common ground in their ideas about a theoretical alternative program. Their failure to propose a paradigmatic alternative is, therefore, often considered to be the main reason why their influence within the field has remained rather marginal.

While there has recently been in economics a distinct revival of the interest in institutional questions, the "new institutionalism" is generally understood not as a legacy of the "old" American institutionalism but rather as a further development of the neo-classical tradition just criticized by the latter. The various interrelated and overlapping theoretical approaches, which can be summarized under the name of new institutionalism (such as the theory of property rights, the public choice theory, or the so-called transaction costs economics), shared with the old institutionalism the intention of including the study of the legal–institutional framework explicitly in the economic research program. Its representatives, however, start generally from the assumption that such an extension of their research program can be easily based on the core of conventional neo-classical theory, and that it is not necessary to turn as radically away from it as was demanded by some of the old institutionalists.[2]

Given this background, it is remarkable that one of the most eminent representatives of the new institutionalism, Oliver Williamson, refers explicitly to John R. Commons as one of the forerunners of his own approach to transaction costs economics (Williamson 1975: 3, 254; 1985: 3, 5, 187). In fact, with the title of one of his books, *The Economic Institutions of Capitalism*, Williamson makes an apparent allusion to Commons's *Legal Foundations of Capitalism*. Even if

Williamson's reference to Commons remains limited to a few general hints, it is still significant that it is Commons who is mentioned in the discussion of whether there is any continuity at all between the old and the new institutionalism. Essentially, Williamson attributes this continuity to the fact that Commons also emphasized transactions as the smallest units of economic analysis.[3] Yet, in Commons's work, more substantial commonalities can be found with contributions from representatives of the new institutionalism.[4]

Commons, in contrast to Veblen, did not wish his institutionalist approach to be understood as a radical alternative to conventional economics; rather, he wanted it to be a complimentary contribution. His concern was, he emphasized, to bestow an appropriate value to the conventionally neglected phenomenon of collective action.[5] Malcolm Rutherford (1994: 1) is referring to the differences between Commons and Veblen when he asserts that in the tradition of American institutionalism there are essentially two distinguishable research programs which can be traced back to these two authors. And, according to Rutherford, it is especially because of the particular orientation of Commons's research program that his work receives more attention in contemporary discussion than that of other representatives of the old institutionalism.[6]

The significance of Commons's approach in the context of more recent discussions about an institution-oriented political economy is also the subject of this chapter. More precisely, what will be dealt with are Commons's ideas with regard to the evolution of the legal–institutional framework within which economic activity takes place. These ideas – paraphrased in the title of this chapter as "Institutional evolution through purposeful selection" – shall be related to two approaches which play a prominent role in the debate on legal and institutional change and between which tension is often noticeable. The first is an approach which emphasizes the role of deliberate design of rules and institutions, an emphasis that can be found, for example, in German ordo-liberalism and in the research program of constitutional economics. The second is an evolutionary view of institutional change as it has been advanced, in particular, by Friedrich A. Hayek. It is my purpose here to demonstrate that, and in which fashion, Commons's concepts about "institutional evolution through purposeful selection" can be considered mediators between the two approaches.

Scarcity, conflict, and social order

As with other writings by Commons, the *Legal Foundations of Capitalism* is generally – and with good reason – considered difficult to understand.[7] This does not mean, however, that one cannot, with a certain investment of effort, discern a coherent theoretical theme in his work.

Just like standard economics, Commons starts from the assumption that the universal problem of scarcity, i.e. the discrepancy between human desires and the means available to satisfy them, constitutes the subject matter of economics. While, however, standard economics goes straight from the problem of scarcity to the ideas of necessity of choice and the role of exchange, Commons emphasizes the connection between scarcity and conflict. The fundamental problem which social theory has to solve in Commons's view lies in the explanation of how social order and peaceful co-operation can emanate from scarcity-induced conflicts.[8] The explanation he offers goes back to the process in which rules are being gradually defined as a result of an ongoing mitigation of conflicts in social groups. These rules define which type of behavior by an individual will be accepted and supported by the group, and which kind of action will be received with criticism and opposition.[9] Commons calls such general regulations "working rules"; and any social grouping in which ordered interaction among the involved individuals results from these working rules he calls a "going concern."[10]

In Commons's work, a central place is taken by the argument that the system of market competition, which is at the core of economic theory, is not a "natural phenomenon," but is actually a societal enterprise in the sense that it presupposes a legal framework which is not a "provision of nature" but rather a product of civilization. The "simple system of natural liberty," of which Adam Smith used to speak and whose functioning he described with the formula of the invisible hand, consists, according to Commons (1924: 137), of nothing else but the framework of rules of an ordered society, as Smith observed it in his time, a framework of rules which was not a gift of nature, but "the fine fruit of evolving centuries of working rules."[11]

Commons does not fail to recognize that Adam Smith was thinking of actions within the framework of "rules of justice" when he talked about the "simple system of natural liberty." Yet Smith had, in Commons's view, concentrated so much on the role of collective action as a threat to individual liberty that the role of collective action in securing rights and liberties had disappeared not only from his own view (Biddle 1991: 96)[12] but even more so from the view of the succeeding advocates of *laissez-faire* liberalism.[13] In the final instance, Commons argues (1924: 323), even the property rights and liberties assumed by Smith would be unthinkable without a certain degree of state activity (Biddle 1991: 96).[14]

Rights and liberties, Commons repeatedly stresses, were not given to individuals by "nature," but by other people. Rights are options for action, which are available to the individual through the support of a social community.[15] Accordingly, from Commons's perspective, the concept of natural rights is misleading if it is meant to imply that there is a pre-social source of immutable rights, i.e. of rights against which the rights created by society could be measured (Commons 1924: 136, 385; 1931: 657). For Commons, rights are necessarily a social category. Rights exist only inasmuch as they are secured through "collective action," be it through formal or informal social support (Commons 1924: 138; 1931: 650). Outside the realm of support through a social community there exist no rights.[16] This view has, as Commons points out, profound consequences for the evaluation of the role of collective action. If one starts with the notion that individuals are endowed with "pre-social" rights, then one may be inclined to interpret collectively enforced rules as an infringement upon one's individual liberty. If, on the other hand, one starts from the assumption that individuals possess rights only inasmuch as they can mobilize social support for their realization, then one will emphasize the role of collective action in the process of defining rights.[17]

Competition and legal order

The thoughts summarized above find expression in Commons's view of the nature of market competition. As he argues, the free competition of economic theory is not a primeval "struggle for survival," but rather a social organizational ideal. What is aimed at is "mitigated" competition, i.e. competition bound by a set of rules which are supposed to bestow upon it the desired functional characteristics (Ramstad 1994: 110).[18]

The co-ordination capacity of market competition is, in Commons's view (1924: 324), not the product of a "natural" interaction between the forces of supply and demand, but the result of an environment structured by certain rules. In the marketplace, people do not encounter each other in a primeval state of anarchy, but meet as legal persons who act out collectively guaranteed liberties.[19] Moreover, economic transactions are not only a mere shifting of commodities between persons. Instead they are transactions that take place within a legal system, i.e. they involve the transfer of property rights, whose contents are defined by the rules of the respective legal community (Commons 1934: 75). It is this very point that Commons stresses when he states that institutional economics differs from conventional views by making the transaction its smallest analytical unit, thus concentrating on the legal aspect of economic action (Commons 1924: 7).[20]

The orientation toward the sphere of property rights instead of the material dimension of economic transactions[21] is what makes Commons's institutional economics relevant for the comparison, noted at the beginning, between ordo-liberalism and constitutional economics on the one side and the evolutionism of Hayek on the other side. It is this orientation which gives his ideas both a constructive–political and an evolutionist touch. There is a constructive–political touch in the sense that the continuous development and reform of the legal–institutional framework represents for Commons the main tool for shaping the economic order. And there is an evolutionist touch in the sense that, according to Commons, it is the evolution of the law by judicative and legislative decisions which holds the key to understanding economic and social change.

When Commons emphasizes strongly that market competition is not a type of natural competition but presupposes a legal order which was achieved as a product of civilization through a laborious process,[22] then this reminds one of the theoretical program of the German ordo-liberals, who stress likewise the idea of a competition–order, i.e. the insight that we are not dealing in the marketplace with unqualified competition but with one defined and limited by rules, and that the characteristics of the market process depend upon the nature of these competition rules.[23]

Whether their interest in the interdependence between the working properties of the market process and its legal framework, which unifies Commons and the ordo-liberals, can be traced back to common roots in history of ideas cannot be discussed here.[24] Irrespective of differences that otherwise separate them, it is apparent that Commons's concept of a market competition order, as an order to be framed in accord with human values, shows similarities to ordo-liberal thinking.[25] In any case, what Yngve Ramstadt (1994: 102) says about Commons applies to the ordo-liberals in a similar way: The market is not a product of nature to which a legal framework was added, but rather it is a competition order which was only made possible through the provision of certain rules. As Ramstadt emphasizes, for Commons, there is no competition *per se*, i.e. independent of the working rules. There are only different orders of competition defined by different rules.[26] What remains where any working rules whatsoever are missing is a state of Hobbesian anarchy, in which competition is acted out "with all possible means" available.

The legal–institutional framework of a market competition order, which standard economics has assumed to be quite "natural," is – and this is what Commons wanted to impress on his colleagues – the product of a historical process. And with his *Legal Foundations of Capitalism*, Commons tried to trace and to illustrate the gradual process of legal evolution from which the social order that we call capitalism emerged, and on whose analysis economics as the study of markets concentrates.

Taking the conditions in England during the time of the Norman conquest as a pragmatic starting point,[27] Commons leads the reader through the process recorded in legislative and judicative documents (Commons 1934: 5; Perlman 1986: 274) which in the course of centuries gave rise to those institutions and rules that characterize the contemporary economic order in the United States (Commons 1924: 313). What drove this process and kept it in motion – a central focus of Commons's interests – were the acts of will of the people involved. Those involved in the process – be it as private people or in official functions (e.g. as politicians or as judges) – were influenced in their behavior by the respective working rules, but, at the same time, through their actions they shaped this framework of rules and changed it, even if only marginally (Commons 1924: 333, 378).[28] In his explanation, Commons repeatedly refers to the special role which, in the case of the United States, falls to the Supreme Court as the protector of the Constitution and as the ultimate authority in the settlement of disputes. In all this, he stresses, it is the actual court decisions that decide what the law, and in this case what the Constitution, mean in reality.[29]

The fact that Commons emphasizes the role of collective action in the process of legal–institutional change does not mean, contrary to widespread misunderstanding, that he is opposed to a methodological individualism. He always traces the dynamics of this process straight back to the actions of the people involved (Rutherford 1990: xxix), and his approach to a theory of institutional evolution through purposeful selection, which will be discussed in more detail below, can be easily interpreted as a methodologically individualistic explanation of institutional change.[30] As Commons notes, when we speak of "customs," "law," or the "state" we always refer to the actions of the people involved, e.g. to the behavior of politicians, judges, policemen, and others (Commons 1924: 125, 140, 363–7, 384). What the law or the state or any other institution actually is – argues Commons – is being defined or "filled in" by all the people who have a certain degree of decision-making power in this sphere, however small it may be (ibid.: 146). Through their actions, they concretize the contents of the working rules (ibid.: 140), and, through their incessant experimenting and calibrating, they subject the working rules to continuous change (ibid.: 354ff.).

Purposeless and "purposeful" selection

Commons (1934: 719) considered an evolutionary approach the adequate analytical tool to understand the process of institutional change which is kept in continual motion by the interplay of harmony and conflict through human interaction. Contrasting his own view to that of Veblen, Commons stresses, though, that his evolutionary approach is not modeled after Darwin's theory of natural selection, but after the latter's arguments concerning artificial selection.[31] Commons (1950: 91, 193) suggests that one should speak of purposeless vs. purposeful selection rather than of natural vs. artificial selection in order to emphasize the role played by the human will in the selection process, which is in Darwin's study the role of the breeder.[32] As Commons (1934: 636) notes on Darwin's concept of artificial selection,[33]

> It is "artificial" simply because it is Purpose, Futurity, Planning, injected into and greatly controlling the struggle for life. Darwin admitted that his own term "natural selection" was a misnomer, and regretted his resort to metaphor. It is more properly blind selection, while the artificial kind is purposeful selection. Natural selection … produces wolves, snakes, poisons, destructive microbes; but artificial selection converts wolves into dogs, nature's poisons into medicine, eliminates the wicked microbes. A Holstein cow could not survive if left to natural selection – she is a monstrosity created by artificial selection for the good she can do for man in the future.[34]

Just as one deals, in the case of genetic evolution, with populations of organisms in which during the process of reproduction new variability is continually generated and subjected to selection, so one can, following Commons, look at the cultural evolution of rules and institutions as a similar process, in which, on the one side, new varieties and diversity are continually injected into "populations" of existing customs and practices and in which, on the other side, human acts of will function as the forces of selection and thus decide which modes of behavior are rejected and which are being spread and passed on as common customs (Commons 1934: 638).[35] Commons comments on this process:

For custom is the mere repetition, duplication, and variability of practices and transactions. No repetition is exactly the same as its predecessor, and no duplication is exactly the same as its contemporary. Hence, there is always a variability of customs in successive times and at the same time. … Thus, there is a continual selection of customs going on. … Since this occurs by operation of the human will, it is much like the artificial selection of Darwin's evolution.

(Commons 1934: 44f.)

According to Commons, a political economy that aims to explain institutional change must be constructed as an evolutionary theory of artificial or purposeful selection because it deals with, as described above, an evolutionary process determined by human acts of will. As Commons (1950: 91) notes: "Political economy belongs to the field of artificial selection, because it deals with human purpose." Natural selection is purposeless. In it, survival and reproduction are the only measure of "success." The question of whether what survives is actually "good" cannot be meaningfully discussed in regard to "the unguided process of nature" (Commons 1924: 377). This is not so in the case of artificial selection, in which human intentions and purposes serve as the criterion of assessment.[36] Here, the question of whether what survives is good in the sense that it serves human ends is meaningful. Neil Chamberlain (1963: 78), commenting on Commons's concept of artificial selection, asserts that people do not simply accept their environment with its respective selection constraints, but adapt it to their needs and purposes. As he notes, artificial selection creates "a social order infused with purpose and subject to continuing tinkering to effect that purpose more completely" (ibid.).

To be sure, the analogy between purposeful selection by a breeder and purposeful selection within the process of cultural evolution of rules and institutions is only valid within limits. The image of the breeder, which suggests a centrally controlled and uniformly executed selection process, would certainly be misleading if transferred to the substantially more complex and heterogeneous process of purposeful selection in the social sphere, where innumerable "selectors" of different kinds, on different levels, and with different purposes, competence and power bring about final results which no one could have originally envisaged or planned. And Commons's treatment of this subject illustrates that he was very much aware of the variety and diversity of purposeful selection in the process of institutional evolution.

Institutional change: conscious design and evolution

That there is no analogue in the evolution of rules and institutions to Darwin's breeder, someone who would bestow a comprehensive plan onto the whole development, does not mean at all that Commons's emphasis on the role of purposeful selection cannot be applied here in an analytically productive fashion. If it is used with the noted limitations, it can help to elucidate a number of basic questions.

In the sense that Commons talks about it, purposeful selection, i.e. purposeful human action, is omnipresent in the process of sociocultural evolution. It constitutes this process and is, so to speak, the substrate or material of which it consists. The trials which generate continually new variation as well as the selective acts which decide upon the upholding, imitation, and passing on of (or upon the ending and rejection of) practices and problem-solving strategies all consist of purposeful human actions.[37] This does not mean, however, that the persons involved always accomplish what they originally intended with their purposeful acts. To be sure, a person uses a problem-solving strategy with the intention of coping with an emerging problem, yet whether he or she will indeed have the desired success is a different story. Irrespective of whether success is intended by the acting party, problem-solving behavior always remains hypothetical: a matter of trial and error.[38] It also does not mean that purposeful actions do not have unintended consequences or that such unintended consequences would not be of importance.[39] Moreover, it does not mean that the final results stemming from the interaction of the different acts of will were, or could have been, planned by anyone. The final result of innumerable single actions which emerges from the process of sociocultural evolution is – to use the well-known phrase of Adam Ferguson – the result of human actions, but not the realization of a human plan (Hayek 1969: 97f). The whole process is open-ended, it leads – as any genuine evolutionary process – into an open future. In this sense, Commons's concept of institutional evolution through purposeful selection can combine the idea of planful design and conscious choice with the idea of an evolutionary open-ended process.[40]

In his analysis of the *Legal Foundations of Capitalism*, Commons directs his attention primarily toward the Anglo-Saxon common law process (Rutherford 1994: 103), whose evolutionary principle he describes as "artificial selection by judges" (Commons 1936: 245, fn. 11): "Since customs change, the evolution of custom is the artificial selection by the judiciary of these customs which shall survive" (Commons 1950: 193).[41] Yet it is apparent that his concept of institutional evolution through purposeful selection can be equally applied to other areas of the complex process in which the rules and the institutional framework of a society develop and change. If, as Commons stresses, purposeful selection is omnipresent in the process of cultural evolution, then the simple contrast between "purposeful design of institutions" and "evolution" does not make sense. The relevant theoretical controversy, then, cannot be about the question of whether human planning and conscious design play a role in the process of evolution, but rather must focus on the question of *how* human intention and planning influence the evolutionary process; whether this occurs through separate individual choices between alternative practices, through judges' choices between alternative interpretations, through collective decisions of law-making bodies, through the behavior of executive agents (police force, bureaucrats, etc.), or in other ways.[42]

The focus of analytical attention must obviously, then, be placed on the manner in which the various individual actions are interrelated and how they generate a structure of rules in their interplay. Only then we can formulate meaningful statements about the relationship between certain forms of purposeful selection and the nature of the aggregate results. Whether, for example, the separate individual choices of problem-solving strategies lead to final results which are desirable for those involved depends upon the existence of a conditioning framework that corresponds to Smith's concept of the invisible hand; or whether, opposingly, conditions prevail that are characteristic of "social traps" such as the "prisoner's dilemma" of game theory. Similarly, the nature of the resulting decisions taken by legislative collective bodies will depend on the terms of the decision-making process and on the conditions prevalent.

Regardless of which forms of "purposeful selection" are effective and in which combination they occur, the entire process in which they are embedded will inevitably be an evolutionary process with an open future. This is true for processes in which collective legislative decisions play an important role, as well as for processes which are determined by separate individual choices among alternative practices; it is obvious, though, that the potential for experimental variation and innovation is bigger under the conditions of decentralized "purposeful selection."

Despite the restrictions that have to be accounted for when the concept of purposeful selection is applied to the process of sociocultural evolution, it can still help to clarify certain ambiguities which have accompanied the reception of Hayek's ideas on cultural evolution. This is especially the case with regard to the question of whether – and, if so, how – Hayek's evolutionism can be reconciled with a constitutional constructive approach as advocated by the ordo-liberalism of the Freiburg school or Buchanan's constitutional economics, which both emphasize the role of conscious institutional design. What caused irritations in Hayek's treatment of the issue were, in particular, statements which seem to describe the evolutionary process as one that happens, so to speak, behind the backs of the individuals involved and whose "efficiency" would actually depend on its unfolding without disturbances from conscious human intervention.[43] Even though it is recognizable from various of Hayek's statements that he had a much more complex view of the relationship between evolution and design in mind, one finds precious few explicit arguments of his which would actually spell out such a more complex outlook.[44]

The idea of purposeful selection and the analogy to the process of purposeful breeding point out that one can seek to "guide" an evolutionary process without wanting to direct it toward a predetermined goal. Hayek is certainly right with his criticism that it would be presumptuous to seek to control the process of sociocultural evolution in the sense of determining at the outset what its detailed results should be. Such a project would not only be doomed to failure. Its attempted implementation would be likely to have highly undesirable consequences for everyone involved. This does not mean, however, that an evolutionary process could not be subjected to certain constraints or to a conditioning framework in order to utilize its exploratory potential while, simultaneously, steering it into an overall direction desirable from a human perspective. By "cultivating" the evolutionary process in such a fashion, one would seek to shape its general working properties, but not to predetermine its concrete results.

"Cultivated" evolution: the market process example

Hayek maintains rightly that we cannot "control" the sociocultural evolutionary process in the sense that we determine its outcome. This does not mean, however, that we have to bear it passively as a given destiny and that we simply have to accept its working rules as we find them. Just as people have not simply accepted their "natural" environment, but have always tried to transform it in accordance with their wishes, so can they also make efforts to bestow upon their "social environment" characteristics they desire without forgetting, however, that there are certain limiting conditions that cannot be changed. In fact, it is not clear at all what it would mean to let the process of cultural evolution "take its course." Wherever such processes are under way, they still occur within the framework of certain defining factors which condition the process of selection. To let evolution "take its course" really means, then, to simply accept whatever working rules exist. In other words, even by staying passive we cannot avoid to opt for a framework of rules. We then only make the decision to accept the existing working rules, whatever they may be. If one wants to prevent such a "passive choice," it is not only legitimate, but even necessary, to examine whether the given working rules actually need improvement and just how they can be ameliorated. To let evolution "take its course" means to close one's eyes to this question.

Hayek did not deal explicitly and systematically with the question of how the process of sociocultural evolution needs to be "cultivated" in order to be beneficial in the sense of serving human interests. This omission is astounding as his own ideas concerning the nature of market competition easily lend themselves as a prime example for this purpose. In his writings on the evolutionary market process, Hayek stressed explicitly that one could not expect just any kind of competitive process to possess the desired working properties attributable to the market, but that this is only true for a more qualified type of competition, "cultivated" by adequate rules. Such a "cultivation" is by no means meant to guide the market process toward certain results and thus to annihilate its explorative potential as a process of evolutionary discovery. Its purpose is, instead, to influence its general characteristics in a way more in line with human interests. The process remains one with an open future. Which concrete results it will generate cannot be predicted. The goal of "cultivation" is to raise the chances that the results, whatever they be, will be desirable for those concerned.

As mentioned above, the German ordo-liberals have, although not in explicit relation to evolutionary theory, worked extensively on the idea of a market competition process "cultivated" by an adequate conditioning framework. Under the catchword of "performance competition" (*Leistungswettbewerb*), they systematically analyzed the question of which kind of legal–institutional framework would raise the prospects of market competition really being of benefit to the people concerned. Their answer was that this could be realized through a process in which consumer interests operate as the decisive selection force and thus act as the central steering element of the process.

A more generalized modern counterpart to the ordo-political approach is the research program of constitutional political economy, which – partly with and partly without reference to evolutionary theory – deals with the question of how decision processes can be institutionally "cultivated" in the various areas, and at the different levels, of social action so as to serve the interests of the respective "sovereigns," i.e. the persons involved (Buchanan 1990a). An important part of this research program is devoted to exploring in more detail, under which conditions, and in which way evolutionary dynamics and conscious institutional "cultivation" can be advantageously combined in order to achieve this goal. In the absence of a universal and definite answer to this question, the task remains to analyze, for different kinds of rules and action contexts, how the "purposeful selections" of the various parties involved interact in producing overall outcomes.

The question that Commons's concept of evolution by purposeful selection suggests for this research program is whether one can – in analogy to the strategy of the breeder – impose constraints on the process of sociocultural evolution in order to raise the chances of the continuation and spreading of rules–institutions serving the interests of the individuals involved, while reducing, simultaneously, the respective chances of rules–institutions with an adverse impact. In other words, the efforts at a desirable "cultivation" of evolutionary processes would be an attempt to create beneficial invisible-hand structures and to eliminate destructive prisoners'-dilemma structures.

Conclusion: J. R. Commons as constitutional economist

The idea of the active "cultivation" of sociocultural evolution processes described above goes further, in several respects, than what Commons had in mind with his thoughts on institutional evolution by purposeful selection. His interest was mainly directed toward an explicative description of the historical process of institutional evolution, and less toward the constructive–political question of designing a framework for future development. But his idea of purposeful selection points, without question, in the direction of such a constructive approach, and in his writings one can easily find arguments that can be interpreted in this sense.[45]

For Commons, the design of the legal–institutional framework is the main instrument with which people can improve their economic and social living conditions. Just as the contemporary framework is the result of past efforts in constitutional construction (Commons 1924: 378), so is it the task of the present to shape the institutional framework for the future. And it is obvious that Commons views the role of political economy, as an applied social science, as acting in an advisory role in this process.[46] Commons's understanding of the political task, to which an economist can contribute, is not based on a belief in the wisdom of government planning (Rutherford 1994: 148), nor is it motivated by utopian visions. It aims rather at a pragmatic and sober attempt to help those involved in the economic and social process to find better instruments and methods for working out, among their conflicting interests, compromises that are mutually acceptable and socially productive (Rutherford 1994: 145). One could argue that his ideal political economist is one who acts as a "constitutional advisor," quite similar to notions advanced in constitutional political economy, and reminiscent of Adam Smith's (1981: 468) view of political economy as the *science of legislation*. The task of constitutional advisors that Commons assigns to political economists does not consist of telling people what they should do and which goals they should pursue, but of showing them ways in which they can pursue their interests more effectively in a mutually compatible fashion.[47] The political economist does not carry preconceived criteria of what is "desirable" to the existing order, but asks how the individuals involved can better realize their own concepts of what is desirable in a world in which they do not live as monads but together with other people with ambitions of their own.[48]

The above interpretation of Commons as a constitutional economist relies, of course, on a selective evaluation of his work: an evaluation which emphasizes certain aspects and neglects other important elements. As proof, however, that this interpretation is not too idiosyncratic, I would like to close with a quotation which comes from an author who is hardly biased toward the views presented here. In his contribution on "The institutionalism of John R. Commons," Ramstad (1990: 86ff.) notes the following about Commons's view of the political economists' task:

> The central problem of political economy becomes that of determining which rules promise to best govern the transactions of individuals in sharing among themselves in the contemporary setting the burdens and benefits of the production of wealth. ... Commons perceived the appropriate task of the economist, qua economist, to be that of showing how the existing structure of working rules must be altered if the evolving purposes of the principals' collective will are to be attained. ... [I]n suggesting modifications of the existing rules, one must show, if the proposed rules are actually to be found acceptable by those with whom ultimate authority resides, that they allow the purposes of the sovereign to be achieved more effectively, or at least that they do not undermine those purposes.[49]

7 The market as a creative process[1]

James M. Buchanan
and Viktor J. Vanberg

Introduction

Contributions in modern theoretical physics and chemistry on the behavior of
non-linear systems, exemplified by Ilya Prigogine's work on the thermodynamics
of open systems (Prigogine and Stengers 1984), have attracted considerable
attention in economics (Anderson *et al.* 1988; Baumol and Benhabib 1989;
Arthur 1990; Mirowski 1990; Radzicki 1990). Our purpose here, which is to
put this orientation in the natural sciences in relation to a particular non-
orthodox strand of thought within economics, does not require a detailed review
of these theoretical developments. What is essential is some appreciation of
the general thrust of the enterprise which involves a shift of perspective from
the determinism of conventional physics, which inspired the neo-classical
research program, to a perspective that emphasizes the non-teleological open-
endedness, the creative and non-determined nature of evolutionary processes.

Prigogine and Stengers (1984: 177) refer to this shift in perspective as "a
reconceptualization of the physical sciences," as a move "from deterministic,
reversible processes to stochastic and irreversible ones." The emphasis is shifted
from equilibrium to non-equilibrium as a "source of spontaneous self-
organization" (Prigogine 1985: 108) to self-organizing processes in open systems
far from thermodynamic equilibrium. A characteristic feature of such systems
is the presence of non-linearities which can amplify "small causes" into "large
effects." At critical points (referred to as "bifurcations"), very small events can
have significant macroeffects, in the sense that they "decide" which particular
path – among a number of equally possible paths – the system will take, a fact
that introduces a stochastic element and renders self-organizing processes in
far-from-equilibrium conditions inherently undetermined.[2] Such processes
exhibit a "mixture of necessity and chance" that, as Prigogine and Stengers
(1984: 169f.) note, produces a unique and irreversible "'history' path along
which the system evolves."

What is suggested here is a generalized perspective which brings into focus
the "creativity" and open-endedness in the evolution of non-equilibrium systems,
a perspective which has as its *leitmotiv* "that the future is not given" (Prigogine
1986: 493) but is "created" in an unfolding evolutionary process.[3] Authors

such as P. M. Allen (1988: 99) and J. S. Wicken (1987: 3) speak of a "new evolutionary synthesis," a "unified view of the world which bridges the gap between the physical and the human sciences" (Allen 1988: 118). In his discussion on the relevance of the "new evolutionary synthesis" for economic theory, Allen stresses the concern with *microscopic diversity* as the critical feature. The "cloudy, confused complexity of the real world" (ibid.: 99) is the essential subject of an evolutionary approach – in contrast to a perspective that looks for types and classes, and that views microscopic diversity and variation as negligible aberrations, to be averaged out through classification and aggregation.[4] Variability and individual diversity at the microscopic level drive evolutionary processes; they are the crucial ingredient to the "creativity" of these processes, of their potential to generate novelty. As Allen (1988: 108) puts it:

> The fluctuations, mutations and apparently random movements which are naturally present in real complex systems constitute a sort of "imaginative" and creative force which will explore around whatever exists at present.

Allen sees here the critical difference between an evolutionary perspective and one that centers around the notion of predetermined equilibrium states, the difference between the new self-organization paradigm and a "Newtonian paradigm" in which any "representation of 'creative processes' was entirely absent" (ibid.: 97).[5]

Our purpose in this chapter is, first, to identify a body of criticism addressed against orthodox equilibrium theory in economics that seems to correspond closely with the developments noted in the natural sciences, and, second, to elaborate on the implications of this (the *radical subjectivist*) criticism in some detail, and particularly in its relation to its "near neighbor," the entrepreneurial conceptualization of Israel Kirzner.

Subjectivism, the growth of knowledge, and indeterminedness

Allen's article is but one example of a growing number of comments on the apparent relevance of the "new evolutionary synthesis" for a reorientation of economic theory. The reasons that limit the applicability of equilibrium models, even in the traditional realm of physics and chemistry, apply *a fortiori* to the domain of economics. The equilibrium concept is associated with a worldview that treats the future as implied in the present. In principle, future states could be predicted based on sufficient knowledge of the present; if it were not for *de facto* limits on our knowledge of an immensely complex reality. By contrast, a core insight of the new paradigm is that nature is "creative," that novelty and genuinely unpredictable outcomes are generated as the evolutionary process unfolds over time. The "creativity" argument has all the more force where concern is with social processes that are driven by human choice and inventiveness.[6]

We want to draw attention to one criticism of economic orthodoxy that has been advanced from a strict *subjectivist* position, a criticism that has, to our knowledge, been developed independently of the literature discussed above, but which has, in some respects, a strikingly similar thrust.[7] It should be said at the outset that there is no clearly delineated body of thought that would fall under the rubric of *subjectivism*. The term has been adopted by, and used as a label for, a number of perspectives in economics which agree in their broad criticism of the neo-classical general equilibrium framework, but which are by no means theoretically homogeneous. With this proviso stated, we want to concentrate the discussion in this section on what is often referred to as "radical subjectivism," a position associated primarily with the name of G. L. S. Shackle as well as with the work of such other authors as L. M. Lachmann, J. Wiseman, and S. C. Littlechild. In the next section, we shall take a closer look at the modern "Austrian" version of subjectivism, represented by I. Kirzner's work on entrepreneurship, and we shall discuss the differences that Kirzner sees between his own position and "radical subjectivism."[8]

At the core of Shackle's attack on the "neo-classical citadel" (Lachmann 1976: 54), and central to the "radical subjectivist" view in general, is the issue of what we can claim to know about the future in our efforts to understand the world of human affairs. The basic objection to neo-classical general equilibrium theory is that it embodies assumptions about the "knowability" of the future which are entirely unfounded not only in their most extreme variant, the assumption of perfect knowledge, but also in their "softer" varieties such as assumptions about rational expectations or Bayesian adaptive rationality. For radical subjectivism, there is simply no way around the fundamental fact that whatever happens in the social realm is dependent on human choices, choices that – if they are *choices* – "could be different," and could, if they were different, have different effects.[9] There can, therefore, be no "given" future, independent of the choices that will be made. Instead, there are innumerable potential futures of which only one will emerge as the choice process unfolds. As Shackle (1983: 33) puts it, "the content of time-to-come is not merely unknown but non-existent, and the notion of foreknowledge of human affairs is vacuous." Or in Wiseman's (1989: 230) terms, "The essence of the radical subjectivist position is that the future is not simply 'unknown', but is 'non-existent' or 'indeterminate' at the point of decision."[10]

The recognition that in human social affairs the future is undetermined but "created" in the process of choice does not imply that the future is "beyond *conjecture*" (Wiseman 1990: 104), nor does it ignore that individuals have *expectations* about the future on which they base their action. The subjectivist's understanding of the nature and role of such expectations is, however, critically different from their interpretation in a neo-classical framework. To the subjectivist, expectations may be more or less reasonable (in the sense of being more or less defendable in the light of past experience), but they can, ultimately, not be more than conjectures about an undetermined and, therefore, unknowable future. To the neo-classical economist, by contrast, expectations are about a future that is, in principle, *knowable*, even if its knowability may be limited by imperfections of the "expectants." Ignorance of the future is essentially seen as a source of inefficiency, as a problem that can, in principle, be remedied by learning.[11] By contrast, from a subjectivist position, such ignorance is simply "an inescapable characteristic of the human condition" (Wiseman 1989: 225). And "the possibility of learning does not imply that through learning the future will become knowable, but only that experience will change behavior" (ibid.: 143).[12]

Arguing on the same theme, Shackle suggests that every person choosing among different courses of action can be seen "to be making history, on however small a scale, in some sense other than mere passive obedience to the play of all-pervasive causes" (Shackle 1983: 28). Every choice can be seen as the beginning of a sequel that "will be partly the work of many people's choices-to-come whose character ... the chooser of present action cannot know" (ibid.: 28f.).[13] Our "un-knowledge" of the future is, from this perspective, not "a deficiency, a falling-short, a failure of search and study" (ibid.: 33). Rather, it reflects a fundamental fact of human existence, "the imaginative and originative source and nature of the choosables, and the endless proliferant creation of hypothetical sequels of choosable action" (ibid.: 36). It reflects, in other words, *"the plurality of rival possibles"* (ibid.: 37).[14]

The emphasis on choice as an *originating* force, the notion of the *creativeness* of the human mind, and the outlook on history as an *open-ended*, evolving process are intimately interconnected aspects of the same general theme that marks the critical difference between the subjectivist perspective and its neo-classical counterpart. It marks the difference between the *non-teleological* outlook on the human social realm that informs the subjectivist notion of an open-ended, creative choice process and the *teleological* thrust that underlies, if only implicitly, the neo-classical notion of an equilibrium solution that is "preordained by patterns of mineral resources, geography, population, consumer tastes and technological possibilities" (Arthur 1990: 99).[15] To Shackle and other radical subjectivists, the whole general equilibrium concept is questionable when applied to a constantly changing social world which has no predeterminable "telos," whether in the pompous sense of a Marxian philosophy of history or in the more pedestrian sense of a conceptually definable "equilibrium" toward which the process of socioeconomic change could be predicted to gravitate. In a world in which creative human choice is a constant source of an "unknowable future," the notion of a "social equilibrium" is, in Wiseman's (1989: 214) words, a "pseudo-concept," one that can "have only the most tenuous general meaning" (ibid.: 265).[16]

Another way of stating the subjectivist objection against the neo-classical equilibrium concept is by saying that the latter does not provide for an adequate account of "real," historical time. It does not take seriously the fact that, as Lachmann puts it, *"Time* and *knowledge* belong together" (Lachmann 1977: 85), that "time cannot pass without modifying knowledge" (ibid.: 93).[17] The common argument in support of the "simplifying assumptions" that, supposedly, allow general equilibrium models to ignore the complexities of the "time and knowledge" problem is rejected by Wiseman as unconvincing. The "simplifying" assumptions about human knowledge are, he argues, "not 'legitimate simplifications' but a gross perversion of the nature of the decision-problem faced by people living in the real world" (Wiseman 1989: 140), a defect that cannot be remedied by sophisticated refinements of the models that are based on such assumptions.[18]

The contrast is between two critically different perspectives by which our efforts better to understand the world can be guided: (1) a *teleological* perspective and (2) a *non-teleological* perspective. We want to argue that it is its uncompromising non-teleological character which marks the critical difference between the understanding of the market process suggested by the subjectivist perspective and various standard conceptions of the market which, if only in a very subliminal fashion, have a teleological undertone. And, as an aside, we want to submit that this "residual teleology" constitutes somewhat of a hidden common link between standard economic teaching on the self-organizing nature of markets and the blatant teleology of the socialist planning mentality.

Kirzner's theory of entrepreneurship

Israel Kirzner's work, with its explicit emphasis on the entrepreneurial role in economic interaction, is of particular interest in the present context because of Kirzner's (1985: 7ff.) claim that his own "alertness" theory of entrepreneurship keeps a balanced middleground between "two extreme views," the neo-classical equilibrium view on the one side and Shackle's subjectivism on the other, or, in our terms, between a teleological and a non-teleological concept of the market process.[19] As we shall argue, however, in spite of his emphasis on innovative entrepreneurial dynamics and in spite of his verbal recognition of the *creative* and *open-ended* nature of the market process, Kirzner's approach fails to escape the subliminal teleology of the equilibrium framework.[20]

There is, as Littlechild (1979) has pointed out in some detail, a disharmonious mixture in Kirzner's work between a basic affinity to and remaining disagreements with the radical subjectivist position. Kirzner explicitly recognizes the creative dynamics of the market process and, indeed, makes this the central theme of his work. He criticizes the neo-classical position for assigning "*no* role … to the creative entrepreneur" (Kirzner 1985: 13); he talks of the role of entrepreneurship "in an open-ended, uncertain world" (ibid.: 52), a world in which we "find scope for the unpredictable, the creative, the imaginative expression of the human mind" (ibid.: 58); and he talks of "new products," "new qualities of products," "new methods of production" and "new forms of organization" that are endlessly generated in the course of the entrepreneurial process.[21] Yet, such emphasis on creativity, imagination and novelty is combined with a theoretical perspective that sees the essence of entrepreneurship in "the discovery of error" (ibid.: 50), and the scope for entrepreneurship "in the possibility of discovering error" (ibid.: 51), a combination that can hardly be called harmonious.

"Discovery of error" means, in the context of Kirzner's theory, such things as the discovery of "erroneously low valuation" (ibid.: 50) of resources, the "alertness to hitherto unperceived opportunities" (ibid.: 52), or the noticing of "situations overlooked until now because of error" (ibid.), phrases that all invite the same questions: if the essence of entrepreneurial discovery is to "provide protection" or "rescue" from "earlier" or "past error" (ibid.: 53), what is then the benchmark or the *reference-base* against which the failure to do something can be judged to be an "error"? And how does the notion of *creativity* square with such definition of entrepreneurial activity? Are creativity and imagination the same as "discovery of errors"?

There is, in our view, a fundamental inconsistency in Kirzner's attempt to integrate the innovativeness of entrepreneurial activity into an equilibrium framework – by modeling it as *discovery* of "erroneously overlooked opportunities."[22] The critical step in Kirzner's argument, the step that is intended – unsuccessfully so, in our view – to establish a "middle ground" between a teleological and a non-teleological understanding of the market process, is his extension of the notion of a divergence between "different parts of the market" (Kirzner 1985: 62) from a *cross-sectional* to an *intertemporal* interpretation.[23] According to the cross-sectional interpretation, the entrepreneur acts essentially as *arbitrageur*: by taking advantage of hitherto unnoticed divergences between different parts in a present market, he helps to bring about greater consistency (ibid.: 61ff.). According to the intertemporal interpretation, the entrepreneur takes advantage of yet unnoticed divergences between *today's* market and *tomorrow's* market, thus helping "to coordinate markets also across time" (ibid.: 62).[24]

Whatever may be said about the "knowability" of divergencies in the cross-sectional interpretation, it should be obvious that the notion of *intertemporal* divergences between markets at different points in time is inherently problematic. If, as we must assume, "divergences" between today's and tomorrow's markets are typically associated with differences between today's and tomorrow's *knowledge*, what does it mean to say that entrepreneurial alertness corrects the "failure to realize" divergences between *present* and *future* markets? What sense does it make to describe today's failure to possess tomorrow's knowledge as *error*?[25] If, to use Lachmann's phrase, "*Time* and *knowledge* belong together," a comparison between present and future markets cannot possibly be made in a sense that would make such terminology meaningful. The kind of comparison that can be made, at least conceptually, across contemporaneous markets cannot be made along the "inter-temporal dimension" (Kirzner 1985: 62). Time is not simply another "dimension," similar to the spatial dimensions. Different parts of a present market exist, they are *present*, and differences in their characteristics can be "discovered." "Future parts" of a market simply do not exist, they are, by definition, not present. There are, at any point in time, many *potential* futures imaginable, based on more or less informed reflections. Yet, which future will come into existence will depend on choices that are yet to be made. Of course, human beings aim to be "prepared for the future" and they act upon their expectations of what lies ahead. The subjectivist argument on the unknowability of the future is certainly not meant as a recommendation to merchants not to anticipate the coming of winter in their storekeeping. Yet, if, and to the extent that, human choices and their complex interactions shape the emerging future, the latter can be a matter of speculation but not of foreknowledge.

The supposition that the future is foreknowable clearly seems implied when, in talking about the problem of intertemporal entrepreneurial alertness, Kirzner speaks of pictures of the future that may or may not "correspond to the truth as it will be realized" (Kirzner 1985: 55), of man's efforts to overcome uncertainty "by more accurate prescience" (ibid.: 58), of "past failure to pierce correctly the fog of uncertainty" (ibid.: 53), and so forth. It is far from obvious how such insinuation of a preknowable future can be consistent with a genuine appreciation of the creativity of the human mind. Indeed, when arriving at this issue, Kirzner simply retreats to the *ex cathedra* claim that his approach does encompass the two notions, without actually showing *how* this can be done. He emphasizes that intertemporal entrepreneurial alertness "does not consist merely in 'seeing' the unfolding of the tapestry of the future in the sense of seeing a preordained flow of events" (ibid.: 56). Indeed, he insists, that such alertness must "embrace the awareness of the ways in which the human agent can ... in fact *create* the future" (ibid.). Yet, as if the compatibility of the two arguments were obvious, he also insists that "the function of market entrepreneurship in the multi-period context is nonetheless still" that of "discovery of errors" in the sense explained above (ibid.).[26] And he leaves undiscussed the issue of what one entrepreneur's creativity means for the "truthfulness" of another entrepreneur's "picture of the future."[27]

If, as Kirzner's construction seems to suggest, today's failure to possess tomorrow's knowledge qualifies as *error* from which entrepreneurial alertness is to provide rescue, one could conclude that the ultimate benchmark or reference base for such judgement is an imagined world in which everything that humans may ever imagine, think or know will be "revealed."[28] Judged against such a benchmark, every act, however imaginative and creative, can be seen as a "discovery" of something that was already waiting to be found. And "failure to discover" may be discussed in terms of "error" and "overlooked opportunities." It seems questionable, however, whether the mental construct of such an imagined world is a helpful analytical guide when applied to the study of socioeconomic change, of human history.

What might be misleadingly suggestive here is the analogy to the scientific "discovery process." To the extent that science is concerned with an "objective" reality "out there," our conjectural knowledge of this reality can be expected to grow over time, through a process of discovery. Although we cannot know at present what we will know in the future, any future increase in knowledge can, in some sense, be viewed as a "finding" of something that could, in principle, be currently discovered. There is something "knowable" out there, to be discovered sooner or later. To be sure, such account of the discovery process in science may itself be seen to be challenged by the new conceptions advanced by Prigogine and others because of its neglect of real time. Yet, even if, for purpose of our discussion here, we should leave this issue aside, the analogous challenge advanced by the radical subjectivists to neo-classical equilibrium economics applies with full force to the concept of the market as a discovery process. Entrepreneurial activity, in particular, is not to be modeled as "discovery" of that which is "out there." Such activity, by contrast, *creates* a reality that will be different subsequent upon differing choices. Hence, the reality of the future must be shaped by choices yet to be made and this reality has no existence independent of these choices. With regard to a "yet to be created" reality, it is surely confusing to consider its emergence in terms of the discovery of "overlooked opportunities."[29]

Conceptions and misconceptions of the market

The essential characteristic of the "radical subjectivist" position which marks its critical departure from a neo-classical framework is, at the same time, the feature that it shares with the "new evolutionary synthesis" discussed at the beginning of this chapter: the conception of "a world in which time plays a vital role" (Littlechild 1979: 38), of history as an open-ended evolving process, and of a future that is not predetermined, merely waiting to be revealed, but that is "continuously *originated* by the pattern and sequence of human choice" (ibid.). Such a conception has clear implications for the theory of the market which set it apart from various theoretical constructs that have been used to explain or to illustrate the adaptive nature of the market process. If the emphasis on the creativity of human choice is taken seriously, it is not only the standard neo-classical equilibrium notion which seems questionable but also less orthodox conceptions of the market process, including Kirzner's more subliminally teleological perspective on markets and entrepreneurship. By stating this, we certainly do not want to suggest that "radical subjectivism" exists as a well-specified theoretical paradigm ready for adoption – it clearly is not. What we want to suggest, however, is that the creativity of human choice poses a problem that a sincere socioeconomic theory has to cope with and cannot evade.

The critical shift in perspective may be further illustrated by reference to three separate "understandings" of the spontaneous order of the market which have been advanced by scholars who have been generally supportive of market organization of the economy, no one of whom would have ever referred to the market as an "analog computer" for the "computation of equilibrium prices."

1   One of us (Buchanan) learned basic price theory at the University of Chicago in the 1940s, when all students, undergraduate and graduate, were required

to master the syllabus written by Henry Simons.[30] This syllabus contained three well-known rent problems that were designed to provide an understanding of how a competitive economy allocates scarce resources among uses. And, as a test of the efficacy of competitive adjustment, one task given to the students was that of comparing the total product of the economy in competitive equilibrium with that which might be achieved under allocation by a benevolent and omniscient planner.

2   In a deservedly famous paper, "The logic of liberty," Michael Polanyi introduced the metaphor of a sack of potatoes which need only to be shaken to insure minimization of volume in order to demonstrate how localized, decentralized adjustment, akin to that which is characteristic of market organization, works better than centralized adjustment.[31]

3   In a monograph-length essay devoted to an explication of the spontaneous order of the market, Norman Barry (1982) stated that the results of a market "appear to be a product of some omniscient, designing mind."[32]

In each of these illustrative examples, there is revealed, at least by inference, an understanding of the spontaneous ordering properties of a market process that is sharply different from the understanding held by the radical subjectivists. In each example, the efficacy of market adjustment is measured *teleologically* in terms of the relative achievement of some predefined goal or objective. In Simons's problems, the objective is, simply, economic product, which is wheat in his one-good economy. In Polanyi's case, the objective is explicitly stated to be minimization of volume. In Barry's essay, the argument is more sophisticated, but any conceptualization of an omniscient, designing mind must imply some well-defined objective that exists independently from the separate participants' own *creative* choices.

If the efficacy of market organization is, as insinuated in the above examples, evaluated teleologically, in terms of its capacity to approach an independently – i.e. "independent" of the choice process itself – determinable goal state, then there remains only an ambiguous discourse over comparative performance as between such an organization and centralized economic planning. Even if Simons, Polanyi, and Barry, along with others, may have succeeded in demonstrating that decentralized arrangements are superior in achieving some objectively identifiable goal, their conceptualization of the market process forces them into a line of comparative defense, which a radical subjectivist understanding of the market would have rendered unnecessary from the outset.

If the market is genuinely perceived as an open-ended, non-determined evolutionary process in which the essential driving forces are human choices, any insinuation, however subtle, of a "telos" toward which the process can be predicted to move must be inherently misleading. There is, in our view, no systematically sustainable "middle ground" between a teleological and a non-teleological perspective. And all conceptualizations of the market process that suppose, whether explicitly or implicitly, a "something" toward which the process is moving are, by this very fact, *teleological*, whether the "something" is specified as an "equilibrium" or otherwise. This applies to the notion of a mechanical equilibrium as implied in the standard textbook models of intersecting demand and supply curves, as well as to the thermodynamic equilibrium concept that is implied where the market process is interpreted in terms of exhaustion of potential gains from trade. And it also applies to images of the market that are intended to capture the constant change in the equilibrium telos, such as Kenneth Boulding's image of the "dog chasing a cat" (Littlechild 1986: 32).

It should be noted that to question the appropriateness of teleological conceptions of the market is not the same as denying the apparent fact that the human participants in the "catallaxy," the game of the market, reasonably *adapt* to the circumstances that they confront and to changes that they expect to occur. The predictive potential of microeconomic theory lies in the uniformity of such adaptive response among persons. But such adaptive behavior does not imply that the overall process is moving toward some determined goal, whether conceived as a predetermined equilibrium or as a "moving cat." The game described by the market may be misunderstood if interpreted in a teleological mind-set. The market economy, *as an aggregation*, neither maximizes nor minimizes anything. It simply allows participants to pursue that which they value, subject to the preferences and endowments of others and within the constraints of general "rules of the game" which allow, and provide incentives for, individuals to try out new ways of doing things. There simply is no "external," independently defined objective against which the results of market processes can be evaluated.

We may illustrate the non-teleological perspective on market interaction by dropping the familiar presupposition that potential traders initially possess quantities of well-defined marketable goods. Assume that no goods exist, and that persons are described by certain talents, capacities, and skills that enable them to produce consumable goods from nature. Assume that the rules of the game allow persons to claim enforceable rights to shares in natural endowments and to their own capacities and skills. In this model, trade will take place when persons recognize that their well-being can be enhanced by producing *and* exchanging rather than producing for own consumption only. The chain of choices is extended, and, also, there is an added requirement that any participant exercises *imagination* in choosing to specialize in production with the ultimate purpose of achieving an increase in well-being through exchange.

Think of the choice calculus of a person in this setting. What can I produce that will prove of exchange value to others? Response to this question allows the participant not only to select among a pre-existing set of goods, but also, and importantly, to *create* new goods that are expected to be of potential exchangeable value. Once the creative–inventive–imaginative element in choice is introduced into the game here, then any idealized omniscience on the part of a planner who might attempt to duplicate the market result would become patently absurd. Individuals would use their own imagination, their own assessment of the potential evaluations of others, in producing goods wholly divorced from own consumption; goods that are anticipated to yield values when put on the market; values which, as income to the producers, can be used to purchase goods from others in the nexus. This seeking to satisfy others through producing marketable value as an indirect means of producing value for themselves – this characteristic behavioral element in a market order – was central to Adam Smith's insight. And it is this feature that allows us to compare the performance of market organization with alternative social arrangements, even in the absence of an independently existing scalar. Markets tend to satisfy the preferences of persons, regardless of what their preferences might be, and even when we acknowledge that preferences emerge only within the process of choice itself.

The market conceived as a "game without goods" also suggests the tenuousness of the whole notion of equilibrium, defined as the exhaustion of gains from trade, which looms so important in the alternative teleological perspective. In the production and exchange of pre-existing and well-defined goods, it is relatively easy to think of the game as having a definitive and final outcome once the goods have been so allocated that no participant seeks out further trades. Goods are, by definition, then allocated to their highest valued uses. But the usefulness of this equilibrium notion becomes less clear when we assume that there is no definite set of goods to be allocated. Conceptually, it remains possible to "freeze" the imaginative elements in individual choice at some point and allow the production–exchange process to work itself out to an equilibrium, in which no further gains from trade, *and from imagination of new trading prospects*, are possible. The artificiality of such an equilibrium construction is apparent, however, as there seems nothing in the mind that is even remotely analogous to the cessation of exchange. There is no determinate limit to the potential of market value to be created as the process of human interaction proceeds.

What has made, and continues to make, the equilibrium concept attractive even to economists who, like Kirzner, are explicitly critical of the neo-classical orthodoxy is, it seems, its perceived capacity to capture readily the co-ordination properties of markets, and the suspicion that one may be left incapable to account systematically for the orderliness of markets if one were to take the radical subjectivist argument too seriously. Even if such suspicion may have been invited by some of the radical subjectivists' testimonies, the emerging new "evolutionary synthesis" suggests a theoretical perspective that allows one to do both: to take seriously the subjectivist emphasis on the creativity of human choice, with all its implications, and, at the same time, to provide a non-teleological explanations for the adaptiveness and co-ordination properties that markets exhibit. If there is a consistent way to spell out a radical subjectivist research program it is, we presume, as an evolutionary economics.

Conclusion

We have suggested in this chapter that a perceptual vision that looks on "the market" as a *creative process* offers more insight and understanding than the alternative visions that elicit interpretations of the market as a *discovery process*,[33] or, more familiarly, as an *allocative process*. In either of the last alternatives, there is a telos imposed by the scientist's own perception, a telos that is non-existent in the first stance. And removal of the teleological inference from the way of looking at economic interaction carries with it significant implications for any diagnosis of failure or success, diagnosis that is necessarily preliminary to any normative usage of scientific analysis.

We may illustrate the differing implications in application to the observed failure of the centrally planned economies of Eastern Europe and elsewhere. The neo-classical economist, trapped in the allocationist perception, tends to locate the source of failure in the distorted incentive structure that causes persons to be confronted with choice alternatives that do not reflect authentically derived evaluations. Resources do not flow to their most highly valued uses because persons who make decisions about resource use do not find it privately in their own interest to shift allocation in such fashion as to accomplish this conceptually definable, and desirable, result.

Some of the modern "Austrian" economists, and notably Kirzner, add an important element to the neo-classical critique. They suggest that, even if the incentive problems could somehow be ignored or assumed corrected, there would still remain the epistemological or knowledge problem. Only a decentralized market structure of economic interaction can exploit fully the knowledge of localized circumstances required to allow a definition of the ultimate valuation that is placed on resource use. Only the market can allow persons the effective liberty to discover the particular localized eccentricities that give form to value. This extension of the neo-classical emphasis on incentive structures is important and relevant to any overall assessment of the central planning model for an economy.

We suggest, however, that the critique, even as extended, falls short of capturing an essential element in any comparative assessment of the market and the planning alternatives. The teleological feature remains to be exorcised. In the neo-classical setting, even as extended by Kirzner, an *omniscient* and *benevolent* monolithic planner could secure the ideally defined result. Omniscience would, of course, insure access to any and all knowledge; benevolence could be such as to match the objective function precisely with whatever it is that individuals desire. But even the planner so idealized cannot create that which is not there and will not be there save through the exercise of the creative choices of individuals, who themselves have no idea in advance concerning the ideas that their own imaginations will yield.

The fundamental misunderstandings of the theory of the market economy that provided the analytical–intellectual foundations for socialism as a principle for socioeconomic organization are exposed by any one of the three interpretations contrasted here. The market as an allocative process, responding to the structure of incentives that confront choice makers; the market as a discovery process, utilizing localized information; or the market as a creative process that exploits man's imaginative potential – socialism cannot, organizationally, be made equivalent to any of these idealized perceptions. But, the "fatal conceit" that was socialism, to use Hayek's descriptive term here, would have surely faced more difficulty in achieving dominance as an idea if the creative spontaneity of the market process had been more fully appreciated.

8 A constitutional economics perspective on international trade

Introduction

The purpose of this chapter is not to enter the long-standing debate on the *economics of international trade*, a debate that is concerned with the economic consequences of free trade compared with various forms of protection (Vousen 1990). Nor do I intend to enter the growing discussion on the *political economy of protection* which looks at the political determinants of protectionist regimes and seeks to explain the latter in terms of an equilibrium between conflicting interests in a *political market* (Magee *et al.* 1989). Instead, taking as undisputed what seems to me to be the main thrust of the economics of international trade and of the political economy of protection, I want to approach, if only in a preliminary and sketchy fashion, some of the more fundamental issues of free trade and protection from a *constitutional political economy perspective*.

What is a constitutional political economy of international trade about? For my purposes here, I want to interpret the notion of international trade in the broad sense in which it includes all across-border economic activities, i.e. all activities that involve movements of goods and services, of capital and of persons across national boundaries. Accordingly, the particular subject of a constitutional approach are the *rules* which pertain to such across-border activities, or, as I shall call them here, the international rules.[1] In what follows, I shall first identify the two main problems which may give rise to international rules: The problem of the enforcement of border-crossing contracts and the problem of protection. I shall, then, address in more detail the enforcement problem in international trade, whereas the role of international rules in dealing with protection will be discussed in the following section. The concluding section provides a brief discussion on the relation between free trade – as a general principle of free movement of goods, capital, and persons – and competition between governments.

Problems and rules in international trade

One of the most noticeable developments in the study of social rules and institutions is the increased use of game theoretical concepts, most notably the *prisoners' dilemma* concept. The perspective of game theory helps to sharpen a notion that has always played a central role in institutional analysis, namely the idea that rules can be usefully looked at as "social tools" which serve to provide standard solutions to recurrent problems. Just as we have tools, in the ordinary sense, for solving problems that we face recurrently, for instance a saw for cutting wood, we can think of social rules as devices that help us to deal with recurrent problems in social interaction, such as the rules of the road that allow for a smoother flow of traffic than would otherwise be possible.

If we look at international trade from such a perspective, two problems immediately come to mind that tend to create obstacles to the realization of potential gains from trade. The first problem is linked with the fact that economic exchanges often cannot be transacted strictly simultaneously, but require one party to move first and to give up a valuable resource before the other half of the transaction can be concluded. In order for such transactions to be carried out, and the gains that they promise to the potential traders to be realized, the party which is to move first has to have a sufficient reason to trust in the other party's compliance. In settings where the prospective traders are involved in continuous dealings and/or directly know each other, *personal trust* can provide such a reason. It is obvious, though, that, if personal trust were the only remedy for the problem, the extent of the market over which trade expands would be very limited, and so would, in Adam Smith's terms, the division of labor which is the source of the gains that can be realized through trade.

While technological advancements, for instance in transportation and communication, are relevant in expanding the size of markets, the most important step in this process is, as economic historians such as Douglass North (1987: 421) argue, the "development of a third party to exchanges, namely government," which enforces contracts that extend beyond the narrow bounds defined by personal trust and continuous dealings. Yet, the effectiveness of government as enforcing agent finds its own limitations in the territorially defined boundaries of national jurisdictions. And the problem arises of how, in the international realm, a foundation can be provided for the kind of trust that is required for potential traders to be able to realize gains from trade across jurisdictional borders. Before I return to this issue, I want to discuss, first, the other problem in border-crossing trade, the problem that is, indeed, the major theme of international trade theory, namely the obstacles that arise from the various forms of *protection* with which national governments intervene in the trading process.

The problem of protectionism

There is an often noted, seeming paradox in international trade, a striking contrast between the lessons of economic theory and observed political practice. On the one side, there is the theory of international trade which, basically since Adam Smith's arguments on the nature and causes of the wealth of nations, teaches that free trade is the best policy if the general welfare of a nation is to be promoted (Bhagwati 1989: 23ff.).[2] On the other hand, we find that protectionist policies are pervasively practiced, that they are the rule rather than the exception, throughout history and across the world. If one is not content with simply attributing such a paradox to the irrationality of politics, the question arises of how a systematic account may be provided from within the standard economic paradigm of rational, self-interested behavior.

Game theory suggests a prime candidate for such an account, namely the concept of the prisoners' dilemma, which is the paradigm case for situations where the separate, rational pursuit of individual interests generates an overall outcome that makes all participants worse off than they could have been; or, in the jargon of game theory, by choosing their – individually rational – dominant strategies the players produce an outcome that is inferior to what would have resulted had they chosen their – individually irrational – dominated strategies. Explanations of the "protection paradox" in terms of the prisoners' dilemma (PD) concept have indeed been proposed, although they come in two critically different versions; the one diagnosing the paradox as an *inter*-national PD, the other tracing it back to an *intra*-national PD.

The international version of the PD argument can be found, for instance, in Robert Axelrod's justly famous book on the *Evolution of Cooperation*. Axelrod (1984: 7) cites the issue of trade barriers among two industrial nations as a "good example of the fundamental problem of cooperation," arguing that, even though the countries would be better off if there were no barriers, this does not bring about free trade because "whatever one country does, the other country is better off retaining its own trade barriers." This view, which Axelrod is certainly not the only one to hold, is dubious for, at least, two reasons. The first is its implied assumption that free trade is advantageous only if *generally* practiced, whereas unilateral free trade would be self-damaging to a country. International trade theory teaches in essence (i.e. except for certain special contingencies) the exact opposite. Although the gains from free trade are the greater the larger the set of free traders, free trade enhances the welfare of a nation even if practiced unilaterally. Or, as Jan Tumlir, the late research director of the General Agreement on Tariffs and Trade (GATT) secretariat in Geneva, put it (Tumlir 1983: 75):

> It is, of course, the case that free trade would benefit even a single country, or a small group of them, in a generally protectionist world. But it is also true that the extent of the benefit to each depends on the number of countries participating in the system of such trade.

The second problem with the "international PD" theory of protectionism is its implied treatment of nations as unit actors who rationally pursue their interests, a perspective that is quite common in the "game theory of international politics."[3] Such a perspective can either be interpreted in an organicist way which would be blatantly inconsistent with the methodological individualism that is generally regarded as the paradigmatic trademark of economic theory. Or it can be read as reflecting the assumption that governments generally act as benevolent and reliable maximizers of their nations' common good. Although, to be sure, the latter assumption has its tradition in welfare economics, the advent of public choice theory has dramatically reduced the number of economists who continue to consider it a useful device for the study of economic policy. Public choice theory has done so by pointing to, and systematically drawing the conclusions from, the simple fact that governments are made up of individual persons who have their own interests, no less than ordinary economic actors, and that they pursue these interests within the constraints that the institutional–constitutional framework imposes on them.

The modern political economy of protection can be understood as an application of public choice theory to the realm of trade politics. By systematically disaggregating the political process into the underlying interplay of particular interests, it is able to provide a quite straightforward explanation for the "paradox of protection" (Frey 1984: 20ff.; Weck-Hannemann 1989: 3ff.; Krueger 1990). It can show that the principal obstacles to the realization of free trade lie at the intra- (rather than the inter-) national level, namely in the differential benefits that government can provide to special interests by granting protection for particular industries or trades. The problem of protection is indeed diagnosed as a prisoners' dilemma, but as one that has its roots on the intranational level rather than in conflicts of interests among nations. As an aside, in this regard, the problem of protection in international trade is critically different from problems, such as environmental pollution, which may justly be classified as international PDs (von Witzke and Livingston 1990).

The theory of protectionism as an intranational prisoners' dilemma problem (Schuknecht 1990) explains protectionist policies as a result of rent-seeking. It states, in short, the following: although, as traditional trade theory argues, free trade is the "best policy" for a country overall, any particular industry can benefit from being protected against foreign competition, and, therefore, has an incentive to seek to achieve such protection. While all would be better off if nobody were protected, to seek protection is the dominant choice for each industry acting separately. Being protected is preferable, independent of what is true for the other industries: if nobody else is protected, one's own protection yields a differential advantage, and so it does if a few or all others are protected as well.

From a constitutional economics perspective, the argument can be restated in terms of the distinction between the constitutional and the in-period level of choice: if we were made to choose between alternative institutional–constitutional regimes, a free-trade regime on the one side, and a regime characterized by pervasive protectionism on the other side, we would certainly prefer to live in the former because it would promise to be the wealthier society. Such choice at the level of regimes would reflect what one may call our *constitutional preferences*, our preferences over alternative constitutional rules, preferences that are informed by our perception of the working properties of alternative constitutional systems (Vanberg and Buchanan 1989). The prisoners' dilemma nature of the problem lies in the fact that our constitutional preference for a free-trade regime does by no means assure that in the arena of ordinary politics we would all have an incentive to refrain from protectionist lobbying. What requires us to draw a careful distinction here is the different nature of constitutional choices among regimes as opposed to strategic choices within regimes. There is nothing inherently inconsistent about advocating free trade on the *constitutional* level, and to seek, at the same time, protection for one's own particular trade on the *sub-constitutional* level of in-period politics. These are simply two different levels of choice, involving fundamentally different choice alternatives: alternative regimes in the one case, and alternative strategies within regimes in the other.

The recognition that if required to choose to live either in a free-trade or a protectionist environment we would rationally opt for the former does, for the reasons explained, by no means imply that we could be expected to abstain voluntarily from protectionist rent-seeking in ordinary politics. Nor does it imply that, within existing regimes, characterized by varying institutional mixtures of free trade and protection, we could easily reach agreement in support of general constitutional prohibitions of protection. The interests that drive protectionist rent-seeking in ordinary politics cannot be expected to evaporate mysteriously as we move up to the level of constitutional politics. The differences between particular industries with regard to their previous success in securing protection create, of course, vested interests which, despite the overall wealth increase that movements toward a free-trade constitution should promise, may still expect to be differentially advantaged by the *status quo* regime. Yet, although certainly driven by interests too, the dynamics of constitutional politics is not just a mere duplication of the conflicts that characterize ordinary politics. For reasons amply discussed under such labels as "veil of uncertainty" or "veil of ignorance" (Vanberg and Buchanan 1991), the prospects for agreement are enhanced as we move to the more generalized reflections that constitutional decisions on rules command. And for the free-trade issue, in particular, it could well be that a fuller account of all the direct and indirect wealth effects of protectionist restrictions may show that a constitutional prohibition of protection is likely to promise net gains – and, therefore, be agreeable – even for the current "beneficiaries" of protectionist regimes because of their dual affectedness as producers and consumers (Buchanan and Lee 1991).

If, as my argument so far suggests, there are indeed constitutional interests in free trade hidden behind, or buried by protectionist policies, the question arises of how these constitutional interests may be effectively implemented. Before discussing this question, I want to return, however, to the enforcement problem in international trade, i.e. the enforcement of contracts that cut across jurisdictional boundaries.

Protective state and trade protection

In an article, already referred to earlier, on "Institutions, transaction costs and economic growth," North (1987) draws a useful distinction between three types of trade arrangements, namely *personal exchange, impersonal exchange,* and *impersonal exchange with third party enforcement.* In personal exchange, the traders possess, because of repeated dealings or otherwise, "a great deal of personal knowledge about the attributes, characteristics, and features of each other" (ibid.: 420). This makes for low transaction costs, but, since such conditions are confined to dense social networks, personal exchange sets rather narrow limits to the extent of the market and, therefore, to the potential for specialization and division of labor.

Going beyond the confines of personal exchange, and entering the "world of impersonal exchange" (ibid.), means increasing potential for specialization and division of labor and, as a result, significant gains in productivity or, in other terms, a significant decrease in production costs. But it also means a significant increase in transaction costs because of the increased difficulties in enforcing the terms of exchange. It is, North argues, the emergence of an enforcing third party, namely government, which allows for the reduction in transaction costs that is required if the potential gains from impersonal exchange are to be fully realized.

North's notion of government as a third party enforcer corresponds to what Buchanan (1975: 68f.) has called the *protective state;* in distinction from the conceptually different *productive state,* the agency through which politically organized individuals provide themselves with public goods. Ideally, the protective state operates as a strictly neutral and impartial enforcer of agreed-on rules and of contractual obligations voluntarily entered into by trading parties. Its essential function is to provide and enforce an institutional framework which facilitates voluntary trade. In other words, the protective state's proper role is to *remove obstacles* to voluntary exchange, such as fraud and coercion. Yet, as Buchanan as well as North note, the emergence of government as an enforcing agent is a double-edged sword. With the concentration of power in the hand of the state comes the potential for this power to be used to impose and enforce rules which favor certain interest groups at the expense of others. Applied to the problem of protectionism: while the protective state plays an essential role in facilitating free trade, its coercive power can also be used to inhibit free trade through protectionist measures. Or, stated somewhat more poetically, the protective state and the state as a protection-granting agent are twin brothers that work to offset partly each other's efforts: the one removing obstacles to voluntary trade, the other erecting new ones. In the state as protection-granting agent, we find, again, the principal subject of the political economy of protection, and of the theory of rent-seeking more generally. And the problem of how this agent can be tamed brings us back to the question of how our constitutional interest in free trade can be effectively implemented, the question that I raised earlier and to which I shall return in the next section.

In the remainder of this section, I want to concentrate on the "pure" role of the protective state and, in particular, on the question of what the territorial confines of its jurisdictional domain imply for the issue of international trade. Put simply, the question is whether the fragmentation in national jurisdictions or, in short, the "territoriality of law" (Schmidtchen and Schmidt-Trenz 1990) leaves obstacles to border-crossing trade, the effective removal of which would require an enforcing agent with transnational or supranational authority.

The international realm, the world of international relations, is often described as a state of anarchy, not unlike the "state of nature" in the Hobbesian sense (Oye 1986).[4] If this were an adequate characterization, one should expect that voluntary trade in the international arena would be subject to the same limitations that hamper co-operation in the Hobbesian arena. That is, we should expect that, in the terms of North's argument, any effective extension of trade beyond the confines of personal exchange would require the emergence of an enforcing agency on the international level in order to bring about the decrease in transaction costs that is needed for the potential gains from impersonal exchange to be realized. Prima facie evidence contradicts such reasoning. Although we have not witnessed the emergence of a world Leviathan, international trade has been successfully carried out through known history and its volume in today's world is obviously gigantic, covering the whole globe.

It is not too difficult to propose an answer for why impersonal exchange is very feasible in the international realm despite the absence of an international enforcing agency. Going back to the original issue of impersonal exchange, one can locate the essential problem in the difficulty for potential traders to make credible commitments, commitments which would assure their respective counterparts that they will indeed conclude their part of the deal. In personal exchange, such credibility derives from personal knowledge. In impersonal exchange, traders can make their commitments credible by mutually submitting to the dictum and enforcement of a third party. This is what gives, as North argues, governmental enforcement such an essential role in expanding the extent of the market, and in providing for the gains from specialization and division of labor that come with it.

On a "first level," so to speak, the emergence of government as third party enforcer is apparently essential in providing a low-cost method for making credible commitments. Once national governments exist, and we move into the realm of international impersonal exchange, the commitment problem takes on a critically different nature. On the first, the national level, there is apparently no fully fledged substitute for government enforcement; although, I should add here, there have been effective "partial," non-government substitutes which have helped through history to facilitate impersonal trade, such as private commercial law, the so-called "law merchant" (Trakman 1983; Benson 1990). In the realm of international trade, there is, however, a potential substitute for an international enforcement agency available, namely the existing national governments. Traders can make credible commitments in international transactions if the enforcement systems in their respective home countries can be used by their foreign counterparts to enforce compliance with the terms of a contract.

The credibility that a national enforcement system provides to contractual commitments exchanged among domestic traders can easily and effectively be extended to international transactions by granting equal enforceability to contracts between domestic and foreign traders. This is, indeed, what we observe – even if only imperfectly realized – and what allows for a rather smooth operation of international trade; although, to be sure, differences between different national legal systems introduce ambiguities which pose obstacles that are absent within national jurisdictions.[5] And there are apparent reasons why traders may find it in their constitutional interest to have their domestic courts enforce foreign claims; or, stated differently, why, if faced with a choice between a regime which insures such enforceability and one which does not, they would choose the former. The reason is, of course, that traders who can back up their commitments by the enforcement power of their own domestic jurisdictions are more attractive trading partners for foreigners than those who cannot, and they will, therefore, encounter more and better opportunities for profitable exchange (Vanberg and Buchanan 1988: 152; Moser 1990: 13ff.).

The above implies that the absence of an international enforcement agency need not pose a real obstacle to international trade. The credibility of commitments in international transactions can be effectively provided through national jurisdictions. In other words, the commitment problems that arise on the international level can be solved with the institutional devices available at the national level. Indeed, the enforceability of international contracts is a direct function of the effectiveness and reliability of national jurisdictions, so that, in a sense, the international order may be said to be, in essence, a "reflection of national constitutional order" (Tumlir 1983: 80; Moser 1990: 139).[6]

Anti-protection commitments and their enforcement

Players who face a prisoners' dilemma-type situation can escape the dilemma if they can exchange credible commitments not to use their dominant, "defection" strategy. In fact, commitments are credible and effective to the extent that they introduce incentives which eliminate the dominance of the non-co-operative choice. Commitments serve as constraints on behavior. They are intended effectively to eliminate certain strategy options from a player's choice set by increasing the costs of choosing them. The prisoners' dilemma is a paradigmatic example of the kinds of situations in which an exchange of commitments, the deliberate adoption of mutual constraints on one's choice set, allows players to realize gains that otherwise would not be attainable.

I have argued above that the problem of protectionism is a prisoners' dilemma-type problem, yet an *intra*-national rather than an *inter*-national one. Such diagnosis would suggest that commitments on the national rather than the international level would be required to solve the problem. If it is indeed intranational rent-seeking – rather than conflicting interests on the international level – that drive protectionist politics, it would seem that the proper remedy would have to come from an exchange of commitments among intranational interest groups rather than from an exchange of commitments between nations. What we observe in reality seems to reflect the exact opposite: free-trade issues are typically the subject of international agreements, rather than of intranational constitutional politics. In the remainder of this section, I shall comment on some of the questions that are raised by this seeming puzzle.

There are basically two questions that arise in this context. First, why is it that we find the problem of protectionism to be a concern of international politics? And, second, given that they have become a subject of international agreements, can such agreements provide effective solutions to the problem of protection? Concerning the first question, one has to keep in mind that, although protectionism is essentially an intranational problem, it is still the case that a nation's economic wealth is negatively affected by other nations' protectionist policies. To be sure, the protectionism of other countries does not change the fact that a nation's overall welfare is still better served by free trade rather than by a protectionist policy. Yet, its gains from trade are clearly reduced compared with what they could be if the other countries were free traders too. There are, in this sense, negative external effects from protectionist policies, and these negative effects create a mutual interest among nations in their respective trade policies. This fact alone could explain why we find protectionism to be a subject of international politics; yet the political economy of protection has added, as a further reason, the observation that, because of the dynamics of intranational democratic politics, domestic support for free-trade commitments may be easier for politicians to secure if such commitments come in the form of a negotiated "exchange" with other governments rather than in the form of unilateral constitutional guarantees.[7]

The second question, concerning the effectiveness of international agreements as a substitute for national constitutional prohibitions of protectionist policies, has a "yes, but" answer. Yes, international agreements could, in principle, serve the same purpose as national constitutional provisions. But, there is a problem of enforceability. There is no third party enforcer out there to whom the contracting governments could turn in order to give credibility to their anti-protection commitments, and it is far from clear how sovereign nations should be able to create an appropriate international enforcement agency, one that is powerful enough to force individual nations into compliance with agreed on commitments and at the same time is safeguarded "against any abuse of that very substantial power" (Tumlir 1983: 83). While the recourse to the national level, as explained above, makes an international agency for the enforcement of privately negotiated trades dispensable, it seems hardly workable for contracts among governments who would be required to act as their own guardians.

It appears as if we were left with the following dilemma: free-trade commitments are apparently easier to achieve in the form of commitment exchanges among governments than in the form of unilateral constitutional guarantees on the national level. And, in principle, such international commitments could serve as genuine substitutes for national constitutional provisions. The problem, however, is that their effective enforcement seems to require an international enforcement agency which is yet absent and unlikely to be created. It is with regard to the enforcement problem for international free-trade agreements that a proposal advanced by Jan Tumlir, whom I mentioned earlier, may promise a feasible solution, a solution which capitalizes on the fact that protectionism is ultimately, indeed, a matter of intranational conflicts of interest. Tumlir's proposal (Hauser *et al.* 1988: 226ff.; Moser 1990: 33ff.) is that internationally negotiated commitments among governments should be translated or incorporated into the respective domestic legal-constitutional order in such a way that they create rights for individual citizens, enforceable in domestic courts, e.g. the right to import goods without governmental interference. In Tumlir's (1983: 82) own words:

> One can imagine the international economic policy commitments of a government to be undertaken in the form of self-executing or directly effective treaty provisions, creating immediate private rights enforceable against one's own government … . These rights would be enforceable in national courts only, with no sacrifice of legal sovereignty.

Tumlir's last remark on national sovereignty points to an issue that deserves somewhat closer examination, namely the question of what effective free-trade commitments imply for the distribution of rights among governments and between governments and citizens.

Free trade and inter-governmental competition

The essence of protectionist measures is that they inhibit voluntary transactions that otherwise would take place among domestic producers/consumers and foreign producers/consumers. This means that free-trade commitments are, in the first instance, not concessions that governments make to each other. They are, instead, about the distribution of rights between governments and their citizens. They are constraints on the discretionary power with which governments can interfere in the economic activities of their citizens. They provide assurances to citizens that they can engage in economic transactions with foreigners free from politically imposed obstacles. Again, in the words of Jan Tumlir (1983: 83):

> International economic policy rules under which governments commit themselves to maintain freedom of and non-discrimination in legitimate international transactions of their citizens represent important additional protection of private property rights – "the second line of national constitutional entrenchment."[8]

Free trade in the general sense of free movement of goods and services, capital and persons is a principle that is not only important with regard to economic efficiency as traditionally understood. It is an essential device through which individuals can secure their rights from government encroachment, a device through which they can effectively control governmental powers. The rights of participation in collective political decision-making that liberal democracies provide for their citizens are, without any doubt, extremely important in keeping governments responsive to the interests of those whom they govern, as a comparison with alternative forms of government clearly reveals. Yet, public choice theory has made us aware of the limits of democratic collective choice mechanisms in large constituencies as to their capacity to establish a sensitive link between citizens' interests and governmental policies. These limits characterize the operation of ordinary politics, and they characterize in no lesser way the realm of constitutional politics.

It is notable with regard to the latter realm that the principle of free trade can considerably strengthen the power of control that citizens, *as individuals*, are able to exercise vis-à-vis their governments.[9] In their capacity as voters–citizens, they can *co*-determine the choice among constitutional regimes, with their vote rapidly becoming insignificant as the size of the constituency increases. It is their freedom to move with their economic activities, with their investments and their human capital between locations that allows them to choose individually and separately among alternative constitutional regimes. In this sense, free trade introduces an important element of competition into the relation between governments. If individuals are free to move with their resources between different jurisdictions, governments have to compete for these resources in much the same way in which firms have to compete for the funds of consumers, the financial contributions of investors, and the human inputs of employees.[10]

Such competition can help to establish, in the political realm, a responsiveness of governments to citizens' interests that is similar to the responsiveness that market competition induces in the relation between producers and consumers, an observation that in Tiebout's classic essay on the "Theory of local expenditures" is summarized in the statement: "Spatial mobility provides the local public-goods counterpart to the private market's shopping trip" (Tiebout 1956: 23). Stefan Sinn (1989; 1992) has elaborated the notion that the allocation of capital among different countries can be compared to Tiebout's voting-by-feet mechanism, and that both

> ... tend to produce the result that government policies (at the national or local level) are more in line with private preferences than would be the case if a centralized solution prevents firms or residents from "shopping around."
>
> (Sinn 1992: 3).

As Sinn points out, the need for governments to "compete for financial capital and other internationally mobile resources" (Sinn 1989: 3) imposes constraints on their policy choices that may substitute for explicit constitutional constraints, "as long as openness is constitutionally guaranteed" (Sinn 1992: 13). Demands for international policy co-ordination should, in this light, be met with suspicion, as potential instruments of "collusion among governments" (ibid.: 14) aimed at escaping such competitive constraints.[11]

The competitive constraints that result from the mobility of resources between jurisdictions clearly impose limits on what governments can do (Hayek 1948b: 258ff.), and they may, in this sense, be said to "reduce national sovereignty." It should, however, be obvious that limitations on the power of government that result from inter-governmental competition are critically different from "reductions in sovereignty" that would result from a transfer of political power to an international authority. Whereas the latter would, in fact, mean a shift of national sovereignty to a common authority, the discretionary power that national governments lose as a consequence of inter-governmental competition is not shifted to some other political body but is returned to the "ultimate sovereigns," the individual citizens, whose freedom of choice and control is enhanced. An effective international market order can, in this sense, be created without any sacrifice in national sovereignty, other than the limitation of governmental power that results from the increased freedom of individuals to move with their resources to jurisdictions of their free choice. The essential requirement would be that such freedom be secured by commitments of governments to allow for the free movement of goods, capital, and persons across national boundaries, commitments that can be enforced in national and/or international courts.

The notion that the right and the capacity of individuals to move with their resources between jurisdictions imposes effective constraints on the power of governments has, for obvious reasons, been an important theme in discussions on federalism in general (Hayek 1948), and on fiscal federalism in particular (Brennan and Buchanan 1980: 168ff.; Wiseman 1990). It has found renewed attention in a number of recent contributions on the concept of *competitive federalism*, on federalism as inter-governmental competition (Breton 1987: 268ff.; Dye 1990a; 1990b; Wildavsky 1990: 43f.; Kenyon and Kincaid 1991: 9ff.; Kincaid 1991).[12] The thrust of this literature is that competition can help to curb, control, and dissipate governmental power in the political arena, just as it helps to control and dissipate private power in the market arena. An aspect that has been given particular attention is the significance of exit costs in interjurisdictional competition, and the role of federal organization in reducing these costs.[13] The lower the costs of moving resources between jurisdictions, the stronger the competitive pressure on the respective governments, and, therefore, their responsiveness to constituents' preferences. Federal arrangements tend to reduce these costs by eliminating "impediments as to the movement of men, goods, and capital" (Hayek 1948b: 255) between polities.[14]

Critics of the concept of "federalism as inter-governmental competition" have argued that it is inappropriate to suppose generally that such competition is benign, and they have pointed to various instances where competition – in matters of taxation, regulation, etc. – between jurisdictions may lead to detrimental results. There is no room, in the present context, for a detailed discussion of this issue (see, however, Kenyon and Kincaid 1991), beyond pointing out that, in this regard, the situation for inter-governmental competition is not entirely different from that for ordinary market competition. To advocate free markets is not the same as claiming that competition *"per se"* is generally and unconditionally beneficial, independent of the means by which it is carried out (e.g. by using coercion, deception, etc.). What is endorsed is appropriately constrained competition. In fact, the notion of market competition implies the understanding that competition is carried out within a framework of rules that serve to promote its beneficial working. In the same sense, and for the same reasons, inter-governmental competition cannot be expected to produce generally and unconditionally desirable outcomes – "desirable" in terms of constituents' preferences. Advocacy of competitive federalism does not mean to recommend for states

> ... to engage in unbridled competition, but rather to compete and cooperate within the bounds of the civil order established by the constitution and within the agreed-upon rules enforced by an overarching government (i.e. the federal government).
>
> (Kenyon and Kincaid 1991: 15)[15]

The question of what are the "appropriate rules" for constraining competition may, here as in the case of ordinary markets, not always be easy to decide, and there is probably no simple formula that would provide a once-and-for-all answer.[16] Furthermore, it may not always be easy to draw the line between appropriate constraints on competition and collusive agreements aimed at eliminating competition. But such difficulties should not distract attention from the principal issue, namely the role of competition as an instrument for promoting responsive government.

The above discussion on inter-governmental competition and responsiveness of governments to citizens' preferences has focused on the role of competition in controlling power. There is, however, a second aspect of competition that is relevant in this context and that should, at least, be briefly mentioned, namely the role of competition as "discovery procedure" (Hayek 1978a). Responsiveness to constituents' preferences has two ingredients: the incentive to respect what citizens want, and the knowledge of what it may be that they want. Market competition does not only induce producers of goods and services to be responsive to predefined consumer preferences. Competition is also a process of exploration and experimentation in which new ways of doing things are constantly tried out, and new goods and services are constantly offered that seek prospectively to provide what consumers may want once they see it but which they – for lack of knowledge – could not have demanded independently. In a similar fashion, inter-governmental competition can be said not only to provide inducements for governments to respect predefined citizens' preferences but also to be a process in which alternative ways of providing services, alternative ways of organizing political institutions, or new kinds of publicly provided goods can be explored and experimented with. That is, in the realm of politics as well as in ordinary markets, a principal argument for relying on competition is that we typically cannot know in advance what is the best way to serve consumers' or citizens' interests, that we do not know in advance what the best way is of organizing political activities or of providing market goods, and that competition provides a framework for exploration and "desirable experimentation" (Hayek 1948b: 268) in these matters.[17] This explorative function of competition also applies to the rules of competition themselves (Vaubel 1985: 416).

Conclusion

The overall thrust of the argument advanced in this chapter is that the principle of free trade, understood in the general sense of free movement of goods, capital and persons, can be made workable with constitutional commitments at the level of existing nation-states and without the need to create supranational governmental authorities, and that it can work as an effective constraint on governments to the benefit of their constituencies. Such a general free-trade regime would extend the working principles of ordinary market exchange into the realm of politics, as competition of policies as well as competition of institutions.[18] It could be viewed as a real world approximation to what Robert Nozick has described as a "framework for utopia" (Nozick 1974: 317ff.), a liberal framework that offers maximal freedom for persons voluntarily to choose and create the kind of communities or institutional arrangements that they find desirable.

To show how a free-trade framework could, in principle, be made workable and to describe its desirable working properties is, of course, not the same as showing how it might be brought into existence. Nor is it meant to imply that movements in the direction of such a framework could easily win popular support. In fact, as far as the prospects for the realization of a free-trade regime are concerned, a quite straightforward public choice argument suggests that the political decision-makers who would have to orchestrate such a constitutional shift have few incentives to do so because it would result in a dramatic decrease in their discretionary power. Nevertheless, the kind of analysis that this chapter exemplifies does need not to remain a mere academic exercise. It may have an effect on public policy by imposing constraints on the rhetoric that can be used in the political arena to justify anti-free-trade measures. As far as the question of popular support is concerned, casual observation reveals that the principle of free movement of persons across jurisdictions is the most sensitive, and potentially controversial, aspect of the free-trade principle. Kindleberger (1986: 4) reports that he regularly used to ask students on examinations, as an aside, questions testing their attitudes toward free trade, separating between the issues of free movement of goods, of capital, and of persons. He found the support for free trade to diminish significantly as his questions proceeded from free trade in goods to free movement of persons. And with regard to the latter, he found the principle of free immigration to enjoy significantly less support than the generally approved principle of free emigration. Much of the anti-immigration sentiments that are evidenced amply beyond Kindleberger's findings can, undoubtedly, be attributed to problems that result from certain attributes of modern welfare states, attributes that produce non-viable incentive structures. Yet, it may also be that there are other ingredients to the problem that defy such straightforward diagnosis. Disturbing questions may be buried here.[19]

Notes

Preface

1   To cite just one out of many possible examples, R. B. Ekelund, Jr., and R. D. Tollison (1994: 96) note: "A *market* is any area in which demand and supply prices of products and services tend toward equality through the continuous interactions of buyers and sellers."

2   Institutional specifics are abstracted from when G. S. Becker (1976: 5) notes: The "economic approach assumes the existence of markets that with varying degrees of efficiency coordinate the action of different participants ... so that their behavior becomes mutually consistent." Exemplifying the kind of "theorems associated with this approach," Becker (1976: 5f.) mentions that "a rise in prices reduces quantity demanded, be it a rise in the market price of eggs, a rise in the 'shadow' price of children reducing the demand for children, or a rise in the office waiting time for physicians ... reducing the demand for their services."

3   From the domain of "pure economics," Walras explicitly wanted to exclude phenomena that are "to be classified under the heading of institutions" (Walras 1954: 63); in particular, phenomena concerned with the "problem of property" or "the mode of appropriation" of scarce things (ibid.: 77). His "pure economics" was to be concerned only with value in exchange as "a *natural* phenomenon" (ibid.: 70) that results "naturally under given conditions of supply and demand" (ibid.: 69). The "theory of property" or the "theory of institutions" he assigned, by contrast, to the domain of "moral science or ethics" (ibid.: 63, 70).

4   G. Debreu (1959: vii), for instance, explicitly notes that his "Axiomatic Analysis of Economic Equilibrium" seeks to explain how prices result "from the interaction of the agents of a private ownership economy," although without going into any further detail about the kind of institutions that are meant to constitute a "private ownership economy."

5   The journal *Constitutional Political Economy*, published by Kluwer Academic Publishers, serves as an outlet for this research program.

1 Constitutionally constrained and safeguarded competition in markets and politics

1   I am indebted to James M. Buchanan and Peter Bernholz for helpful comments on an earlier draft. The article was originally prepared for the Workshop on

Economics and Politics, International School of Economic Research, University of Siena, 4–10 July 1993.

2   With reference to the classical liberal critique of a producer-oriented economic system of privileges and monopoly, Böhm (1982: 109) notes: "The quest for profit ought not to operate to the detriment of a helpless consumer tied to the apron-strings of the producers. On the contrary, the consumers should be liberated and enabled to choose from among the suppliers the one who met their requirements most thoroughly and willingly. This link between the profit motive and competition placed the entrepreneur's pursuit of profit in the direct service of the consumer. Only those with something to offer the consumers could realize a gain and this in turn became an automatic, precise and sensitive criterion for assessing a producer's economic qualities."

3   Böhm (1980: 202): "Daher die große Bedeutung, die dem *Wettbewerb* zukommt, der keineswegs nur ein Leistungsansporn, sondern vor allem auch ein *Entmachtungsinstrument* ist."

4   Eucken (1982: 123) argued similarly: "It is only under a competitive system that the much cited proposition applies: private property benefits not only the owner but also the non-owner." Hayek (1988: 35) pointed in the same direction when he noted that "we need the general practice of competition to prevent abuse of property."

5   Hayek (1978: 149): "(C)ompetition is the most effective discovery procedure which will lead to the finding of better ways for the pursuit of human aims."

6   The effectiveness of functioning competitive markets in catering to consumer preferences is, as Hayek (1979a: 75) points out, "demonstrated by the difficulty of discovering opportunities for making a living by serving the customers better than is already being done."

7   Hayek (1948: 101): "The solution of the economic problem of society is in this respect always a voyage of exploration into the unknown, an attempt to discover new ways of doing things better than they have been done before. This must always remain so as long as there are any economic problems to be solved at all, because all economic problems are created by unforeseen changes which require adaptation."

8   In the words of Alchian (1977: 127): "In *every* society conflicts of interest among members of that society must be resolved. The process by which that resolution (not elimination!) occurs is known as *competition*. Since, by definition, there is no way to eliminate competition, the relevant question is what kind of competition shall be used in the resolution of the conflicts of interest."

9   In reference to well-meant but misguided governmental interventions in the economy, Smith (1981: 687) notes: "All systems either of preference or of restraint, therefore, being thus completely taken away, the obvious and simple system of natural liberty establishes itself of its own accord. Every man, as long as he does not violate the laws of justice, is left perfectly free to pursue his own interest his own way, and to bring both his industry and capital into competition with those of any other man, or order of men."

10   As Knight (1982: 449) phrased it: "A free market means simply ... that every man as buyer or seller (or potentially one or the other) is in a position to offer terms of exchange to every other, and any pair are free to agree on the most

favorable terms acceptable for both parties." Von Mises (1940: 261) argues similarly: "Wettbewerb äussert sich auf dem Markte in der Weise, daß die Käufer den übrigen Kauflustigen durch das Angebot höherer Preise, und daß die Verkäufer den übrigen Verkaufslustigen durch das Fordern niedrigerer Preise bei gleicher Leistung oder durch Erhöhung der Leistung bei gleicher Preisforderung zuvorzukommen haben."

11 A beneficially working market economy requires, as Röpke (1949: 76) notes, "Maßnahmen und Institutionen, die dem Wettbeweb denjenigen Rahmen, diejenigen Spielregeln und denjenigen Apparat unparteiischer Überwachung dieser Spielregeln geben, denen der Wettbewerb so gut wie ein Wettspiel bedarf, wenn er nicht in eine wüste Schlägerei ausarten soll."

12 Böhm (1980: 200) notes on this issue: "Denn eine rational ablaufende Marktwirtschaft kommt nicht etwa dadurch zustande, daß man durch Gesetz die Gewerbefreiheit einführt und sodann die Dinge laufen läßt, wie sie laufen. Vielmehr fordert dieses sich selbst steuernde System das Vorhandensein und die dauernde Pflege und Verbesserung einer ganzen Reihe von politischen, rechtlichen, sozialen, zivilisatorischen Vorbedingungen, das Vorhandensein einer ziemlich hochgezüchteten sozialen Parklandschaft." Röpke (1942: 364) had argued similarly about a "desirable economic constitution": "Der Kern dieser Wirtschaftsverfassung wird … der freie Markt und der unverfälschte Wettbewerb sein müssen, in dem sich unter fairen und gleichen Bedingungen des Wettkampfes der privatwirtschaftliche Erfolg nach der Höhe der Leistung für die Konsumenten bemisst (*Leistungswettbewerb*). Freier Markt und Leistungswettbewerb stellen sich jedoch nicht … von selbst als Ergebnis eines völlig passiven Verhaltens des Staates ein … Sie sind vielmehr ein außerordentlich gebrechliches und von vielen Bedingungen abhängiges Kunstprodukt, das … einen Staat voraussetzt, der … fortgesetzt für die Aufrechterhaltung von Marktfreiheit und Wettbewerb sorgt, indem er das notwendige Rahmenwerk des Rechts und der Institutionen schafft." See also Röpke (1949: 75): "Eine lebensfähige und befriedigende Marktwirtschaft entsteht nämlich nicht dadurch, daß wir geflissentlich nichts tun. Sie ist vielmehr ein kunstvolles Gebilde und ein Artefakt der Zivilisation."

13 In critical reference to certain "*laissez-faire*" versions of liberalism, Hayek (1948a: 111) has noted: "Where the traditional discussion becomes so unsatisfactory is where it is suggested that, with the recognition of the principles of private property and freedom of contract … all the issues where settled, as if the law of property and contract were given once and for all in its final and most appropriate form, i.e., in the form which will make the market economy work at its best. It is only after we have agreed on these principles that the real problems begin." On a version of liberalism that he considers more appropriate, Hayek (1959: 594) comments: "Der neue Liberalismus unterscheidet sich vom alten vor allem darin, daß er sich des engen wechselseitigen Zusammenhangs zwischen wirtschaftlichen und politischen Institutionen bewußter ist … vor allem auch, daß das befriedigende Funktionieren der *Wettbewerbswirtschaft* ganz bestimmte Erfordernisse bezüglich des rechtlichen Rahmenwerkes stelle. … An die Stelle der irreführend gewesenen Formel 'Laissez faire' trat das ausdrückliche Bemühen um eine Gestaltung der Rechtsordnung, die der Erhaltung und dem ersprießlichen Wirken des Wettbewerbs günstig ist und das Entstehen von privaten

Machtpositionen sowohl auf der Seite der Unternehmer wie der Arbeiter zu verhindern sucht."

14 Eucken (1952: 275f.): "Vertragsfreiheit ist offensichtlich eine Voraussetzung für das Zustandekommen der Konkurrenz. … Aber Vertragsfreiheit hat auch dazu gedient, um Konkurrenz zu beseitigen, um monopolistische Positionen herzustellen oder auch um sie zu sichern und auszunutzen." The ordo-liberals' concern with this issue is, in Eucken's (1952: 267) account, in contrast to the politics of *laissez-faire* "in der private Machtgruppen das Recht hatten, sich nicht nur zu konstituieren, sondern auch ihre Märkte mit Kampfmitteln zu schließen."

15 Eucken (1982: 120) notes on this issue: "In many sectors of German industry, cartels would disappear immediately if tariffs were to go. … Despite certain legal precautions, patent law has unexpectedly triggered powerful tendencies towards the formation of monopolies and concentration processes in industry."

16 Despite the differences in emphasis between German ordo-liberals and public choice theorists, the problem of rent-seeking would not have been a matter of controversy. What might have been controversial is the tendency among the latter to be much less concerned than the ordo-liberals with the problems of monopoly in particular and with private power in general. Hayek (1979a: 73) points to the issue that is at stake here when he notes that monopoly power has to be judged differently when it is gained by serving "customers better than anyone else, and not by preventing those who think they could do still better from trying so." Monopoly power, Hayek (ibid.) adds, "does not constitute a privilege so long as the inability of others to do the same is not due to their being prevented from trying."

17 Note that I mean, of course, fundamentally different things when I talk about *constraining* competition on the one side and *restricting* competition on the other. While the first is about the "*how*" of competition, the second is about the "*how much*"; and while the first must be a necessary requirement for beneficially working market competition, the second works as an inhibition on competition. I should add, though, that this distinction may be often more difficult to apply in practice than it can be stated conceptually. The difficulties that may exist in political practice reliably to distinguish provisions that *restrict* competition from those that serve to *constrain* competition invite, of course, attempts of anti-competitive interests to camouflage their intentions to restrict competition to their favor as concerns for generally desirable constraints.

18 Hayek's above quote continues: "In particular, the direct effects will be felt by the members of the same trade who see how competition is operating, while the consumer will generally have little idea to whose actions the reduction of prices or the improvement in quality is due" (Hayek 1979a: 77). Böhm (1980: 209) comments on this issue: "Denn die Marktwirtschaft ist eine Ordnung, die den Unternehmer zum Nutzen der ganzen Gesellschaft steuert, nicht eine Ordnung, in der die Gesellschaft den undomestizierten Interessen der Unternehmer huldigt. Die Unternehmer freuen sich immer des Gewinns, was ihr gutes Recht ist; aber sie freuen sich keineswegs immer der Marktkontrollen und befinden sich bei dem Versuch, sich ihnen zu entziehen, durchaus nicht in Übereinstimmung mit der Gesellschaft."

19 Böhm (1982: 107): "The fundamental assumptions on which the teachings of the classical economists hung were that … the consumer's interests represented

the sole directly justifiable economic interests and that in particular the producer's interests ... rested on a *derived* economic justification." What Böhm has in mind here is, specifically, the following passage from Smith's (1981: 660) *Wealth of Nations*: "Consumption is the sole end and purpose of all production; and the interest of the producer ought to be attended to, only so far as it may be necessary for promoting that of the consumer. The maxim is so perfectly self-evident, that it would be absurd to attempt to prove it. But in the mercantile system, the interest of the consumer is almost constantly sacrificed to that of the producer; and it seems to consider production, and not consumption, as the ultimate end and object of all industry and commerce."

20 For an exemplification of this issue, see Habermann's (1990) study of the German "Handwerksordnung" (Crafts Regulation Act).

21 For a brief discussion, see Vanberg (1992).

22 For a comparative discussion of the two kinds of "competition in politics," see Vanberg and Buchanan (1991) and Vanberg Ch. 8 of the present volume, pp. 115ff.

23 As Dye (1990a: 14) puts it: "Competitive federalism envisions a marketplace for governments where consumer–taxpayers can voluntarily choose the public goods and services they prefer, at the cost they wish to pay, by locating in the governmental jurisdiction that best fits their policy preferences. In this model of federalism, state and local governments compete for consumer–taxpayers by offering the best array of public goods and services at the lowest possible costs."

24 Another significant difference is that for ordinary market firms there is a bottom line for bad performance, namely bankruptcy, whereas for polities and governments formal bankruptcy procedures do not exist. The existence of such provisions would clearly impose an effective constraint on governments, yet it is not easy to imagine how, in the political realm, a formal analog to bankruptcy in the business world could be devised.

25 As indicated here, one obvious difference between the two kinds of political competition is the fact that, by casting a vote, a person cannot control what government he gets. That will be decided, instead, by the vote count; in large constituencies, the impact of a single vote is, of course, insignificant. The only way for a person effectively to choose his government is, as a rule, by his choice of residence.

26 The case of financial capital exemplifies the fact that, in terms of Hirschman's (1970) distinction, a viable exit option can be a valuable substitute for a lacking voice option. Although in modern democracies votes are assigned to persons (one person one vote), whereas capital does not carry formal voting rights, the mobility of capital certainly provides considerable protection to capital owners.

27 This aspect is commented on by Hayek when, in reference to *local government*, he argues that "... people can escape exploitation by voting with their feet" (Hayek 1979a: 16), and when he notes about the classical liberal's preference for local government over central arrangements as being based on "a hope that competition between the different local authorities would effectively control and direct the development ... on desirable lines" (Hayek 1978: 144).

28 Professor Jordi Bacaria from the University of Barcelona drew my attention to this issue.

29   While the right to exit is, for any polity, clearly a viable constitutional provision, independent of what other polities practice, it is not so obvious whether a unilaterally granted right of entry is in the constitutional interest of the constituents of a polity, or whether it is even viable. Yet, whatever may be true for unilateral right-of-entry provisions, it should be apparent that mutual commitments between governments to allow for free entry should increase the responsiveness of these governments to citizens' interests. In such case, the "free entry" provision could be seen as part of a social contract among the inclusive group of citizens in the participating polities.

30   On the potential relevance of secession rights for a European constitution, see Buchanan (1990a: 5ff.) and Bernholz (1992).

31   Röpke (1963: 22) notes on this issue: "Leveling a revolver at someone is one of the quickest but also one of the riskiest ways of getting something for nothing. Much safer and more efficient are the devices of special privilege and monopoly for they can be tricked out in ideological trappings which may make them seem not only innocuous but even beneficial to the general interest."

32   As Dye (1990a: 14, 19, 32) notes: "Matching public policy to citizen preferences is the essence of responsive government. Competitive elections and political parties were designed to achieve this goal. But decentralized government is also a way to match citizen preferences with public policies. ... Democracy itself, with competing parties and periodic free elections, is a powerful inducement to policy responsiveness, at least to majority policy preferences, even in a monopoly government. But if multiple governments are both democratic and competitive, citizens have two separate mechanisms to help achieve congruence between their preferences and public policy. ... [C]ompetitive federalism operates independently of the type of political system to encourage responsiveness. Theoretically, even authoritarian governments, if they were forced to compete with each other and if citizens could migrate to the government of their choice with little cost to themselves, would be responsive to citizen preferences."

33   Hayek points to this issue when, in his aforementioned article, he notes that competition between the individual states in a federation forms "a salutary check on their activities and, while leaving the door open for desirable experimentation, would keep it roughly within the appropriate limits" (Hayek 1948b: 268).

34   Dye (1990a: 15) notes: "Competition in the marketplace promotes discoveries of new products. Competition among governments promotes policy innovation."

35   In this sense of the term, even the Soviet Union was an "experimenting" polity, but such experimenting, if carried out in a unitary "closed" system, cannot serve the knowledge function that parallel experimenting allows for in a decentralized open system.

36   As Kenyon and Kincaid (1991: 19) put it, to advocate competitive federalism does not mean to recommend for states "to engage in unbridled competition, but rather to compete and cooperate within the bounds of the civil order established by the constitution and within the agreed-upon rules enforced by an overarching government (i.e. the federal government)." Dye (1990a: 26) comments on this issue: "Competition is not anarchy; it is restrained, disciplined, orderly behavior. Just as the marketplace requires rules ... so also inter-governmental competition requires rules." For the case of the United States, Dye

(1990a 27f.) discusses various provisions in the Constitution that "set forth a series of basic rules of competition among the states."

37 Dye (1990a: 114f.) notes on this issue: "Competitive federalism requires that states and communities have significant and autonomous responsibility for the welfare of people living in their jurisdictions. It requires that these governments be free to pursue a wide range of public policies. Most important, competitive federalism requires that the costs of state and local government goods and services be fully reflected in the revenues collected by these governments. Federal grants-in-aid create distortions in the relationships between the preferences of citizens–taxpayers in the states and the policies of state and local governments." On this issue, see also Bernholz and Faber (1988: 245), Marlow (1992: 81), and Holcombe (1993).

38 What Smith (1981: 145) has said about the collusive inclination of private business can be assumed to apply to politicians as well: "People of the same trade seldom meet together, even for merriment and diversion, but the conversation ends in a conspiracy against the public, or in some contrivance to raise prices."

39 This is, unfortunately, also a reason why one can expect not only politicians at the federal level but also national politicians to have a natural preference for the centralist over the competitive version because it provides, at least, a new arena for political activity, while competitive federalism means a definite reduction in the politicized realm.

2 Markets and regulation: the contrast between free-market liberalism and constitutional liberalism

1 This article was originally prepared for the 1998 General Meeting of the Mont Pelerin Society in Washington DC. I would like to thank James M. Buchanan and Israel M. Kirzner for their comments on the original version of this article.

2 In 1975, R. H. Coase (1975: 183f.) reported: "There have been more serious studies made of government regulation of industry in the last fifteen years or so, particularly in the United States, than in the whole preceding period. ... The main lesson to be drawn from these studies is clear: they all tend to suggest that the regulation is either ineffective or that when it has a noticeable impact, on balance the effect is bad."

3 W. Röpke's (1961: 10f.) brief report reads: "Es kam zu Zusammenstößen, unter denen derjenige besonders schwer und eindrucksvoll war, der sich zwischen Walter Eucken und Ludwig v. Mises ereignete. Auf den von dem letzteren erhobenen Anspruch, in seiner Person den allein maßgeblichen Liberalismus zu repräsentieren, war Eucken die Antwort nicht schuldig geblieben, und so wäre es denn nicht leicht gewesen, einen halbwegs versöhnlichen Ausgang zu erreichen, wenn nicht Ludwig v. Mises mit seiner Ritterlichkeit eingelenkt hätte. Jene Diskussion, in der es vor allem um das Monopolproblem und um die dem Staat und der Rechtsordnung dadurch zufallende Aufgabe ging, ist symbolisch für einen Richtungsstreit im liberalen Lager geblieben, der innerhalb der Mont-Pèlerin-Gesellschaft immer wieder hervortrat."

4 In Max Hartwell's (1995) history of the MPS, the incident is not mentioned.

5 L. von Mises's (1949: 238f.) definition: "The imaginary construction of a pure or unhampered market economy ... assumes that the operation of the market is not obstructed by institutional factors. It assumes that the government ... is intent upon preserving the operation of the market system, abstains from hindering its functioning, and protects it against encroachments on the part of other people." [On the "method of imaginary constructions," von Mises (1949: 237) notes: "An imaginary construction ... is a product of deduction, ultimately derived from the fundamental category of action. ... In designing such an imaginary construction the economist is not concerned with the question of whether or not it depicts the conditions of reality which he wants to analyze."] As von Mises (1949: 239) notes: "The classical economists and their epigones used to call the system of unhampered market economy 'natural' and government meddling with market phenomena 'artificial' and 'disturbing.' But this terminology also was the product of their careful scrutiny of the problems of interventionism."

6 As Kirzner (1985: 141) puts it, "Nothing within the regulatory process seems able to simulate even remotely the discovery process that is so integral to the unregulated market."

7 In a more recent contribution, Kirzner (1994) explicitly distinguishes between governmental enforcement of what he calls the "outer limits of the market" and governmental "suspension of or interference with the market" (ibid.: 108). By "outer limits" he means the "institutional pre-requisites for the very existence of the market" (ibid.: 101) or "the rights system" (ibid.: 108) that constitutes the institutional framework within which market activities take place. Kirzner sees this "rights system" as based on society-wide "shared ethical perspectives" (ibid.), and he states that it is "only in the context of a given pattern of individual rights" (ibid.: 105) that "the function of the market" (ibid.) can be defined. In this context, government intervention is then to be understood as interference with the process of voluntary co-ordination of individual activities as it unfolds within this framework *of a given rights system*. I shall return to Kirzner's argument in the next section.

8 The liberals claim, von Mises (1949: 240) says, "that the operation of an unhampered market ... brings about more satisfactory results than the decrees of anointed rulers."

9 Hayek (1976a: 115): "It is a wealth-creating game (and not what game theory calls a zero-sum game), that is, one that leads to an increase of the stream of goods and of the prospects of all participants to satisfy their needs."

10 Hayek (1976a: 129): "The particular results that will be determined by altering particular actions of the system will always be inconsistent with its overall order: if they were not, they could have been achieved by changing the rules on which the system was henceforth to operate. Interference, if the term is properly used, is therefore by definition an isolated act of coercion, undertaken for the purpose of achieving a particular result, and without committing oneself to do the same in all instances where some circumstances, defined by a rule, are the same."

11 In this sense, Kirzner (1985: 139) justly asks: "But what is the likelihood that government officials ... will *know* what imposed prices, say, might evoke the 'correct,' desired actions by market participants? ... How do government officials know what prices to set (or qualities to require, and so forth)?"

12 Hayek (1976a: 129): "Every act of interference thus creates a privilege in the sense that it will secure benefits to some at the expense of others, in a manner which cannot be justified by principles capable of general application."

13 Hayek (1960: 228): "Strictly speaking, then, there are two reasons why all controls of prices and quantities are incompatible with a free system: one is that all such controls must be arbitrary, and the other is that it is impossible to exercise them in such manner as to allow the market to function adequately."

14 Hayek (1944: 37): "Any attempt to control prices or quantities of particular commodities deprives competition of its power of bringing about an effective coordination of individual efforts ... This is not necessarily true, however, of measures merely restricting the allowed methods of production, so long as these restrictions affect all potential producers equally ... To prohibit the use of certain poisonous substances or to require special precautions in their use, to limit working hours or to require certain sanitary arrangements, is fully compatible with the preservation of competition. The only question here is whether in the particular instance the advantages gained are greater than the social costs which they impose."

15 Hayek (1960: 225): "But if, for instance, the production and sale of phosphorous matches is generally prohibited for reasons of health or permitted only if certain precautions are taken, or if night work is generally prohibited, the appropriateness of such measures must be judged by comparing the over-all costs with the gain; it cannot be conclusively determined by appeal to a general principle."

16 Hayek (1960: 222) suggests "... that the rule of law provides the criterion which enables us to distinguish between those measures which are and those which are not compatible with a free system. Those that are may be examined further on the grounds of expediency."

17 When, as quoted above, von Mises (1949: 238f.) says about the operation of the unhampered market that it is "not obstructed by institutional factors," he cannot mean to imply that in the unhampered market any institutional factors are absent. As K. R. Popper (1997: 312) has remarked in critical reference to von Mises: "[I]n a complex society, anything approaching a free market could only exist if it enjoyed the protection of laws, and therefore of the state. Thus the term 'free market' should always be placed in inverted commas, since it was always bound, or limited, by a legal framework and made possible only by this framework."

18 Kirzner (1994: 101): "We wish to emphasize the insight that, for its very emergence and existence, the market must rely on the presence of extra-market institutions, without which the idea of a market process must be a mere dream." "The uniquely valuable character of the spontaneous forces of the market process rests entirely on non-market-generated institutions which frame the market" (ibid.: 109).

19 Kirzner (1994: 106) speaks of "opportunities inherent in the given set of rights."

20 From a passing reference, one may conclude that Kirzner considers "citizens' preferences" (Kirzner, 1994: 105) as a criterion. He explicitly refers to "shared ethical perspectives" as a criterion when he notes: "Our affirmation of outer limits to markets should drive home the need for society-wide acceptance of shared ethical perspectives (and most likely, for governmental, extra-market enforcement of the rights system implied in such shared ethical perspectives" (ibid.: 108).

21   The fact that opting for the market system is a matter of *constitutional choice*, a choice that can be recommended because of its attractiveness compared with alternative arrangements, is obfuscated by some of von Mises's arguments that make it appear as if there is no choice. Under a chapter heading "Capitalism: the only possible system of social organization," von Mises (1985: 88f.) argues, for instance, "Liberalism is derived from the pure sciences of economics and sociology, which make no value judgements. ... [T]hese sciences show us that of all the conceivable alternative ways of organizing society only one, viz., the system based on private ownership of the means of production, is capable of being realized, because all other conceivable systems of social organization are unworkable. ... [E]very system of social organization that could be conceived as a substitute for the capitalist system is self-contradictory and unavailing."

22   As Buchanan (1977: 5) notes on the "market economy": "But the economy cannot function *in vacuo*, it must be incorporated in, and must be understood to be incorporated in, a structure of 'laws and institutions.' Modern economists have grossly neglected the constitutional–institutional or framework requirements of an economic system."

23   von Mises (1949: 678): "Private ownership ... is the fundamental institution of the market economy."

24   von Mises (1985: 88): "One may undertake to modify one or another of its [the market system's, V.V.] features as long as in doing so one does not affect the essence and foundation of the whole social order, viz. private property."

25   R. Cooter and T. Ulen (1995: 153): "Regulations restrict the use of the property without taking title from the owner."

26   That property rights are always circumscribed in some manner is, of course, one of the basic premises of the economics of property rights. As P. Milgrom and J. Roberts (1992: 289) note: "For economic analysis, it is often useful to interpret 'owning an asset' to mean having the *residual rights of control* – that is, the right to make any decisions concerning the asset's use that are not explicitly controlled by law or assigned to another by contract."

27   R. A. Epstein (1985: 93): "Taxation, regulation, and modifications of liability rules ... cannot be kept in a watertight compartment separate from takings of private property." About "government's efforts to regulate the possession, use, and disposition of private property," Epstein (1985: 100f.) says: "Some regulations require owners to allow others to gain access and entry to their property. Land use regulation can limit land to residential, commercial or industrial uses; ... it can prohibit certain types of activities ... Regulations limit the goods that can be sold in commerce and the prices charged for them. The differences between these various forms of regulation are sure to be important in any assessment of their economic consequences or their legal justification. Yet these protean forms of regulation all amount to partial takings of private property."

28   Epstein (1986: 15): "When resources, which are subject to well-defined private rights, are placed into common pools, then the presumption is that their value diminishes."

29   Epstein (1985: 96): "That the common law is malleable is, within important limits, correct. ... Ownership is a social concept. ... The basic rules of ownership state in general form the types of actions by others that constitute wrongs."

30 Goldberg (1976a: 429): "Conceptually, we can treat judges and legislators as agents enforcing and revising the rules under which individual transactions take place."

31 Goldberg (1976a: 429): "The common law is embedded in a social contract which establishes a procedure for adjusting the specific terms of the contract over time."

32 In his distinction between the "catallactic notion of ownership and property rights" and "the legal definition of ownership and property rights as stated in the laws of various countries," von Mises (1949: 678) may seem to suggest that such an immutable standard can be defined. Yet, at least with regard to the notion that the "natural law" may provide for such a standard, he flatly states: "There is, however, no such thing as natural law and a perennial standard of what is just and what is unjust."

33 Epstein (1986: 11): "The zoning ordinance that masquerades as an antipollution device could easily be an effort to prevent (legitimate) competitive injury."

34 Hayek (1944: IXf.): "The essence of the liberal position, however, is the denial of all privilege, if privilege is understood in its proper and original meaning of the state granting and protecting rights to some which are not available on equal terms to others." For a general discussion on the role of the generality constraint, see Buchanan and Congleton (1998).

35 Epstein (1985: 211): "Government action may be very general in its articulation and application, but it may impose all of the burdens on one class and all of the benefits on another, imposing uncompensated takings of private property on a grand scale."

36 M. N. Rothbard (1970: 77): "A society based on voluntary exchanges is called a *contractual society*. ... [T]he contractual type of society is based on freely entered contractual relations between individuals. ... It is the society of the unhampered market."

37 Rothbard (1970: 84): "The contractual society of the market is a genuinely *co-operative society*."

38 von Mises (1949: 258): "There is in the operation of the market no compulsion and coercion. The state ... does not interfere with the market and with the citizens' activities directed by the market. It employs its power to beat people into submission solely for the prevention of actions destructive to the preservation and the smooth operation of the market economy. It protects the individuals' life, health, and property against violent and fraudulent aggression on the part of domestic gangsters and external foes. ... Thus the state creates and preserves the environment in which the market economy can safely operate." There are, of course, a number of libertarian authors who seek to avoid the conclusion that "the protective state" is a necessary institution for securing the market as an arena of purely voluntary co-operation. For a discussion of this literature, see G. Habermann (1996).

39 Rothbard (1970: 766): "Intervention is the intrusion of aggressive physical force into society; it means the substitution of coercion for voluntary actions."

40 Rothbard (1970: 72): "The major form of voluntary interaction is voluntary interpersonal exchange." Also, Rothbard (1970: 152f.): "Contract must be considered as an agreed-upon exchange between two persons of two goods, present or future."

41   About the types of contracts that I call *constitutional* contracts, Goldberg (1976a: 428) says that they are concerned with "the establishment, in effect, of a 'constitution' governing the ongoing relationship."

42   Kirzner (1994: 105f.): "Where cooperation is of a real or imagined mutual benefit to a group of individuals, the market will of course provide scope for such cooperation. The market does, as has often been recognized, make it possible for groups within it to organize themselves in communes or other organizations on strictly socialist principles, if they choose (This, let us not forget, is how capitalist firms come into existence.)."

43   Also on this issue, see Rothbard (1956: 255).

44   Rothbard (1970: 560): "Rather than 'consumers' sovereignty,' it would be more accurate to state that in the free market there is a *sovereignty of the individual:* ... *individual self-sovereignty.*"

45   For more details, see Ch. 3, p. 37. To the Freiburg scholars, the constitutional choice in favor of market competition implies a commitment to submit to the constraints of competition, and they considered it incompatible with such constitutional choice to allow the players in this game to seek to exempt themselves from these constraints by private contracts. They would have strictly disagreed with the statement of B. R. Tucker that Rothbard (1970: 584) quotes approvingly: "The right to cooperate is as unquestionable as the right to compete; the right to compete involves the right to refrain from competition ... To assail or control or deny this form of cooperation [cartel, V.V.] on the ground that it is itself a denial of competition is an absurdity."

46   Buchanan (1991a: 112; 1991b: 125ff., 129). The issue of the relation between "private" and "public" constitutional contracts is raised when Buchanan (1991b: 129) notes: "The libertarian who defends private, cartel-like agreements among contracting parties on the same side of the market, as long as such agreement is voluntary, must have difficulty arguing against politically orchestrated cartel-like restrictions in particular markets."

47   Epstein (1985: 202) clearly appears to argue in this sense when he places "antitrust laws, which prevent monopoly and foster competition" in the class of regulations that potentially make for a "positive-sum game." As he puts it, "Monopoly therefore can be understood as a negative-sum game which the antitrust laws, at least in their prospective application, are designed to overcome."

48   H. Demsetz (1995: 157f., 166).

49   von Mises (1949: 310) appeals to the very same performance criterion when he notes: "So far as the operation of the market is not sabotaged by the interference of government and other factors of coercion, success in business is the proof of services rendered to the consumers."

50   As for the rules of the "system of natural liberty," Smith (1981: 308) noted that the "obligation of building party walls, in order to prevent the communication of fire, is (not) a violation of natural liberty."

51   Rothbard (1970: 562) criticizes as "inconsistent" Hutt's appeal to "'consumer's sovereignty' as an *ethical ideal against which the activities of the free market are to be judged.*"

52   Rothbard (1970: 561) credits Hutt for being "the originator of this concept."

53   On Hutt's concept, see also Vanberg (1998b: 639).

54 Indeed, Rothbard's reasoning is in this regard not entirely unambiguous. On the one hand, his claim seems to be that the concept of consumer sovereignty is not the adequate "ethical ideal against which the activities of the free market are to be judged" (Rothbard 1970: 562). On the other hand, it seems as if he accepts the ideal, but wants to argue that, as a matter of fact, cartel agreements are not obstacles to the capacity of the "free market" to work for the benefit of consumers (ibid.: 76, 574, 578, 581f.). My concern here is not with the second but only with the first claim. It may be noted as an aside that Rothbard (1970: 620) does not extend his sanguine view of cartels to unions: "It is clear that while cartels, to be successful, must be economically more efficient in serving the consumer, no such justification can be found for unions."

55 The issue of whether "voluntary enslavement" should be permitted may also be used to illustrate the difference between a free-market approach and a constitutional approach. To the latter, this question cannot be answered in terms of the abstract principle of freedom of contract, and the fact that the parties to such contracts would indicate, by their voluntary agreement, that they expect to be made better off does not provide a sufficient argument for permitting such contracts. Instead, the issue has to be examined in terms of the working properties of a constitutional order within which such contracts are permitted, compared with one in which they are prohibited. And the relevant criteria of evaluation in this comparison are the interests of the constituents of the jurisdiction for which such constitutional choice is to be made.

56 See Buchanan (1991c).

57 For further discussion, see Vanberg (1998c; 1998d).

58 He can only be said to implicitly agree, given the rules of the game, if he chooses not to pay his neighbor for not putting up the sign.

59 On this issue, see Buchanan and Vanberg (1988).

60 For a detailed discussion of this issue, see Buchanan (1986b).

61 That there is such a standard seems to be implied when Rothbard (1970: 653) describes the "purely free market" as the arena "where the individual person and property are not subject to molestation," and when he defines: "'Free' ... is used in the interpersonal sense of being unmolested by other persons" (ibid.: 581).

62 Rothbard (1956: 259fn.): "The famous 'external diseconomy' problems (noise, smoke nuisance, fishing, etc.) are ... due to insufficient defense of private property against invasion. Rather than a defect of the free market, therefore they are the result of invasions of property, invasions which are ruled out of the free market by definition." See also Rothbard (1970: 156) and von Mises (1949: 653). Hayek (1960: 229) comments on this issue: "Though the principle of private property raises comparatively few problems as far as movable things are concerned, it does raise exceedingly difficult ones where property in land is concerned. The effect which the use of any piece of land often has on neighboring land clearly makes it undesirable to give the owner unlimited power to use or abuse his property as he likes." See also Hayek (1944: 38f.; 1948: 113).

63 That we need to distinguish between the transactions carried out within markets and the social processes that shape the institutions that frame markets is explicitly stressed by Kirzner. He speaks of "the sharp difference ... separating the character of market processes from the character of the processes leading up to the

crystallization of the institutions upon which markets must rest for their very existence" (Kirzner 1994: 107). He comments: "The institutions upon which the market must depend must have been created or have evolved through processes different from those spontaneous coordinative processes which we have seen to constitute the essence of the market's operation."

64   Rothbard (1956: 250): "Such an exchange is voluntarily undertaken by both parties. Therefore, the very fact that an exchange takes place demonstrates that both parties benefit ... from the exchange. ... The free market is the name for the array of all the voluntary exchanges that take place in the world. Since every exchange demonstrates a unanimity of benefit for both parties concerned, we must conclude that *the free market benefits all its participants.*"

65   von Mises (1985: 68): "Governments must be forced into adopting liberalism by the power of the unanimous opinion of the people." See also von Mises (1985: 46).

66   von Mises (1949: 271) points to the symmetry between the issue of "the sovereignty of the individual" in the market and in the political arena when he notes: "It would be more correct to say that a democratic constitution is a scheme to assign to the citizen in the conduct of government the same supremacy the market economy gives them in their capacity as consumers. However, the comparison is imperfect. ... [O]n the market no vote is cast in vain." See also von Mises (1985: xvi).

67   Rothbard (1956: 260).

68   See part three of Nozick (1974).

69   Vanberg and Kerber (1994); Frey and Eichenberger (1999).

3 The Freiburg school of law and economics: predecessor of constitutional economics

1   On the history of the founding, see Böhm's account: "Die Forschungs- und Lehrgemeinschaft zwischen Juristen und Volkswirten an der Universität Freiburg in den dreißiger und vierziger Jahren des 20. Jahrhunderts," (Böhm 1960: 158–75).

2   Sally (1996: 252): "The Freiburg school, unbeknown to or overlooked by most Anglo-Saxons, centrally addresses the question of institutions and property rights." (Only after completing this chapter did I become aware of a most instructive contribution on this subject by D.J. Gerber.) Because the writings of the founders of the Freiburg school are almost unaccessible in most parts of the world, I use this article also to document (in the notes) their views by extensive quotations from their original German publications. Even for readers who are not familiar with German, and who may just want to skip over them, these quotations can serve as a potential source for future reference.

3   Sally (1996: 250f.): "It can be argued quite credibly that German ordo-liberalism ... anticipates concerns and theoretical explorations that have recently been in vogue in the Anglo-American world, although partially and relatively unsystematically. This applies in particular to the New Political Economy, ... constitutional economics, and the New Institutional Economics. ... Many of the insights of Mancur Olson, Anne Krueger, George Stigler, James Buchanan and

others on 'market failure' and 'government failure' ... were expounded with force by the German neoliberals, albeit in a less precise manner." Tumlir (1989: 126) notes that "the growing interest in law and economics and constitutional economics in the English-speaking world will be served by a review of the work [of Böhm, V.V.] which lies at the beginning of both lines of analysis." Kasper and Streit (1993: 13) note: "In many respects, Böhm and Eucken anticipated Mancur Olson (1982) and some of the contributions of the public-choice school."

4   Eucken (1940: 504): "To criticize Schmoller is to criticize a considerable part of economic doctrine of our time."

5   Eucken (1938: 79): "Unter seiner [Schmoller's, V.V.] Führung verloren die meisten deutschen Nationalökonomen die Fähigkeit, die wirtschaftspolitischen Einzelfragen als Teilfragen der gesamten Wirtschaftsverfassung zu sehen. Zugleich verlernten sie, theoretisch zu arbeiten."

6   As Eucken (1940: 503) notes about Schmoller: "Nur eine Ansicht, seine Grundansicht, vertrat er widerspruchslos und setzte sich mit ihr nirgends in Gegensatz: Eben seine Entwicklungs- und Fortschrittsidee." See also Böhm *et al.* [1989 (1937: XIIIff.)].

7   On speaking of *rules of the game* with regard to an economic constitution Böhm (1980: 126, fn. 3) notes: "Der Begriff der 'Spielregel' ist wichtig, erregt aber bei einigen Autoren Anstoß, denen es offenbar schwer fällt, der Geringschätzung Herr zu werden, die durch die Ideenassoziation: Roulette, Skat oder Fußball nahegelegt wird. Nun läßt sich aber schlechterdings nichts daran ändern, daß es Subordinationsordnungen und Koordinationsordnungen gibt und daß die Lenkung der Beteiligten bei Subordinationsordnungen durch Befehl und Weisungen, bei Koordinationsordnungen aber durch Spielregeln erfolgt und daß die moralisch-staatsbürgerliche Tugend dessen, der gelenkt werden soll, bei Subordinationsordnungen der Gehorsam und bei Koordinationsordnungen die Fairneß ist." On the use of the concept of "Spielregeln" (rules of the game) in the Freiburg school, see also Böhm (1937: 120) and Eucken (1989a: 204; 1990: 377).

8   As Johnson (1989: 48) notes about the use of the concept of order in the Freiburg school: "In English, the word has an imperative connotation which accords with the Nazi but not with the neo-liberal usage."

9   Eucken (1990: 23): "Die Wirtschaftsordnung eines Landes besteht in der Gesamtheit der jeweils realisierten Formen, in denen Betriebe und Haushalte miteinander verbunden sind, in denen also der Wirtschaftsprozeß in concreto abläuft." As a definition of what he means by "Wirtschaftsordnung," Eucken (1990: 238) also states: "Sie ist die Gesamtheit der realisierten Formen, in denen in concreto jeweils der alltägliche Wirtschaftsprozeß abläuft."

10   As Eucken (1989a: 58) notes, "... understanding the economic order is the first step toward an understanding of economic reality."

11   Eucken (1990: 377): "Die rechtliche und soziale Ordnung, die den Handlungen der Wirtschaftssubjekte Richtung geben kann und Grenzen setzt, ... muß in einem weiten Sinne aufgefaßt werden: Nicht nur die Gesetze, die Sitten und Gewohnheiten sind gemeint, sondern auch der Geist, in dem die Menschen leben und sich an die Spielregeln halten."

12   Eucken (1989a: 79) speaks of "die beiden reinen konstitutiven Grundformen, auf welche die historische Untersuchung in allen Epochen stieß ...: Das

idealtypische Wirtschaftssystem der verkehrslosen 'Zentralgeleiteten Wirtschaft' und das Wirtschaftssystem der 'Verkehrswirtschaft.'" Böhm (1950: XXIV) characterizes "die Verkehrswirtschaft als eine Koordinationsordnung, die Zentralverwaltungswirtschaft als eine Subordinationsordnung." Böhm (1980: 201): "Die marktwirtschaftliche Ordnung ist außerdem – hierauf hat insbesondere Walter Eucken aufmerksam gemacht – eine *Koordinationsordnung*. D.h. die Beteiligten sind einander *gleichgeordnet*. Verpflichtungen und Ansprüche zwischen Beteiligten können nur auf Grund von Verträgen entstehen. Ohne Vertrag gibt es keine Über- und Unterordnung."

13   Kasper and Streit (1993: 15) note that the Freiburg school "formulated a well-founded, institutionally based criticism of collectivist economic planning. This was done independently of the Austrian School, in the 1930s and 1940s, when most mainstream economists still considered central planning theoretically feasible." About the survival prospects of the soviet economic system, Böhm (1950: XXVII) noted in 1950: "Was geschehen wird, wenn der Friede gewahrt bleibt, läßt sich mit Sicherheit voraussehen: der Zusammenbruch des sowjetischen Wirtschaftssystems, wenn auch erst in vermutlich ferner Zeit und unter überaus schmerzhaften und dramatischen Begleitumständen für die beklagenswerten Völker. *Ob* aber der Frieden gewahrt bleiben wird, dies läßt sich freilich nicht voraussehen."

14   Böhm *et al.* (1989: 23f.): "We wish to bring scientific reasoning, as displayed in jurisprudence and political economy, into effect for the purpose of constructing and reorganizing the economic system. The problem of understanding and fashioning the legal instruments for an economic constitution, however, can only be solved if the lawyer avails himself of the findings of economic research." The original text [Böhm *et al.* 1989 (1937: XVIIIf.)] reads: "… wollen wir die wissenschaftliche Vernunft, wie sie in der Jurisprudenz und der Nationalökonomie zur Entfaltung kommt, zum Aufbau und zur Neugestaltung der Wirtschaftsverfassung zur Wirkung bringen … Die Aufgabe aber, die Rechtsordnung als Wirtschaftsverfassung zu begreifen und zu formen, ist nur lösbar, wenn sich der Jurist der Ergebnisse wirtschaftswissenschaftlicher Forschung bedient."

15   Eucken (1990: 373) speaks of the problem of finding a "… funktionsfähige und menschenwürdige Ordnung der Wirtschaft, der Gesellschaft, des Rechts und des Staates." See also the preface "Die Aufgabe des Jahrbuchs" (The aim of the yearbook) in the first volume of *ORDO* (1948: VII–XI).

16   Kasper and Streit (1993: 7): "The central and defining concern of the Freiburg School … was 'order,' the set of institutional–legal rules for a free society. … They often used the Latin word *ordo* which alluded to the medieval Christian concept of a natural harmonious state of a society, aspiring to the realisation of natural law." As Eucken (1982: 130; 1990: 290) notes about his approach: "However, the regulative framework with which we are concerned here did not emanate from natural law or … dogmatic axioms. … The emphasis among all these principles lies upon their positive aim."

17   As Eucken (1989a: 240) notes, the task of creating a "… funktionsfähige und menschenwürdige Ordnung der Wirtschaft … erfordert die Schaffung einer brauchbaren 'Wirtschaftsverfassung', die zureichende Ordnungsgrundsätze

verwirklicht." As he adds: "Insgesamt hat die Nationalökonomie die Schaffung einer Wirtschaftsverfassung für die ganze moderne Wirtschaft durch Gedankenarbeit einzuleiten" (ibid.: 241).

18 Eucken (1942: 48): "... eine Ordnung zu geben, die wirtschaftlich funktionsfähig *und* menschenwürdig ist. Das ist die Ordnungsaufgabe der Wirtschaftsverfassungspolitik." Eucken (1989a: 242): "Da die Nationalökonomie heute daran arbeitet, brauchbare Ordnungsgrundsätze für den Aufbau einer leistungsfähigen Wirtschaftsverfassung – international und einzelstaatlich – zu entwickeln, ... können nunmehr nationalökonomisches Denken und Rechtsdenken ineinandergreifen,–mag es sich um die Behandlung von Kartellen, um das Recht der Allgemeinen Geschäftsbedingungen, um Fragen der internationalen Währungsordnung oder um eine andere wirtschafts- und rechtspolitische Frage handeln."

19 Eucken (1990: 336). Sally (1996: 8) notes about the ordo-liberal approach: "It is incumbent on the state to set up and maintain the institutional framework of the free economic order, but it should not intervene in the mechanisms of the competitive economic process. This is the essence of *Ordnungspolitik*."

20 Eucken (1990: 360): "Es wird zur großen Aufgabe der Wirtschaftspolitik, die Kräfte, die aus dem Einzelinteresse entstehen, in solche Bahnen zu lenken, daß hierdurch das Gesamtinteresse gefördert wird, daß also eine sinnvolle Koordination der Einzelinteressen stattfindet." Eucken (1990: 365): "Den spontanen Kräften der Menschen zur Entfaltung zu verhelfen und zugleich dafür zu sorgen, daß sie sich nicht gegen das Gesamtinteresse wenden, ist das Ziel, auf das sich die Politik der Wettbewerbsordnung richtet. ... Die Wettbewerbsordnung aber zwingt auch den reinen Egoisten, für das Gesamtinteresse tätig zu werden."

21 Eucken (1990: 360): "Die 'unsichtbare Hand' schafft nicht ohne weiteres Formen, in denen Einzelinteresse und Gesamtinteresse aufeinander abgestimmt werden."

22 Böhm (1980: 236–8) notes about the evolution of the market economy: "Die Marktwirtschaft selbst ist viele Tausend Jahre alt. ... Man kann sagen, die Marktwirtschaft ist von den Menschen und Völkern praktisch angewendet, aber nicht von ihnen erfunden worden. ... Wo immer die Marktwirtschaft entstand, funktionierte sie Jahrtausende hindurch, ohne daß die Beteiligten wußten, daß es sie überhaupt gab. ... Die Entdeckung der Ordnungsstruktur des marktwirtschaftlichen Systems ist seiner praktischen Anwendung um viele Tausend Jahre *nachgefolgt*. Erst in der Mitte des 18. Jahrhunderts ist sie gemacht worden. Sie gehört in der Tat zu den *größten und wichtigsten wissenschaftlichen Leistungen* der Menschheit." See also Böhm (1937: 30f.). Böhm (1937: 31f.) and Eucken (1989a: 52) emphasize, however, the importance of the deliberate constitutional reforms in Europe during the late eighteenth century and early nineteenth century for the emergence of modern market economies.

23 Böhm (1950: XLf.): "Eucken hat seine Zeit instandegesetzt, sich von dem Alpdruck geschichtlichen Entwicklungsdenkens in Zwangsabläufen ... zu befreien, und hat ihr stattdessen eine schlichte, vollständige, übersichtliche und kristallklare Musterkarte von Gestaltungs- und Ordnungsmöglichkeiten dargeboten. ... Es ist wie ein Durchbruch aus lähmender Enge ... in eine Welt der freien und verantwortlichen Wahl." See also Böhm (1937: 16f., 21; 1960: 163f.).

24   Eucken (1989a: 52): "Unter 'Wirtschaftsverfassung' haben wir die
     Gesamtentscheidung über die Ordnung des Wirtschaftslebens eines
     Gemeinwesens zu verstehen." Eucken (1938: 80): "Die Behandlung aller
     wirtschaftspolitischen und wirtschaftsrechtlichen Einzelfragen muß deshalb an
     der Idee der Wirtschaftsverfassung ausgerichtet sein. ... Die Wirtschaftsverfassung
     ist als eine politische Gesamtentscheidung über die Ordnung des nationalen
     Wirtschaftslebens zu verstehen. Aufgabe des Staates ist es, eine funktionsfähige
     Wirtschaftsverfassung zu schaffen."
25   Eucken (1989a: 38f.): "The actual economic policy of many countries is dominated
     today by an *ad hoc* treatment of economic problems. It is probably this *ad hoc* way
     of thinking that mainly obscures the problem of the economic system. The
     interrelationships of all economic activities as a whole is not recognized. Monetary
     policy, policy on cartels, trade policy, policy toward small businesses et cetera, are
     all seen as separate specialized areas to be dealt with discretely. ... For example,
     in many countries company law encourages industrialized concentration while
     cartel policy and policy toward small businesses are discouraging it."
26   Sally (1996: 5): "Eucken clearly opts for thinking in terms of orders, ... all acts
     of policy should be judged in terms of how they fit in with the total economic
     process and its steering mechanism, i.e. with the order of economic activities."
27   In his book of 1937, Böhm emphasizes again and again that "eine freie
     Wirtschaftsverfassung" must be seen "als das Musterbeispiel eines politisch-
     rechtlichen Kunstprodukts" (Böhm 1937: 74), "... daß der Wettbewerb kein
     Naturereignis, sondern eine Veranstaltung der Rechtsordung ist" (ibid.: 120),
     and he states: "Als Veranstaltung der Rechtsordnung ist der Wettbewerb eine
     Einrichtung des öffentlichen Rechts" (ibid.: 121). See also Böhm (1937: 45, 53,
     68–72, 74, 108, 122, 142f., 152f.).
28   Eucken (1990: 374f.): "Die Prinzipien der Wirtschaftspolitik, die hier dargestellt
     wurden, werden bisweilen 'liberal' oder 'neoliberal' genannt. Aber diese
     Bezeichnung ist oft tendenziös und nicht treffend. ... Die Liberalen des 19.
     Jahrhunderts waren zumeist Anhänger einer Politik des Laissez-faire." See also
     Eucken (1938: 81).
29   See Böhm (1950: XXXIX). One may well argue that their image of *laissez-faire*
     liberalism was oversimplified and their critique overstated, but there can be no
     mistake about the substance of the argument that they wanted to make. As
     Tumlir (1989: 130) comments: "Many of Böhm's readers found it difficult to
     understand his strong condemnation of *laissez-faire*. The term is seldom defined
     and is usually used as a red herring. He had a clearly defined meaning of it: an
     approach to legal policy in which all contracts will be enforced, including contracts
     intended to curtail or eliminate competition. ... The standard conclusion of
     economists is that if the state concentrated on the business of preventing force
     and fraud and refused to enforce contracts in restraint of competition, markets
     would be efficient. The lawyer might agree ... but he still faces great practical
     difficulties ... What kinds of contracts are in restraint of competition ... must be
     specified in considerable detail. Nor is the question of 'force and fraud' in economic
     transactions at all self-explanatory." Sally (1996: 6f.) comments on the ordo-
     liberals' critique of *laissez-faire*: "The analysis is faulty in several respects. First it
     is inaccurate to portray the classical theory of the period in terms of unconditional

laissez-faire. ... Second there is an overestimation of the spontaneous emergence of monopoly in the private sector ... and a corresponding underestimation of the creation and promotion of monopoly by discriminating acts of government." Whatever shortcomings their critique of *laissez-faire* liberalism may have, they do not play any significant role as far as the paradigmatic core of the ordo-liberals' approach is concerned.

30 Böhm (1950: LII) mentions as "the most critical error" of the classical liberals: "Sie haben den Anteil der bewußten sozialen Kulturleistung an der Entfaltung der vorgegebenen Ordnungsmöglichkeiten weit unterschätzt und geglaubt, es genüge die Beseitigung der Privilegien, die Einführung der Gewerbefreiheit und die Unterlassung von Staatsinterventionen, um einen politisch-sozialen Rahmen zu schaffen, der es gestattet, alles weitere der 'Natur' zu überlassen. So kam es denn dazu, daß die Ära der Gewerbefreiheit nicht eine Wettbewerbsordnung, sondern bloß die Wirtschaft des laissez-faire, laissez-aller hervorbrachte."

31 Böhm (1937: 74) notes, "... daß man eine freie Wirtschaftsverfassung mit viel größerem Recht als das Musterbeispiel eines politisch-rechtlichen Kunstprodukts bezeichnen könnte."

32 Böhm (1937: 105): "Der Grundgedanke der freien Wirtschaftsverfassung besteht also darin, daß der Staat erstens *nur* den Tausch (bzw. den freiwilligen Vertragsschluß) als Mittel, die wirtschaftliche Mitwirkung anderer zu erlangen, zuläßt, d.h. daß er Gewalt (Raub, Erpressung, Nötigung), Eigenmacht (Diebstahl, Unterschlagung) und List (Betrug) als Wirkungsmethoden ausschließt, und daß er zweitens unter den Anbietenden und Nachfragenden aller erdenklichen Wirtschaftsleistungen Wettbewerb veranstaltet."

33 Böhm (1937: 124f.) argued in response to critics of the Freiburg concept of competition within appropriate rules: "Wenn dieser Auffassung entgegengehalten wird, der wirtschaftliche Kampf sei in Wirklichkeit nicht so regelhaft, so begegnen wir hier wiederum jener in der wirtschaftsverfassungsrechtlichen Diskussion so überaus häufigen Verwechslung von Ordnung und Zustand, von Norm und Tatbestand, von Sein und Sollen. Daß im praktischen Wirtschaftskampf in recht erheblichem Ausmaß gegen das Leistungsprinzip verstoßen wird, muß jeder Beobachter der Verhältnisse zugeben. Die wirtschaftsverfassungsrechtliche Betrachtungsweise hat sich indessen nicht mit der Untersuchung und Beschreibung des tatsächlichen Wettbewerbs, sondern mit der Ermittlung und Ausdeutung der rechtlichen Ordnung zu befassen, der die gewerbliche Wettbewerb zu unterstellen ist, wenn das Ziel erreicht werden soll, mittels Wettbewerb eine freie Verkehrswirtschaft zu ordnen."

34 Böhm (1937: 31f.): "Und das alles ereignete sich in einer Geschichtsepoche, die gerade im Begriff stand, die Feudalgesellschaft in eine Zivilrechtsgesellschaft umzuwandeln, die Grundrechte und Zuständigkeiten der Individuen vor der Staatsgewalt und dem gesellschaftlichen Kollektivwillen in Sicherheit zu bringen und die Staatsgewalt ihrerseits mit Hilfe von Funktionenteilungen, rechtsstaatlichen und demokratischen Kontrollen zu beschränken. Zur Zeit als Adam Smith den Marktmechanismus entdeckte, war das der Marktwirtschaft auf den Leib gezimmerte 'Haus' in England nicht nur bezugsfertig, sondern sogar bereits schon bezogen. In den anderen Nationen bewirkte die französische Revolution mit ihrer nicht-öknomisch begründeten Abschaffung der

Gewerbeprivilegien und mit ihrer rechtsstaatlichen Domestizierung der Staatsgewalt, ... daß der wissenschaftlich mittlerweile bekannt gewordene Marktmechanismus offiziell in seine ... Lenkungsfunktion eingesetzt werden konnte."

35   As Böhm (1980: 109; 1989: 47) emphasizes, this was in itself a constitutional choice, a choice of the *rules of the game* under which social and economic interactions were to proceed: "The decision to abolish all class prerogatives and privileges was justified by the maxim: henceforth in the field of society there shall be only one single legal status for all. ... This postulate that all members of society should have the same status is, of course, not a private law concept but a political one under constitutional law."

36   Eucken (1938: 81): "*Laissez-faire* und Wettbewerb sind nicht im mindesten identisch. ... Und eine staatliche Ordnung der Wirtschaft ist nötig. Als ein Werkzeug dieser staatlichen Ordnung ist aber der Leistungswettbewerb anzusehen, dessen Durchsetzung eine der vielen Aufgaben staatlicher Wirtschaftsverfassungspolitik darstellt." As erroneous Eucken (1989a: 241) criticizes the view, "... daß es zwar notwendig sei, eine Rechtsordnung durchzusetzen und auszubauen, daß sich aber eine brauchbare, natürliche Wirtschaftsordnung aus der Entwicklung heraus spontan bilde. ... Inzwischen ist aber erkannt, daß die moderne industrialisierte Welt im Zuge ihrer Entwicklung nicht von selbst brauchbare Wirtschaftsordnungen erzeugt, daß sie also gewisser Ordnungsgrundsätze oder einer Wirtschaftsverfassung bedarf."

37   Eucken (1982: 116; 1990: 255): "The fundamental principle not only calls for abstinence from certain economic acts such as government subsidies, the establishment of mandatory State monopolies, a general freeze on prices, prohibitions of imports etc. Nor is it enough simply to prohibit cartels, for instance. The principle is not primarily negative in nature. There is, rather, a need for a positive economic policy aimed at developing the marketing structure of unrestricted competition and thus at realising the fundamental principle. This is also a field in which the competitive system differs entirely from the policy of laissez-faire." Eucken (1990: 26f.) notes about the period of *laissez-faire* economic policy: "Der Staat hat gerade in dieser Zeit ein strenges Eigentums-, Vertrags-, Gesellschafts-, Patentrecht usw. geschaffen. ... Aber die Überwachung der Wirtschaftsordnung i.S. der Gesamtentscheidung wurde nicht als besondere staatliche Aufgabe angesehen. Man war der Überzeugung, daß sich im Rahmen des Rechtes eine zureichende Wirtschaftsordnung von selbst entwickeln würde."

38   Böhm (1937: 18) speaks of the "freie Verkehrswirtschaft" as "eine politische und verfassungsrechtliche Ordnung." See also Böhm (1937: 39f., 45, 47f., 71, 73, 75).

39   It is not sufficient for the state to establish freedom of trade, "it is also necessary to ensure that the restricting of the market by private pressure groups does not take place. What is the use of officially decreed freedom of trade if it is annulled in practice by the policies of the pressure groups? ... All kinds of preventive competition should be ruled out" (Eucken 1982: 119; 1990: 267).

40   Eucken (1982: 124; 1990: 276): "Freedom to contract may serve not only to promote but also to destroy competition." Eucken (1990: 267): es ist "nötig, daß auch die Schließung der Märkte durch private Machtgruppen unterbleibt. Was

nützt staatlich gesetzte Gewerbefreiheit, wenn sie durch die Politik der Machtgruppen faktisch aufgehoben wird? ... Die Öffnung der Märkte hat einen wirtschaftsverfassungsrechtlichen Sinn. Deshalb kann privaten Machtgruppen nicht das Recht verliehen werden, sie zu beseitigen. Sie gehört zur Ordnungspolitik, die Privaten nicht überlassen werden darf." See also Eucken (1989a: 57).

41 In an article on "Wettbewerbsfreiheit und Kartellfreiheit," Böhm (1980: 233ff.) discusses, and answers in the negative, the question: "Darf ein Privatrechtssubjekt, das unstreitig im Besitz der Wettbewerbsfreiheit ist, über diese seine Wettbewerbsfreiheit durch Vertrag verfügen, d.h. darf es sich Konkurrenten gegenüber vertraglich verpflichten, von seiner ihm zustehenden Wettbewerbsfreiheit keinen oder nur einen eingeschränkten Gebrauch zu machen?" (ibid.: 233).

42 Eucken (1990: 170): "In einer berühmten Entscheidung vom 4. Februar 1897 hat das Reichsgericht grundsätzlich zur Bildung von Kartellen Stellung genommen. Es hat Kartellverträge für zulässig erklärt, und es hat auch Sperren gegen Außenseiter erlaubt. ... Diese Haltung zum Kartellproblem ist von grundsätzlicher Bedeutung. Das Recht der Vertragsfreiheit durfte auch dazu benutzt werden, um Konkurrenz zu beseitigen."

43 Böhm *et al.* [1989 (1937: X)]; Böhm (1960: 167–71); Eucken (1989a: 56). Streit (1994: 511): "In his inaugural lecture Großmann-Doerth (1933) drew attention to what he called 'self-created law of the business community' and to the fact that, for example, standardised conditions of sale were used to restrain competition and that the state tolerated the general private law's being bent into a law which served the vested interests of the business community." See also Kasper and Streit (1993: 13).

44 As Böhm (1950: LI) argues, such "private rule-making" has "den bereits erreichten Stand der Privatrechtskultur wieder fühlbar zurückgebildet und barbarisiert; man denke nur an die rohen Verfälschungen, die sich die Idee der primitivsten Tauschgerechtigkeit in den Allgemeinen Geschäftsbedingungen der Industrie, des Bank-, des Verkehrs- und des Versicherungsgewerbes einschließlich der staats- und gemeindeeigenen Betriebe hat gefallen lassen müssen und täglich aufs neue gefallen lassen muß." Eucken (1990: 328) notes on this issue: "Diese Übernahme staatlicher Kompetenzen durch private Machtgruppen greift aber noch viel weiter, wohl am stärksten infolge der Selbstverständlichkeit, mit der das autonome Recht der Allgemeinen Geschäftsbedingungen sich durchgesetzt hat."

45 Eucken (1942: 46): "Der Wettbewerb würde viel stärker in der Wirtschaftsordnung hervortreten, wenn er nicht durch organisatorische Maßnahmen der Interessenten und der Staaten immer wieder zurückgedrängt wäre." About the erosion of a competitive economic constitution, Eucken (1989a: 52f.) notes: "Aber auch dann, wenn Wirtschaftsverfassungen die Ordnung der Wirtschaft ... vollziehen wollen, entwickeln sich auf der Grundlage der Wirtschaftsverfassungen *faktisch* oft Wirtschaftsordnungen, welche den Grundgedanken der Wirtschaftsverfassung nicht oder nicht voll entsprechen. Dieser Zustand ist z.B. für das späte 19. und für das beginnende 20. Jahrhundert kennzeichnend."

46 As Röpke (1960: 31) worded it, Leistungswettbewerb means "that the only road to business success is through the narrow gate of better performance in service of the consumer."

47 Eucken (1938: 81) speaks of the principle (Ordnungsprinzip) of "Leistungswettbewerb" as "die Pointe unserer wirtschaftsverfassungsrechtlichen Idee."

48 Creating a suitable framework for 'Leistungswettbewerb' has been, as Eucken (1990: 42) notes, a principal aim of liberal economic policy: "Durch Beseitigung der vielen überkommenen Privilegien, Bann- und Zwangsrechte, Zünfte usw. wollte die liberale Wirtschaftspolitik offene Märkte herstellen, um den Leistungswettbewerb und die Auslese der Unternehmer nach der Leistung zu ermöglichen. ... Die Bewährung für die Versorgung mit Konsumgütern sollte entscheiden."

49 Böhm (1980: 200): "Denn eine rational ablaufende Marktwirtschaft kommt nicht etwa dadurch zustande, daß man durch Gesetz die Gewerbefreiheit einführt und sodann die Dinge laufen läßt, wie sie laufen. Vielmehr fordert dieses sich selbst steuernde System das Vorhandensein und die dauernde Pflege und Verbesserung einer ganzen Reithe von politischen, rechtlichen, sozialen und zivilisatorischen Vorbedingungen, das Vorhandensein einer ziemlich hochgezüchteten Parklandschaft." Böhm (1950: XXXV): "Die Wettbewerbswirtschaft wiederum ist ein kulturelles Wunderwerk, das auf ein hohes Maß von pflegehafter Verwaltungskultur, einsichtiger Grundsatzfestigkeit, Achtung vor der individuellen Freiheit, ... und von Rechtsbewußtsein angewiesen ist, das also nur bei hochgespannter Daueranstrengung eines politisch geschulten, freiheitsliebenden Volkes vor Verfall geschützt werden kann." See also Böhm (1980: 115): "Die Privatrechtsgesellschaft bedarf ... einer Mitwirkung politischer Herrschaftsfunktionen, wenn auch nur in bescheidenem Umfang und wenn auch bloß pfleghaft-gärtnerischen Charakters." Tumlir (1989: 135) notes about Böhm: "All his work consists of describing and analysing the conditions that must be satisfied for the competitive system of free enterprise to function satisfactorily and be secured against drift. ... Maintenance of these conditions is a matter of constant attention."

50 Böhm (1950: XXXIII): "Wenn man wünscht, die ordnende Kraft einer verkehrswirtschaftlichen Verfassung voll zum Zuge kommen zu lassen, so muß man mit allen zu Gebote stehenden Mitteln versuchen, die Bedingungen der vollständigen Konkurrenz auf allen Märkten herzustellen, eine entsprechende Geldordnung zu schaffen, muß es ferner unterlassen, in diese Wirtschaft mit irgendwelchen Interventionen einzugreifen." See also Böhm (1950: XLIf.).

51 Eucken (1989a: 241) argued, for instance, that an economic constitution based on the principle of *Leistungswettbewerb* should include unlimited liability as one of its essential elements.

52 Böhm et al. [1989: 24f. (1937: XX)]: "Free competition must not be stopped on the erroneous grounds of alleged unfair practice. On the other hand, it must not be allowed to degenerate into truly unfair competition either. How the line is to be drawn between unfair and permissible competition, whether there is free competition or not, whether competition is restricted, whether competition is efficient or obstructive, whether or not price-cutting contradicts the principle of

the system – all these issues can only be decided by investigations conducted by economists into the various states of the market."

53 Böhm *et al.* [1989 (1937: XX)].

54 In his book of 1937, Böhm (1937: 105f.) even said about markets where these conditions of complete competition are not realized on both sides that they ought to be subject to direct state control: [Dort] "kann das System der freien Marktwirtschaft nicht funktionieren. Diese Märkte sind daher der unmittelbaren Marktlenkung durch den Staat zu unterstellen." Böhm was, however, at the same time very skeptical as to the likely effects of such state supervision: "Hierzu ist zu sagen, daß die Methode der staatlichen Marktlenkung nur dann gewählt werden sollte, wenn ihre Anwendung praktisch den *gleichen Ordnungserfolg* verspricht, wie der Wettbewerb. ... [Wenn diese Voraussetzung nicht gegeben ist, V.V.] dann ist die Methode der Staatslenkung ... die schwächere Form der Ordnung. Die Folge ist, daß eine Flucht der Wirtschaft aus der Konkurrenz in die Staatsaufsicht einsetzt, weil es sich unter der Staatsaufsicht bequemer lebt als unter der Konkurrenz" (Böhm 1937: 147). See also Böhm (1960: 64f.). Sally (1996: 10f.) notes on this aspect of the Freiburg message: "This is perhaps the most unrealistic and faulty aspect of Eucken's work and that of the early Freiburg School. ... Monopoly is bound to exist in large measure in real-life conditions. The problem is not one of monopoly *per se*, but of the prevention of competition, which can be tackled by general rules. ... The perfect competition assumption however, can be used ... for discretionary powers of government."

55 Böhm (1937: 70) invokes both concepts when he argues: "Nach der Konstruktionsidee der richtig verstandenen freien Wirtschaftsverfassung kommt der privatwirtschaftliche Sachverstand des einzelnen Unternehmers der Gesamtwirtschaft nur unter der Voraussetzung zugute, daß sich der Markt, auf dem der Unternehmer tätig ist, im Zustande der doppelseitigen Konkurrenz befindet und daß der Wettbewerb unter Einhaltung der Spielregel (Leistungsprinzip!) ausgetragen wird." See also Eucken (1989a: 256; 1990: 247).

56 Willgerodt and Peacock (1989: 7f.) note: "The theoretical concept of competition for Ordo-liberals has changed considerably ... In general, however, it was always more realistic than some static concepts of 'perfect' competition." They also note that modern-day ordo-liberals consider the policy goal of perfect competition both impossible to achieve in all markets and an undesirable goal to pursue (Peacock and Willgerodt 1989: 7).

57 Kasper and Streit (1993: 21): "The original Freiburg School developed its basic position between the 1930s and the 1950s, at a time when national economic systems were relatively closed. ... This induced the Freiburgers to seek strong support for proper competitiveness from the government and legislation. It has been pointed out that nowadays, in a system that is open to international competition and innovation, a strong government is no longer all that necessary to ensure a proper competitive order. ... Worldwide competition and innovation are now breaking monopolies." Tumlir (1989: 127): "Whether competition has to be protected or enforced by a special effort of government, beyond its elementary duty of preventing force and fraud, is a perennial problem in economic as well as legal theory. It was Franz Böhm's central preoccupation and he shaped the Ordo doctrine in this most important respect. His views can only be understood from German history."

58   By "market competition," Böhm (1950: L) argues, a competition is meant, "der nicht ein prinzipienindifferenter Wirtschaftskrieg, sondern ein rechtlich geordnetes, von einer sinnvollen Spielregel beherrschtes Leistungs-und Bewährungsausleseverfahren ist." Böhm (1937: 126): "Ein nicht 'regelhafter' Wettbewerb hat jedenfalls keinen Daseinsanspruch im Rahmen einer Wirtschaftsverfassung, die Anspruch darauf erhebt, eine Ordnung der Wirtschaft zu sein."

59   Böhm (1960): "An diesem Punkte wird es deutlich, daß die Lehre von der Vertragsfreiheit die Vorstellung von einer auf freier Konkurrenz beruhenden Wirtschafts- und Marktverfassung zur Voraussetzung hat; denn wo Wettbewerbsfreiheit verwirklicht ist, da fehlt dem schlechteren Anbieter jede Möglichkeit der Zufügung von Nachteilen. ... In der Möglichkeit, als schlechterer Anbieter den Partner von der Annahme besserer Angebote abzuhalten oder ihn für deren Annahme zu bestrafen, beruht das Wesen der wirtschaftlichen Macht; in der Ausnützung dieser Möglichkeit aber das Wesen des wirtschaftlichen Zwangs."

60   Tumlir (1989: 138) notes in critical reference to Böhm's focus on the problem of private economic power: "What deserves at least equal emphasis is the fact, or at least the strong presumption, that already in its emergence, private economic power depends on public, political power."

61   Eucken (1942: 43) points to the "Wirtschafts- und Rechtspolitik der meisten Industriestaaten" as a major source of concentration in the economy: "Durch unzählige Bestimmungen und Maßnahmen des Gesellschaftsrechts, des Steuerrechts, des Patentrechts, des Konkursrechts, der Handelspolitik, der Kreditpolitik usw. ist der Konzentrationsprozeß und sind die monopolistischen oder oligopolistischen Machtballungen vor allem in der Industrie entscheidend gefördert, vielfach überhaupt erst angeregt worden." See also Eucken (1982: 120): "In many sectors of German industry, cartels would disappear immediately if tariffs were to go. ... Despite certain legal precautions, patent law has unexpectedly triggered powerful tendencies toward the formation of monopolies and concentration processes in industry." Commenting on the Freiburg school, Tumlir (1989: 138) notes on this issue that, in a protectionist regime, "maintaining competition at home becomes difficult both in theory and in practice. In this sense, liberal trade policy, legally secured against lobbying and pressure of legislative coalitions ... is the most effective competition policy."

62   Tumlir (1989: 135) notes about Böhm's (1989) essay "Privatrechtsgesellschaft und Marktwirtschaft": "The last part of this essay could easily be translated into the contemporary analytical language of rent-seeking."

63   Böhm (1980: 164) speaks of the "verfassungspolitischen Grundentscheidung, die mit der Option für das marktwirtschaftliche System und die privilegienlose Zivilrechtsgesellschaft getroffen worden ist."

64   Böhm (1937: 41) also clearly described the asymmetry in the political dynamics that makes it easy for politicians to grant privileges, but very difficult to take them away: "Durch Interventionen werden *private Besitzstände* geschaffen. Man denke insbesondere an spezifisch protektionistische Interventionen, wie etwa Zölle, Einfuhrverbote, Prämien, Subventionen. Die Einführung solcher Maßnahmen ist leicht, besonders da die öffentliche Meinung regelmäßig mit dem Hinweis

darauf beschwichtigt wird, daß es sich um Eingriffe von nur vorübergehender Art handelt. Die Wiederaufhebung dagegen stößt bei den Begünstigten auf einen leidenschaftlichen Widerstand. Sie kommen sich vor und stellen sich an, als ob sie enteignet würden. Kurz, der politische Effekt von Interventionen ist, daß auf die Wirtschaftenden ein starker Anreiz ausgeübt wird, sich zum Behuf der Erlangung und Beibehaltung von Interventionen *politisch* zu organisieren."

65 Using theft as a metaphor, Böhm (1960: 165) notes: "Der Diebstahl ist ein Störungsfaktor in einer Eigentumsordnung, kann aber trotzdem nur in einer Eigentumsordnung vorkommen. Er ist – als Technik des Kooperierens – nicht fähig, konstituierender Baustein einer selbständigen Ordnung zu sein. Eine auf Diebstahl ... gegründete Gesellschaftsordnung würde im günstigsten Fall eine sehr unpraktische Ordnung sein und sich nicht behaupten können. Insbesondere würde sie den Dieben von Geblüt nicht die mindeste Freude machen. Ein Dieb ist kein Revolutionär, sondern ein konservativer Ordnungsfreund. Er wünscht sich eine Ordnung, an die sich alle halten, bloß er nicht."

66 Böhm (1980: 164f.): "Die 'Sünde', von der hier die Rede ist, besteht nun darin, daß die Wirtschaftsbeteiligten der Versuchung erliegen, die Einkommenserwartungen, die sie bei ordnungskonformer Handhabung des Systems haben, dadurch zu verbessern, daß sie – soweit ihnen das objektiv möglich ist – für ihre eigene Person ordnungs*inkonform* handeln oder daß sie ihre politischen Mitbestimmungsrechte und ihren politischen Einfluß verwerten, um die amtierende Staatsgewalt zu veranlassen, zugunsten einer bestimmten Gruppe von Bürgern *eine ordnungsinkonforme Ausnahme zuzulassen, und daß die amtierende Staatsgewalt diesem Einfluß nachgibt.*"

67 As Böhm (1980: 165) phrases it: "Die Folge ist ein Überhandnehmen von Interventionen, deren Wirkungen sich gegenseitig im Wege stehen."

68 Böhm (1950: XXXVI) describes the dilemma when he speaks of the necessity "to exploit, in order not to be exploited."

69 Kasper and Streit (1993: 26): "The main purpose of 'order policy' [is] ... to ensure that enterprise is directed away from seeking a return on its assets by securing politically sanctioned rents and privileges."

70 Eucken (1932: 323) noted in reference to advocates of state control of the economy: "Stillschweigend wird meist ein allmächtiger und allwissender Staat als vorhanden angenommen – also ein Gebilde, das keinerlei Ähnlichkeit mit einem wirklichen Staat besitzt und niemals als ordnende Kraft der Volkswirtschaft tätig sein kann." Eucken (1990: 331): "Üblich ist folgender Gedankengang: Weil die freie Wirtschaft versage, müsse der Staat die Lenkung des Wirtschaftsprozesses übernehmen. Ohne sich den Kopf über die Schwierigkeit des Lenkungsproblems zu zerbrechen, bejaht man vorschnell die Frage, ob der Staat die Aufgabe bewältigen kann."

71 Eucken (1990: 338): "So falsch es ist, im vorhandenen Staat einen allweisen und allmächtigen Betreuer allen wirtschaftlichen Geschehens zu erblicken, so unrichtig ist es auch, den faktisch vorhandenen, von Machtgruppen zersetzten Staat als Datum hinzunehmen und dann – folgerichtig – an der Möglichkeit der Bewältigung des wirtschaftspolitischen Ordnungsproblems zu verzweifeln."

72 Eucken (1940: 490f.): "Darin besteht der empfindlichste Stachel aller großen wirtschaftspolitischen und wirtschaftsverfassungsrechtlichen Probleme: Eigennützige Menschen, einflußreiche und eigennützige Machtgruppen sind da,

– auf der anderen Seite darf der staatlichen Verwaltung und den Beamten in der Leitung des Wirtschaftsprozesses nicht zu viel zugemutet werden. Trotzdem ist eine brauchbare Ordnung der Gesamtwirtschaft und ihrer Teilbereiche zu schaffen. ... Wäre tatsächlich das Gebot der Nächstenliebe zur höchsten Macht auf Erden geworden und richteten sich die Menschen nach ihm, so würden sich alle wirtschaftsverfassungsrechtlichen Fragen anders stellen. – Aber wir müssen uns hüten, am Schreibtisch eine solche fortgeschrittene Welt zu schildern und für sie wirtschaftspolitische Vorschläge zu ersinnen – in der Meinung, die Welt sehe wirklich so aus."

73   Eucken (1990: 327): "Und so wird man wieder auf die Frage zurückgeworfen: Wie kann der moderne Staat eine Potenz werden, die eine brauchbare Wirtschaftsverfassung verwirklicht?" Eucken (1990: 331): "Die Ordnung des Staates ist ebenso eine Aufgabe, wie die Ordnung der Wirtschaft." Eucken (1990: 332): "Und so bedarf der Aufbau des Staates abermals von Grund aus ordnungspolitischer Durchdenkung, ... weil ohne die ordnende Potenz des Staates eine zureichende Wirtschaftsordnung nicht aufgebaut werden kann., und weil umgekehrt eine neue Staatsbildung im Zusammenhang mit dem Aufbau der Wirtschaftsordnung steht."

74   Eucken (1990: 334): "Weil aber diese allgemeine Interdependenz besteht, kann die Frage nach dem Aufbau des Staates, der die neufeudalen Abhängigkeiten überwindet, nur so gestellt werden, daß die Probleme der Staatsordnung und der Wirtschaftsordnung in Zusammenhang gebracht werden."

75   Eucken (1990: 338): "Die Interdependenz von Staatsordnung und Wirtschaftsordnung zwingt dazu, den Ordnungsaufbau von beiden in einem Zug in Angriff zu nehmen. ... Ohne Wettbewerbsordnung kann kein aktionsfähiger Staat entstehen und ohne einen aktionsfähigen Staat keine Wettbewerbsordnung."

76   Böhm (1980: 258): "Was sich ereignen wird, ist etwas ganz anderes, nämlich der *schwache Staat, der sich in alles einmischt*, der schwache Staat, der zum Spielball rivalisierender organisierter Gruppeninteressen wird." Eucken (1990: 327): "Doch der weitaus wichtigste Wesenszug staatlicher Entwicklung im 20. Jahrhundert ist *die Zunahme im Umfang der Staatstätigkeit und die gleichzeitige Abnahme der staatlichen Autorität*." Eucken (1990: 329): "Überall handelt es sich um die Unterhöhlung der Staatsautorität durch partikulare Gewalten, die partikulare Interessen vertreten. Und eine Eigenart der modernen Entwicklung ist es eben, daß mit diesem Autoritätsverlust eine rasche Expansion der Staatstätigkeit verbunden ist." Eucken (1932: 307): "Die Umwandlung des liberalen Staates zum Wirtschaftsstaat bedeut für das staatliche, wie für das wirtschaftliche Leben sehr viel. Daß mit diesem Prozeß die Größe des Staatsapparates außerordentlich wächst, daß sein Etat mächtig anschwillt, daß er mit seinen Subventionen, Zöllen, Einfuhrverboten, Kontingenten, Moratorien usw. ... viel tiefer als früher in die Einkommensgestaltung des einzelnen eingreift, daß sich also eine entschiedene Expansion der Staatstätigkeiten vollzieht, ist oft geschildert worden. Solche Tatsachen dürfen aber nicht eine andere Seite der Sache übersehen lassen; diese Expansion nämlich ... bedeutet nicht etwa eine Stärkung, sondern ganz im Gegenteil eine Schwächung des Staates."

77   As a "strong state" in this sense, a state would qualify that meets Böhm's (1980: 148; 1989: 61) description: "The situation in a private law society, which is combined with a democratically structured constitutional state favors the

realisation of a social structure which makes the attempt by social groups to exploit other social groups a more and more hopeless undertaking."

78 Eucken (1990: 337): "Die beiden Grundsätze der Staatspolitik, die darauf zielen, den Staat als ordnende Potenz wirksam werden zu lassen, harmonisieren aber auch vollständig mit den Prinzipien, die für den Aufbau einer zureichenden Wirtschaftsordnung gelten." The "two principles" to which Eucken refers are the following: "Erster Grundsatz: Die Politik des Staates sollte darauf gerichtet sein, wirtschaftliche Machtgruppen aufzulösen oder ihre Funktion zu begrenzen" (Eucken 1990: 334). "Zweiter Grundsatz: Die wirtschaftspolitische Tätigkeit des Staates sollte auf die Gestaltung der Ordnungsformen der Wirtschaft gerichtet sein, nicht auf die Lenkung des Wirtschaftprozesses."

79 Eucken (1990: 331f.): "Die Ordnung des Staates ist ebenso eine Aufgabe wie die Ordnung der Wirtschaft. ... Denn es ist auch die ordnungspolitische Frage zu stellen: Wie kann ein leistungsfähiger Rechtsstaat aufgebaut werden? ... Und so bedarf der Aufbau des Staates abermals von Grund auf ordnungspolitischer Durchdenkung."

4 Hayek's legacy and the future of liberal thought: rational liberalism versus evolutionary agnosticism

1 This article was first presented as a paper at the Mont Pelerin Society General Meeting, Cannes, France, 1994. Support of this research by the Earhart Foundation is gratefully acknowledged. I also wish to thank Georg Vanberg for helpful comments.

2 In its subtitle, Hayek calls his major, three-volume treatise on *Law, Legislation and Liberty* (Hayek 1973; 1976a; 1979a) *A New Statement of the Liberal Principles of Justice and Political Economy*.

3 In the same spirit, Hayek (1960: 30) also declares: "So far as possible, our aim should be to improve human institutions."

4 Kukathas (1990: vii) sums up his view as follows: "The central dilemma of Hayek's political philosophy is, given his view of the limited role reason can play in social life, how is it possible to mount a systematic defense of liberalism without falling victim to the very kinds of rationalism he criticizes? This difficulty stays unresolved in Hayek's political thought because it is informed by two incompatible assumptions about what reason can achieve."

5 See also Wilhelm (1991: 169), who refers to the same issue when he notes that "(t)wo major themes in Hayek's political thought seem ... to conflict with each other."

6 As Kukathas notes, throughout his work Hayek's "primary concern has been to elucidate and defend the principles of a liberal social order" (Kukathas 1990: 166), to articulate "the normative principles which underlie the liberal ideal of a free society" (ibid.: 13).

7 For a discussion of this issue, see, for instance, Hayek (1969: 172; 1973: 4; 1978: 136); West (1990: 118); Albert (1979: 27).

8 In his 1947 "Opening address to a conference at Mont Pelerin" (reprinted in Hayek 1992: 237–48), Hayek noted that to achieve a revival of liberal ideals would require "purging traditional liberal theory of certain accidental accretions

... and also facing up to some real problems which an over-simplified liberalism has shirked" (ibid.: 237f.).

9 As Kukathas (1990: 212f.) observes: "Hayek is not a simple advocate of *laissez-faire* but maintains that the important problems for liberals concern the rules or laws which define property and freedom of contract. ... If there is a reason why Hayek turns out to be a constructivist of sorts it may be that it is difficult for liberals in general, and classical liberals in particular, not to be."

10 This pamphlet was a prelude to *The Road to Serfdom*, as Hayek notes in the 1976 "Preface" [Hayek 1976b (1944): xix].

11 Hayek [1976b (1944): 35]: "The dispute between the modern planners and their opponents is ... *not* on whether we ought to choose intelligently between the various possible organizations of society; it is not a dispute on whether we ought to employ foresight and systematic thinking in planning our common affairs. It is a dispute about what is the best way of so doing." In his article on "The new confusion about 'planning'" (Hayek 1978: 232–46) quotes, at some length, his argument in *The Road to Serfdom* on this issue (ibid.: 233–4).

12 Hayek (1939: 8f.): "We can 'plan' a system of general rules, equally applicable to all people and intended to be permanent (even if subject to revision with the growth of knowledge), which provides an institutional framework within which the decisions as to what to do and how to earn a living are left to the individuals."

13 In a handbook article on "liberalism" Hayek (1959: 594f.) comments on the difference between the 'new' and the 'old' liberalism: "Der neue Liberalismus unterscheidet sich vom alten vor allem darin, dass er sich des engen wechselseitigen Zusammenhangs zwischen wirtschaftlichen und politischen Institutionen bewusster ist ..., vor allem auch, dass das befriedigende Funktionieren der *Wettbewerbswirtschaft* ganz bestimmte Erfordernisse bezüglich des rechtlichen Rahmenwerks stelle. ... An die Stelle der irreführend gewesenen Formel 'Laissez—faire' trat das ausdrückliche Bemühen um eine Gestaltung der Rechtsordnung, die der Erhaltung und dem erspriesslichen Wirken des Wettbewerbs günstig ist und das Entstehen von privaten Machtpositionen sowohl auf Seiten der Unternehmer wie der Arbeiter zu verhindern sucht."

14 See Ch. 3. in this volume.

15 See also Hayek (1956/57: 524). Using a similar image, F. Böhm (1980: 200) argues that a well-functioning market economy requires "die dauernde Pflege und Verbesserung einer ganzen Reihe von politischen, rechtlichen, sozialen und zivilisatorischen Vorbedingungen, das Vorhandensein einer ziemlich hochgezüchteten sozialen Parklandschaft."

16 Hayek (1976b[1944]: 38): "The functioning of competition ... depends, above all, on the existence of an appropriate legal system, a legal system designed both to preserve competition and to make it operate as beneficial as possible. ... The systematic study of the forms of legal institutions which will make the competitive system work efficiently has been sadly neglected."

17 For a more detailed discussion, see Vanberg (1994a; 1994b, Ch. 5).

18 U. Witt (1994: 184) concludes from his discussion of Hayek's evolutionary argument: "[O]n a closer look it turns out that the theory of societal evolution appears rather unfinished and leaves several questions open."

19 Hayek makes a number of remarks which sound as if he thinks of cultural evolution as a totally unconstrained process in the sense that it includes all conceivable

competitive strategies. He notes, for instance: "Although the displacement of one group by another, and of one set of practices by another, has often been bloody, it does not need always to be so" (Hayek 1988: 121).

20 Hayek (1979b: 17): "Nicht was vom Menschen als nützlich verstanden wurde, sondern nur was sich ohne sein Verständnis für die Förderung seiner Vermehrung als wirksam erwiesen hat, regiert tatsächlich die Geschichte, ob wir dies nun mögen oder nicht; und wahrscheinlich hat dieser Umstand auch bestimmt, was die Werte sind, die zumindest in der Vergangenheit die Mehrzahl der Menschen geleitet haben." In *The Fatal Conceit*, Hayek even makes the somewhat obscure claim that it *"is not the present number of lives that evolution will tend to maximize but the prospective stream of future lives"* (Hayek 1988: 132; emphasis in original). In evaluating this or other quotes from *The Fatal Conceit*, one should always keep in mind that this last book by Hayek was edited by W. Bartley. And there are many indications that Bartley's editing may have been quite heavy. This is one more reason not to give too much weight to *The Fatal Conceit* in evaluating Hayek's life work.

21 The ambiguity of Hayek's argument on this issue is visible, for instance, when he reasons: "It would however be wrong to conclude, strictly from such evolutionary premises, that whatever rules have evolved are always or necessarily conducive to the survival and increase of the populations following them. We need to show, with the help of economic analysis ... how rules that emerge spontaneously tend to promote human survival. Recognizing that rules generally tend to be selected, via competition, on the basis of their human survival-value certainly does not protect those rules from critical scrutiny. This is so, if for no other reasons, because there has so often been coercive interference in the process of cultural evolution" (Hayek 1988: 20). It is very difficult to identify what claims are actually made in this statement as it raises, and confounds, a number of different issues such as: What kind of "competition" is meant? What is meant by "coercive interference in the process of cultural evolution"? What would characterize a process of cultural evolution *without* coercive interference? What is meant by the claim that evolved rules "tend to promote human survival"?

22 On this issue, see, for instance, Hayek's (1988: 155) reference to the Smithian notion "that division of labor is limited by the extent of the market, and that population increase is crucial to the prosperity of a country."

23 This seems to be what Hayek means when he speaks of "beneficial traditions" that enable "groups following them to grow" (Hayek 1988: 136), or when he talks about rules that evolved "not because men recognized by reason that they were better but because they made possible the growth of an extended order ... in which more effective collaboration enabled its members, however blindly, to maintain more people and to displace other groups" (ibid.: 23).

24 Hayek seems to have this claim in mind when he notes about the competitive selection among institutions: "Many of these processes may then have happened entirely peacefully, although the greater military strength of commercially organized people will often have accelerated the process" (Hayek 1988: 121).

25 On this issue, Hayek notes that groups "following market practices would, as they grew in numbers, displace others who followed different customs" (Hayek 1988: 120).

26 Hayek (1988: 121): "I have been contending that socialism constitutes a threat to the present and future welfare of the human race in the sense that neither socialism nor any other known substitute for the market order could sustain the current population of the world."

27 Hayek (1988: 20f.): "While it [an understanding of cultural evolution, V.V.] cannot prove the superiority of market institutions, a historical and evolutionary survey of the emergence of capitalism ... helps to explain how such productive ... traditions happened to emerge."

28 As noted earlier, the claim that the results of cultural evolution are desirable can be meaningful only if one knows what *kinds of results* the evolutionary process can be expected to produce. In other words, only on the basis of an evolutionary theory with *empirical* content can the issue of the desirability of evolutionary outcomes be meaningfully discussed. In discussing the issue of the normative content of Hayek's evolutionary argument, I disregard here the problems identified by my foregoing analysis of its empirical content.

29 Even if in some global, eternal sense one might say that not our wishes but the forces of evolution have the last word (whatever that may mean), this could hardly be a serious argument for abstaining from efforts in institutional improvement. Hayek invokes in this context also the argument that human values are themselves a product of evolution. He notes, for instance: "But the basic conclusion that the whole of our civilization and all human values are the result of a long process of evolution in the course of which values ... continue to change, seems inescapable in the light of our present knowledge" (Hayek 1978: 38). This argument is certainly correct, yet the question is what Hayek's point in using it is. Is it supposed to suggest that, in matters of social organization, our 'human values' cannot serve as a meaningful guide? And, if so, what other guide, if any, could be used in legislative reform?

30 The context from which the above quotes are taken indicates that, here again, Hayek's real argument is about the superior wealth-creating potential of market institutions, and the disastrous consequences that can be predicted to result from their destruction. As he notes: "So many people already exist; and only a market economy can keep the bulk of them alive. ... Since we can preserve and secure even our present numbers only by adhering to the same general kinds of principles, it is our duty – unless we truly wish to condemn millions to starvation – to resist the claims of creeds that tend to destroy the basic principles of these morals, such as the institution of several property. In any case, our desires and wishes are largely irrelevant. Whether we desire further increases of production and population or not, we must – merely to maintain existing numbers and wealth, and to protect them as best we can against calamity – strive after what, under favorable conditions, will continue to lead, at least for some time, and in many places, to further increases" (Hayek 1988: 134). It should be apparent, that the essential content of these arguments can well be defended on rational grounds, without the need to employ any of Hayek's evolutionary notions.

31 For a more detailed discussion of the normative implications of Hayek's theory of cultural evolution, see Vanberg (1994a: 180ff.).

32 As a follow-up on the above discussion on the population size issue: we can assume that Hayek does not consider population size in itself of normative relevance.

Even if his suggestion were true that cultural evolution favors institutions in proportion to population size, it would be strange for him to claim that evolutionary 'successful' institutions are 'beneficial' *because* of their population attributes.

33 Note that "better off" can be interpreted in a subjective as well as an objective sense. In its subjective interpretation, the (necessarily subjective) *interests* of the persons involved are the relevant measuring rod. In its objective interpretation, by contrast, some "objective" measure of wealth would be the standard. It is not always unambiguously clear which version Hayek wants to apply. It seems to me that only the subjective interpretation is consistent with his overall philosophy; yet, it would go beyond the scope of this article to discuss this issue here. I shall presume for the purposes of my discussion here that the subjective interpretation applies.

34 Hayek (1978: 37): "Since Adam Smith ... a market economy has ... been likened to a game in which the results for each depend partly on his skill and effort and partly on chance. The individuals have reason to agree to play this game because it makes the pool from which the individual shares are drawn larger than it can be made by any other method."

35 Hayek (1976a: 132) defines a "beneficial social order" as "one in which the chances of anyone selected at random are likely to be as great as possible," and he notes that the aim of institutional reform "should be to improve as much as possible the chances of anyone selected at random" (ibid.: 129f.). For similar statements, see Hayek (1967: 165, 173; 1978: 63f., 184, 186).

36 Hayek (1979a: 168): "Man has been civilized very much against his wishes. It was the price he had to pay for being able to raise a larger number of children."

37 See also Hayek (1988: 7): "But if mankind owes its existence to one particular rule-guided form of conduct of proven effectiveness, it simply does not have the option of choosing another merely for the sake of the apparent pleasantness of its immediately visible effects."

38 I should point out that my interest here is not in exegesis but in explicating what, in my view, is the most useful reading of some of Hayek's arguments. I do not claim that everything in Hayek's writings can be brought under my interpretation. In fact, some of his arguments on cultural evolution, in particular in *The Fatal Conceit*, I find quite elusive, such as the following paragraph: "Civilization is not only a product of evolution – it is a process; by establishing a framework of general rules and individual freedom it allows itself to continue to evolve. This evolution cannot be guided by and often will not produce what men demand. Men may find some previously unfulfilled wishes satisfied, but only at the price of disappointing many others. Though by moral conduct an individual may increase his opportunities, the resulting evolution will not gratify all his moral desires. Evolution *cannot be just*" (Hayek 1988: 74).

39 To argue that a *rational, constitutional* argument in favor of a liberal order can be made is not the same as claiming that people can, as a matter of fact, be easily convinced of the preferability of a liberal order by general and abstract arguments. Hayek is clearly skeptical about the latter issue, and rightly so. It may well be that people, when given a chance to compare the actual working properties of alternative constitutional systems, can easily recognize the preferability of a liberal

order, but that they may have difficulties doing so when they face a choice among alternative regimes in the abstract, e.g. in political elections. The migration streams between socialist and liberal Western societies, before the collapse of communism, and some of the recent voting results in former communist countries illustrate this point.

40 For a more detailed discussion of this theme, see Vanberg and Kerber (1994).

41 Hayek (1978: 124f., 135): "Adam Smith's decisive contribution was the account of a self-generating order which formed itself spontaneously if the individuals were restrained by appropriate rules of law. ... David Hume and Adam Smith did not assume a natural harmony of interests, but rather contended that the divergent interests of different individuals could be reconciled by the observance of appropriate rules of conduct."

42 As a minimal requirement, Hayek (1988: 19) notes: "To operate beneficially, competition requires that those involved observe rules rather than resort to physical force. Rules alone can unite an extended order."

43 Hayek [1976b (1944): 38]: "It is by no means sufficient that the law should recognize the principle of private property and freedom of contract; much depends on the precise definition of the right of property as applied to different things. The systematic study of the forms of legal institutions which will make the competitive system work efficiently has been sadly neglected." The general criterion that Hayek sees for "an appropriate legal system" is expressed in his statement: "[T]he main condition on which the usefulness of the system of competition and private property depends: namely, that the owner benefits from all the useful services rendered by his property and suffers all the damages caused to others by it" (ibid.). See also Hayek (1978: 145).

44 Hayek (1978: 184): "Therefore it clearly makes sense to try to produce conditions under which the chances for any individual taken at random to achieve his ends as effectively as possible will be very high." See also Hayek (1967: 173): "An optimal policy in a catallaxy may aim, and ought to aim, at increasing the chances of any member of society taken at random."

45 As noted earlier, a principal, and acceptable, assumption in Hayek's theory of cultural evolution is that the gradual improvement in market rules was, to a large extent, a spontaneous process: "The rules which gradually developed, because they made this game [the game of catallaxy, V.V.] more effective, were essentially those of the law of property and contract. These rules in turn made possible the progressive division of labor, and the mutual adjustment of independent efforts, which a functioning division of labor demands" (Hayek 1978: 62). Note that the issue relevant in the context of this article is *not* whether "beneficial" institutions can result from spontaneous evolutionary processes. The issue is whether evolutionary processes can be *relied* upon to select in favor of "beneficial" institutions.

46 Hayek speaks of "the task of gradually amending our legal system to make it more conducive to the smooth working of competition" (Hayek 1960: 230).

47 As Hayek (1967: 174) adds: "It should also be specially observed that this modest and achievable goal has never yet been fully achieved because at all times and everywhere governments have both restricted access to some occupations and tolerated persons and organizations deterring others from entering occupations."

48 In the course of this discussion, I hope to clarify the issue that Kukathas (1990: 103f.) raises: "Hayek is not an anarchist. He sees a place for politics in the development of the institutions of justice, he does not present what might be termed a 'pure theory of spontaneous order'. Indeed, the market can only flourish, in his view, if sound institutions of justice, law, and property are put in place. Yet it is obscure how far these institutions arise 'spontaneously', when it is permissible to alter them, or what criteria we may use to evaluate their functioning. ... [W]hile Hayek has developed a theory of the spontaneous ordering forces of society, he has not come up with an explanation of the extent to which reason can criticize and try to alter the direction of social development." I seek to show that what Kukathas sees lacking can be reconstructed from Hayek's own argument.

49 Hayek (1960: 63): "[A]lthough we must always strive to improve our institutions, we can never aim to remake them as a whole."

50 See also Hayek (1988: 8): "By 'reason properly used' I mean reason that recognizes its own limitations. ... How, after all, could I be attacking reason in a book arguing that socialism is factually and even logically untenable? Nor do I dispute that reason may, although with caution and humility, and in a piecemeal way, be directed to the examination, criticism and rejection of traditional institutions and moral principles. ... Thus I wish neither to deny reason the power to improve norms and institutions."

51 Hayek (1988: 53): "I am entirely in favor of experimentation. ... What I object to among rationalist intellectuals ... [is that they, V.V.] shelter their own 'experiments' from scrutiny."

52 Using the image of the gardener (see Ch. 4, fn. xx) to characterize the nature of this task, Hayek (1956/7: 524) notes, "daß wir statt von Beherrschung besser von *Kultivierung* sprechen sollten – in dem Sinn, wie der Gärtner seine Blumen kultiviert und der Staatsmann oder Politiker die gesellschaftlichen Bildungen kultivieren und nicht beherrschen sollte."

53 Hayek (1969: 13): "Die Hauptaufgabe der Wirtschaftspolitik ist daher, ein Rahmenwerk zu schaffen, innerhalb dessen der einzelne nicht nur frei entscheiden kann, sondern seine auf Ausnützung seiner persönlichen Kenntnisse gegründete Entscheidung soviel wie möglich zum Gesamterfolg beitragen wird."

54 Hayek (1969: 51): "Es ist irreführend, wenn man das Rahmenwerk von Regeln ... 'Interventionen' nennt. Keiner der großen Theoretiker der Wirtschaftsfreiheit hätte das getan. Für sie alle war Freiheit immer 'freedom under the law'. Ganz anders steht es freilich mit den echten Interventionen, deren sich die moderne Wirtschaftspolitik in so hohem Maße bedient. ... Sie erfordern alle, daß die Behörden dem einen erlauben, etwas zu tun, was sie dem anderen verbieten, und sie wären daher unzulässig unter einem System, das Zwangsanwendung nur nach allgemeinen Regeln erlaubt."

55 Hayek (1973: 51): "[W]e can preserve an order of such complexity not by the method of directing the members, but only indirectly by enforcing and improving the rules conducive to the formation of a spontaneous order. ... This is the gist of the argument against 'interference' or 'intervention' in the market order. ... What the general argument against 'interference' thus amounts to is that, although we can endeavor to improve a spontaneous order by revising the general rules on which it rests, ... we cannot improve the results by specific commands that deprive its members of the possibility of using their knowledge for their purposes."

5 Hayek's theory of rules and the modern state

1   Hayek (1973: 13): "It will be one of our chief contentions that most of the rules of conduct which govern our actions, and most of the institutions which arise out of this regularity, are adaptations to the impossibility of anyone taking conscious account of all the particular facts which enter into the order of society." Hayek (1973: 19): "(T)he constructivist approach denies that it can be rational to observe such rules."

2   Hayek (1978: 124f.): "Adam Smith's decisive contribution was the account of a self-generating order which formed itself spontaneously if the individuals were restrained by appropriate rules of law. His *Inquiry into the Nature and Causes of the Wealth of Nations* marks perhaps more than any other single work the beginning of the development of modern liberalism."

3   Hayek (1967: 162): "The central concept of liberalism is that under the enforcement of universal rules of just conduct, protecting a recognizable private domain of individuals, a spontaneous order of human activities of much greater complexity will form itself than could ever be produced by deliberate arrangement." Hayek (1978: 136): "The great advantage of such a self-generating order was thought to be, not only that it left the individuals free to pursue their own purposes ... . It was also that it made possible the ... utilization of more knowledge of particular facts than would be possible under any system of central direction of economic activity." Hayek (1978: 236): "The chief reason why we cannot hope by central direction to achieve anything like the efficiency in the use of resources which the market makes possible is that the economic order of any large society rests on a utilization of the knowledge of particular circumstances widely dispersed among thousands or millions of individuals."

4   Hayek (1973: 51): "We shall see that it is impossible, not only to replace the spontaneous order by organization and at the same time to utilize as much of the dispersed knowledge of all its members as possible, but also to improve or correct this order by interfering in it by direct commands."

5   See, in particular, Hayek's essay "Rechtsordnung und Handelsordnung" in Hayek (1969: 161–98).

6   Hayek (1948: 19f.): "But, if our main conclusion is that an individualist order must rest on the enforcement of abstract principles rather than on the enforcement of specific orders, this still leaves open the question of the kind of general rules which we want. ... [I]t still allows almost unlimited scope to human ingenuity in the designing of the most effective set of rules. ... [T]here is a good deal ... we can learn ... with regard to the desirable nature and contents of these rules." Hayek (1960: 229): "The relation between the character of the legal order and the functioning of the market system has received comparatively little study. ... How well the market will function depends on the character of the particular rules. The decision to rely on voluntary contracts as the main instrument for organizing the relations between individuals does not determine what the specific content of the law of contract ought to be; and the recognition of the right of private property does not determine what exactly should be the content of this right in order that the market mechanism will work as effectively and beneficially as possible." See also Hayek (1969: 180).

7   Hayek (1978: 124f., 135).

8   Hayek (1948: 110f.): "That a functioning market presupposes not only prevention of violence and fraud but the protection of certain rights, such as property, and the enforcement of contract, is always taken for granted. Where the traditional discussion becomes so unsatisfactory is where it is suggested that, with the recognition of the principles of private property and freedom of contract, which indeed every liberal must recognize, all the issues were settled, as if the law of property and contract were given once and for all in its final and most appropriate form, i.e., in the form which will make the market economy work at its best. It is only after we have agreed on these principles that the real problem begins." See also Hayek (1939: 11).

9   Hayek (1964: 8): "The question which is of central importance both for social theory and social policy is what rules the individuals must follow so that an order will result ... [and, V.V.] that this order will be of a beneficent character."

10   It should be noted that Hayek does not explicitly distinguish between the two versions of *constructivist rationalism*. Although the two are clearly concerned with systematically different issues, he occasionally even seems to treat them as the same, for instance when he talks about "a particular conception of the formation of social institutions, which I shall call 'constructivist rationalism' – a conception which assumes that all social institutions are, and ought to be, the product of deliberate design. This intellectual tradition can be shown to be false both in its factual and in its normative conclusions, because the existing institutions are not all the product of design, neither would it be possible to make the social order wholly dependent on design without at the same time greatly restricting the utilization of available knowledge" (Hayek 1967: 88). With the last remark, about the "utilization of available knowledge," Hayek apparently refers to the issue of central planning, i.e. the issue that I call constructivist rationalism I. Yet, as Hayek has explicitly acknowledged elsewhere, whether an order is spontaneously formed or is the product of deliberate design and whether the rules on which an order is based have evolved or have been deliberately chosen are two different issues. See Hayek (1973: 45f.): "Although undoubtedly an order originally formed itself spontaneously because the individuals followed rules which had not been deliberately made but had arisen spontaneously, people gradually learned to improve those rules; and it is at least conceivable that the formation of a spontaneous order relies entirely on rules that were deliberately made. The spontaneous character of the resulting order must therefore be distinguished from the spontaneous origin of the rules on which it rests, and it is possible that an order which would still have to be described as spontaneous rests on rules which are entirely the result of deliberate design."

11   Hayek (1973: 51): "[A]lthough we can endeavour to improve a spontaneous order by revising the general rules on which it rests, and can supplement its results by the efforts of various organizations, we cannot improve the results by specific commands that deprive its members of the possibility of using their knowledge for their purposes." On this issue, see also Hayek (1967: 72; 1969: 50f., 86; 1973: 129).

12   Hayek (1978: 234): "According to the modern planners ... it is not sufficient to design the most rational permanent framework within which the various activities would be conducted by different persons according to their individual plans.

This liberal plan, according to them, is no plan ... . What our planners demand is a central direction of all economic activity according to a single plan."

13   Hayek (1967: 92): "[A]ll we can hope for will be a slow experimental process of gradual improvement rather than any opportunity for drastic change." Hayek (1978: 11): "All that man could do was to try to improve bit by bit on a process ... through modifications of some of the inherited rules. All that he could deliberately design, he could and did create only within a system of rules, which he had not invented, and with the aim of improving the existing order." Hayek (1978: 20): "But sudden and complete reconstruction of the whole is not possible at any stage of the process."

14   Hayek adds, however, that "[a]lthough probably all beneficial improvement must be piecemeal," the separate steps need, nonetheless be "guided by a body of coherent principles" (Hayek 1973: 56).

15   I said that this is how Hayek "primarily" understands the notion of cultural evolution because he uses this notion also in a second, more inclusive sense. In the first, and more narrow, sense, cultural evolution can be contrasted to *legislation* as a deliberate process of rule change. In this sense, cultural evolution and legislation can meaningfully be distinguished as the principal alternative mechanisms by which rules may be changed *within a defined group or jurisdiction*, namely either by a decentralized spontaneous process or by explicit collective legislative choice. Yet, Hayek uses the notion of cultural evolution also in a more inclusive sense in which it is not an alternative to, but may comprise, legislation. I am referring here, of course, to his argument on *group selection* by which he suggests an evolutionary process of competitive selection among groups, a process in which rules come into competition as attributes of groups whether they were adopted by deliberate legislation or whether they came to prevail in a spontaneous process.

16   Hayek (1967: 72): "The important question of which of these rules of individual action can be deliberately and profitably altered, and which are likely to evolve gradually with or without such deliberate collective decisions as legislation involves, is rarely systematically considered."

17   Hayek (1973: 88) notes in reference to the common law process: "For a variety of reasons the spontaneous process of growth may lead into an impasse from which it cannot extricate itself by its own forces or which it will at least not correct quickly enough. ... The fact that law that has evolved this way has certain desirable properties does not prove that it will always be good law or even that some of its rules may not be very bad. It therefore does not mean that we can altogether dispense with legislation."

18   Hayek (1964: 8) talks about the "particular class of rules ... which, because we can deliberately shape them, are the chief tool through which we can influence the general character of the order which will form itself: the rules of law."

19   I have examined Hayek's concept of cultural evolution in some detail elsewhere (Vanberg 1986; 1994a).

20   In this definition, the terms "state" and "government" have different meanings. The "state" is defined as the inclusive political organization, including the citizens as its members, whereas the "government" is more narrowly defined as the organized apparatus that acts on behalf of the citizenry. In my discussion here, I shall, however, use the two terms without such distinction.

21 Hayek (1973: 47): "Although it is conceivable that the spontaneous order which we call society may exist without government, if the minimum of rules required for the formation of such an order is observed without an organized apparatus for their enforcement, in most circumstances the organization which we call government becomes indispensable in order to assure that those rules are obeyed."

22 Hayek (1964: 8): "In order to enforce the rules required for the formation of this spontaneous order, and order of the other kind, an organization, is required. ... The task of changing and improving the rules may also, though it need not, be the object of organized effort."

23 The task of enforcing and maintaining the framework of rules is described by Hayek as government's "coercive functions" to indicate that it is only for these functions and not, however, for its service functions that government needs its coercive powers and monopoly role (Hayek 1973: 48). See Hayek (1979a: 138): "The task of government is to create a framework within which individuals and groups can successfully pursue their respective aims, and sometimes to use its coercive powers of raising revenue to provide services which for one reason or other the market cannot supply. But coercion is justified only in order to provide such a framework within which all can use their abilities and knowledge for their own ends so long as they do not interfere with the equally protected individual domains of others." See also Hayek (1967: 162): "The central concept of liberalism is that under the enforcement of universal rules of just conduct, protecting a recognizable private domain of individuals, a spontaneous order of human activities of much greater complexity will form itself than could ever be produced by deliberate arrangement, and that in consequence the coercive activities of government should be limited to the enforcement of such rules."

24 Hayek (1973: 48f.): "To some extent every organization must rely also on rules and not only on specific commands. The reason here is the same as that which makes it necessary for a spontaneous order to rely solely on rules: namely that by guiding the actions of individuals by rules rather than specific commands it is possible to make use of knowledge which nobody possesses as a whole."

25 Hayek (1973: 124f.): "Yet these rules governing the apparatus of government will necessarily possess a character different from that of the universal rules of just conduct which form the basis of the spontaneous order of society at large. They will be rules of organization ... [a]nd they will have to establish a hierarchy of command determining the responsibilities and the range of discretion of the different agents."

26 Hayek (1979a: 37f.) speaks of constitutions as "the formal documents 'constituting' the organization of the state."

27 As Hayek notes, the general rules of just conduct "restrict the range of permitted actions for any member of the society" (Hayek 1973: 127), whereas the limiting rules of the constitution impose constraints "on the members of the organization we call government" (ibid.), they "regulate the powers of the agents of government over the material and personal resources entrusted to them" (ibid.: 125).

28 For a more detailed discussion of Hayek's concept of constitutional rules, in the context of his various distinctions between different kinds of rules, see Vanberg (1994b: Ch. 7).

29 As Hayek notes, the distinction between the rules which determine the organization of government and the rules which "form the basis of the spontaneous

order of society at large" (Hayek 1973: 125) corresponds to the familiar distinction between public law and private law. We can, accordingly, distinguish between, on the one side, the connection between the general rules of conduct of the private law and the resulting order of society and, on the other side, the connection between the organizational rules of public law and the resulting order of the governmental apparatus (Hayek 1969: 116f., 178).

30 A similar view is adopted in J. M. Buchanan's (1986: 22) constitutional economics approach: "How does one 'improve' a market? One does so by facilitating the exchange process, by reorganizing the rules of trade, contract, or agreement. One does not 'improve' or 'reform' a market-like exchange process by arbitrary rearrangement of final outcomes. ... To improve politics it is necessary to improve or reform the *rules*, the framework within which the game of politics is played. There is no suggestion that improvement lies in the selection of morally superior agents, who will use their powers in some 'public interest'. A game is described by its rules, and a better game is produced only by changing the rules."

31 Hayek (1979a: 1): "It appears that the particular process which we have chosen to ascertain what we call the will of the people brings about results which have little to do with anything deserving the name of the common will of any substantial part of the population."

32 Hayek (1979a: 23): "Let us recall once more how different the task of government proper is from that of laying down the universally applicable rules of just conduct. Government is to act on concrete matters, the allocation of particular means to particular purposes. Even so far as its aim is merely to enforce a set of rules of just conduct given to it, this requires the maintenance of an apparatus of courts, police, penal institutions, etc., and the application of particular means to particular purposes."

33 Hayek (1979a: 23): "It is, however, by no means true that a body organized chiefly for the purpose of directing government is also suited for the task of legislation in the strict sense, i.e. to determine the permanent framework of rules under which it has to move its daily tasks."

34 Hayek (1979a: 37): "[T]rue legislation is thus essentially a task requiring the long view ... [I]t must be a continuous task, a persistent effort to improve the law gradually and to adapt it to new conditions ... Though it may require formal decisions only at long intervals, it demands constant application and study of the kind for which politicians busy wooing their supporters and fully occupied with pressing matters demanding rapid solutions will not really have time."

35 Hayek (1969: 53): "Eine einzige 'Legislative' kann dieser doppelten Aufgabe aber ebensowenig gerecht werden, wie ein einzelner imstande waere, gleichzeitig praktische Entscheidungen zu treffen und die Moralregeln festzusetzen, die er in diesen Entscheidungen befolgen soll."

36 Hayek (1979a: 143): "Many of the gravest defects of contemporary government ... are in fact the consequences only of the unlimited character of present democracy."

37 Hayek (1979a: 3): "The tragic illusion was that the adoption of democratic procedures made it possible to dispense with all other limitations on governmental power." See also Hayek (1978: 152f.): "For centuries efforts had been directed towards limiting the powers of government; and the gradual development of

constitutions served no other purpose than this. Suddenly it was believed that the control of government by elected representatives of the majority made any other checks on the powers of government unnecessary, so that all the various constitutional safeguards which had been developed in the course of time could be dispensed with." For similar statements, see Hayek (1960: 403; 1978: 109).

38 Hayek (1967: 161): "Liberalism and democracy, although compatible, are not the same. The first is concerned with the extent of governmental power, the second with who holds this power. The difference is best seen if we consider their opposites: the opposite of liberalism is totalitarianism, while the opposite of democracy is authoritarianism." See also Hayek (1960: 103).

39 Hayek (1978: 153): "All democracy that we know today in the West is more or less unlimited democracy."

40 Hayek (1964: 12): "It is therefore also not really surprising that the consequence of modern democratic legislation which disdains submitting to general rules and attempts to solve each problem as it comes on its specific merits, is probably the most irrational and disorderly arrangement of affairs ever produced by the deliberate decisions of men."

41 Hayek (1978: 156f.): "The apparently paradoxical fact is that a nominally all-powerful assembly – whose authority is not limited to, or rests on its committing itself to, general rules – is necessarily exceedingly weak and wholly dependent on the support of those splinter groups which are bound to hold out for gifts which are at the government's command." Hayek (1979a: 99): "[A]n omnipotent democratic government ... will be forced to bring together and keep together a majority by satisfying the demands of a multitude of special interests, each of which will consent to the special benefits granted to other groups only at the price of their own special interests being equally considered. Such a bargaining democracy has nothing to do with the conceptions used to justify the principle of democracy." See also Hayek (1979a: 3, 10f.).

42 Hayek (1979a: 11): "If no superior judiciary authority can prevent the legislature from granting privileges to particular groups there is no limit to blackmail to which government will be subject." Hayek (1979a: 128): "[T]he very omnipotence conferred on democratic representative assemblies exposes them to irresistible pressures to use their power for the benefit of special interests, a pressure a majority cannot resist if it is to remain a majority." Hayek (1979a: 139): "The root of the trouble is, of course, to sum up, that in an unlimited democracy the holders of discretionary powers are forced to use them, whether they wish it or not, to favour particular groups on whose swing-votes their power depends."

43 Hayek says about the "general rules of the game" on which a spontaneous order rests: "Was sie ausschliessen, ist jede Art vom Staate gefoerderter Privilegien oder von Diskriminierung. Sie wuerden ein fuer alle gleiches Rahmenwerk bieten, innerhalb dessen jeder weiss, dass er das gleiche tun darf wie jeder andere" (Hayek 1969: 50).

44 Hayek (1978: 108): "The root of the evil is the unlimited power of the legislature in modern democracies."

45 The issue is, as Buchanan (1993) has stated in the title of an article: "How can constitutions be designed so that politicians who seek to serve 'public interest' can survive and prosper?" See also Buchanan (1978: 17): "The challenge to us is

one of constructing, or re-constructing, a political order that will channel the self-serving behaviour of participants towards the common good in a manner that comes as close as possible to that described for us by Adam Smith with respect to the economic order."

46   Hayek (1973: 1): "In the form in which we know the division of power between the legislature, the judiciary, and the administration, it has not achieved what it was meant to achieve. Governments everywhere have obtained by constitutional means powers which those men had meant to deny them. The first attempt to secure individual liberty by constitutions has evidently failed." Elsewhere, Hayek (1979a: 21) characterizes "the American attempts to limit in their Constitution the powers of the legislature" more mildly as a "limited success." On a still more positive note, he had commented earlier: "Incredibly successful as the American experiment in constitutionalism has been ... it is still an experiment in a new way of ordering government, and we must not regard it as containing all wisdom in this field" (Hayek 1960: 191f.).

47   Hayek (1979a: 108): "[T]he particular institutions which for a time worked tolerably in the West presuppose the tacit acceptance of certain other principles which were in some measure observed there but which, where they are not yet recognized, must be made as much a part of the written constitution as the rest." See also Hayek (1969: 56).

48   Hayek (1979a: 105): "What can we do today, in the light of the experience gained, to accomplish the aims which, nearly two hundred years ago, the fathers of the Constitution of the United States of America for the first time attempted to secure by a deliberate construction? Though our aims may still be the same, there is much that we ought to have learnt from the great experiment and its numerous imitations. We know now why the hope of the authors of those documents, that through them they could effectively limit the powers of government, has been disappointed."

49   When, with regard to the rules of government or constitutional rules, Hayek speaks of constructivist rationalism, what he criticizes is not the notion of deliberate design in constitutional matters, but, instead, a view that one may call "anti-constitutionalism," i.e. the refusal to bind governmental powers by general rules (Hayek 1973: 34; 1979a: 129).

50   Hayek (1979a: 122f.): "The function of the Legislative Assembly must not be confused with that of a body set up to enact or amend the Constitution. ... [W]hile the Constitution allocates and restricts powers, it should not prescribe positively how these powers are to be used. The substantive law in the sense of rules of just conduct would be developed by the Legislative Assembly. ... The Governmental Assembly and its government as its executive organ on the other hand would be restricted both by the rules of the Constitution and by the rules of just conduct laid down or recognized by the Legislative Assembly." See also Hayek (1979a: 38).

51   Hayek (1969: 53): "Das Ideal des government under the law kann nur erreicht werden, wenn auch die Volksvertretung, die die Regierungstaetigkeit dirigiert, unter Regeln steht, die sie selbst nicht aendern kann, sondern die von einer anderen demokratischen Körperschaft bestimmt werden, die gewissermassen die langfristigen Prinzipien festlegt."

6 John R. Commons: institutional evolution through purposeful selection

1   In his survey of this theory tradition, Gruchy (1947) dealt with the following authors: Th. Veblen, J. R. Commons, W. C. Mitchell, J. M. Clark, R. G. Tugwell, and G. C. Means.

2   For a comparison between "old" and "new" institutionalism, see the contributions in *Review of Political Economy* (1989: 1), including Vanberg (1989).

3   Commons (1934: 117) talks about a possible classification of economists into "commodity economists" and "transactional economists"; this contrast relies on what they regard as the smallest unit of their analysis, i.e. people–goods relations or proprietary relationships between people. With regard to the difference, Commons states: "But the transaction is a proprietary relation – a relation between Man and Man – whereas the commodity, where ownership is omitted from its definition, is a relation between Man and Nature" (ibid.: 118).

4   On this issue see, for example, Goldberg (1976b), Medema (1992; 1994), and Rutherford (1983; 1990).

5   Commons (1934: 5): "Collective action, as well as individual action, has always been there; but from Smith to the Twentieth Century it has been excluded or ignored, except as attacks on trade unions or as postscripts on ethics or public policy. The problem now is not to create a different kind of economics – 'institutional economics' – divorced from preceding schools, but how to give to collective action, in all its varieties, its due place throughout economic theory." With "collective action," Commons referred to the role of organizations in the economic arena (such as companies or professional associations) as well as to the role of socially sanctioned rules and proprietary rights. For details, compare Vanberg (1989).

6   Rutherford (1990: xiii): "Commons is quite alone among the major writers in the American institutionalist tradition in the extent of his interest in law, organizations and their evolution, and it is exactly these interests that give Commons's work its considerable contemporary relevance."

7   Chamberlain (1963: 80), Medema (1992: 298), Ramstad (1990: 90; 1994: 93). Chamberlain notes (1963: 91) that Commons was painfully aware of the problems of understanding that his writings encountered. On the first page of his *Institutional Economics* (Commons 1934), Commons mentions that some readers of his *Legal Foundations of Capitalism* insinuated in talking to him "that they could not understand my theories nor what I was driving at, and that my theories were so personal to myself that perhaps nobody could understand them."

8   Ramstad (1990: 55): "Commons believed the following to be the central puzzle that a science of economics must resolve: Given the existence of manifold conflicts of interests between individuals due to scarcity, how is it that economic order rather than chaos obtains?... By what process is order brought out of conflict of interests?" Compare also Ramstad (1994: 94).

9   Biddle (1991: 91) summarizes Commons's views as follows: "Working rules arose because of the fundamental problem of scarcity, which created conflicts of interests between individuals vying for control of scarce resources. While scarcity created conflict between individuals, it also created interdependence between individuals, for co-operative action was more effective than individual action in alleviating scarcity. To survive, a society required working rules to create order."

10   Commons (1934: 118): "In every transaction there is a Conflict of Interest because each participant is trying to get as much and give as little as possible. ... Hence they must come to a working agreement, and, since such agreements are not always possible voluntarily, there always has been some form of collective compulsion to decide disputes. If these decisions are accepted as precedents and are conformed to as a matter of course in succeeding transactions, then the deciding authority need not intervene and does not usually intervene unless the conflict again reaches the crisis of a dispute between plaintiff and defendant. This process we name the Common-Law Method of Making Law by Deciding Disputes. To the entire process we give the name, Working Rules of Going Concerns, the purpose of which is to bring Order out of Conflict." Similarly to "collective action," Commons also uses "going concerns" with a double meaning; on the one hand, he relates these terms to organizations as units of collective action (Commons 1934: 69), and, on the other hand, he refers by them to any social arrangement governed by normative rules. It is this lack of clarity in terminology that constitutes one of the sources of ambiguity in Commons's work.

11   Commons (1924: 138): "The modern liberty and freedom of individuality emerges as the fine fruit of evolving centuries of working rules."

12   Biddle (1991: 97) remarks in this context: "Perhaps Commons overstated Smith's hostility toward collective action ... Commons's tendency to focus on isolated passages and concepts in Smith's work led him to ignore qualifications and subtleties existing elsewhere. But Commons's interpretation makes more sense when examined in light of his purposes. His theoretical purpose was to integrate a treatment of collective action into an existing body of economic theory that employed many of Smith's ideas."

13   With regard to such "*laissez-faire* economists," Commons remarks (1950: 105): "They thought government was repressive and obnoxious. We also investigate how government acts to lead people into supposedly better economic administration."

14   As a summary of Commons's view, Biddle (1990: 34) notes: "Smith's system of natural liberty was not a divine plan ordained from the beginning of time, but a fabrication of purposeful human action. And it was still evolving in Smith's time, as judges continued to respond to unintended consequences of their past decision."

15   Commons (1924: 82): "Freedom is a social product whereby society opens up for the individual an enlarging world of the potential and possible within which he may construct his own future."

16   In passing, it may be mentioned that L. von Mises, who otherwise has little in common with Commons, states in a quite similar sense: "Freedom and liberty always refer to interhuman relations. ... The self-sufficient individual is independent, but he is not free. He is at the mercy of everybody who is stronger than himself. The stronger fellow has the power to kill him with impunity. It is therefore nonsense to rant about an alleged 'natural' and 'inborn' freedom. ... Man was not created free; what freedom he may possess has been given to him by society. Only societal conditions can present a man with an orbit within the limits of which he can attain liberty" (von Mises 1949: 279).

17   Commons (1924: 126): "If we start with Herbert Spencer's historical or ethical concept of the individual as a free man existing prior to law, then man's liberty has been gradually taken away from him by the common law, by equity and

statute law. But if we start with individuals as subjects of conquest, slavery, serfdom, then liberty has gradually been taken away from the masters and bestowed on the subjects." This quotation as well as other statements by Commons on this subject remind one of Hobbesian descriptions of an anarchic state of nature. Compare Commons (1934: 6), Commons (1950: 104), Ramstad (1990: 94, fn. 13), Rutherford (1990: xxiii), and Rutherford (1994: 101).

18 Commons (1934: 713): "Competition is not Nature's 'struggle for existence' but is an artificial arrangement supported by the moral, economic, and physical sanctions of collective action."

19 Commons (1936: 247, fn. 14): "The individual of economic theory is not the natural individual of biology and psychology; he is that artificial bundle of institutes known as legal person, or citizen. He is made such by sovereignty which grants to him the rights and liberties to buy and sell, borrow and lend, hire and hire out, work and not work, on his own free will. Merely as an individual of classical and hedonistic theory he is a factor of production and consumption like a cow or slave. Economic theory should make him a citizen, or member of the institution under whose rule he acts."

20 Commons (1931: 652): "It is this shift from commodities and individuals to transactions and working rules of collective action that marks the transition from the classical and hedonic schools to the institutional schools of economic thinking. The shift is a change in the ultimate unit of economic investigation. ... The smallest unit of the institutional economist is a unit of activity – a transaction, with its participants. Transactions ... are, not 'the exchange of commodities,' but the alienation and acquisition, between individuals, of the rights of property and liberty created by society." Compare also Commons (1934: 4f., 73; 1936: 241 fn.)

21 Commons (1936: 242) refers to Böhm-Bawerk and his work *Rechte und Verhältnisse* (1881) as an economist who dealt explicitly with the proprietary–institutional side of economic activity who then, however, excluded it from a "pure economics of man's relation to physical nature:" "He limited his pure economics to the physical and psychological process of producing and consuming material things. But if his pure economic man should go along the street picking up groceries, clothing, and shoes according to their marginal utility to him, he would go to jail. He must first negotiate with an owner to whom the policemen, courts, and constitution have given the right to withhold from him what he wants but does not own, until that owner willingly consents to sell his ownership. This is ... a part of what I mean by institutional economics."

22 Commons (1934: 713): "The theory of free competition developed by economists is not a natural tendency toward equilibrium of forces but is an ideal of public purpose adopted by the courts."

23 Ramstad (1990: 91) states about Commons's concept: "As such, competition has no inherent tendencies and operates toward no inherent ends other than those implanted in the specific working rules determining its 'artificial' nature. In short, 'competition' has no essence separate from the character imparted to it by the specific working rules of which it is actually comprised."

24 Grossekettler (1989) stresses the common connection to the German historical school. Commons (1934: 2) says about R.T. Ely, who was directly influenced by this tradition (Biddle 1991: 86): "My first introduction to the problem of the

relation of law to economics was in the classes of Professor Ely at Johns Hopkins University, 1899."

25   Referring to the *Legal Foundations of Capitalism*, Hayek remarks (1960: 229): "The relation between the character of the legal order and the functioning of the market has received comparatively little study, and most of the work in this field has been done by men who were critical of the competitive order rather than by its supporters."

26   Ramstad (1990: 91): "In short, 'competition' has no essence separate from the character imparted to it by the specific working rules of which it is actually comprised."

27   Commons states that one can choose the starting point for an examination of the evolution of a legal order only in a pragmatic way because an ultimate origin of this process cannot be meaningfully defined. "The working rules of human societies have evolved out of the working rules of pre-human societies, and indeed the evolution of individuals is in itself an evolution of capacities to act in concert according to common rules accepted by each individual" (Commons 1924: 136).

28   Ramstad (1994: 101): "Commons's principal 'message' in *Legal Foundations* is that competition is wholly a socially constructed process volitionally crafted out over many centuries by means of authoritative selection of 'good' practices (rules, customs)." Chamberlain (1963: 72) remarks on Commons's view: "Social custom and law are in fact the product of these interactions. People are not simply adapters to a code of property law. ... In the process of dealing with each other, bargaining, negotiating, transacting, compromising, they bend and mold the customs ..., help to create the very customs which affect their economic relationships."

29   Commons (1931: 248): "There is in American economics a written Constitution and an unwritten constitution. The written Constitution was written in 1787 and in succeeding amendments. The unwritten constitution was written piecemeal by the Supreme Court in deciding conflicts of interests between plaintiffs and defendants. We live under this unwritten constitution; we do not even know what the written Constitution means until the Supreme Court decides a case."

30   Biddle (1990: 30): "Commons's artificial selection theory of institutional evolution is a theory in which purposeful choice has a predominant place. In fashioning it, Commons adopted a methodological individualism. ... The institutions existing at a point in time are not explained by the choices of individuals living at the same time – in fact, by shaping individual perceptions of reality they affect the choices of the individuals that make them up. Rather, the institutions of one period are the result of choices made by past individuals, as they pursued their purposes within a different institutional structure."

31   Commons (1934: 657): "But Darwin had two kinds of 'selection' among the variabilities: Natural Selection and Artificial Selection. Ours is a theory of artificial selection. Veblen's is natural selection." Commons (1924: 316f.): "Economic phenomena, as we know them, are the result of artificial selection and not of natural selection. Their evolution is like that of a steam engine or a breed of cattle, rather than like that of a continent, monkey or tiger. If you watch how the steam engine evolved ... you will see how economic institutions evolved. ... The subject-matter is the habits, customs and ways of thinking of producers, consumers, buyers, sellers, borrowers, lenders and all who engage in what we name economic transactions."

32 Darwin (1972: 3f.): "Although man does not cause variability and cannot even prevent it, he can select, preserve, and accumulate the variation given to him by the hand of nature almost in any way in which he chooses. ... Man may select and preserve each successive variation, with the distinct intention of improving and altering a breed, in accordance with a preconceived idea. ... As the will of man thus comes into play, we can understand how it is that domesticated breeds show adaptation to his wants and pleasures."

33 Commons (1924: 375): "All of the phenomena of the human will are, in this sense, 'artificial,' in contrast with phenomena which may be distinguished as 'natural.' That which is 'artificial' is not thereby unnatural, but is the highly 'natural' process of the human will." Compare Commons (1924: 378).

34 Ramstad (1994: 110) remarks on Commons's ideas: "In his view, it is purposeful human action – 'artificial selection' – that has transformed the 'struggle for existence' into the wealth-producing 'machine' we refer to as the 'market system'. ... And just as purpose-driven artificial selection has produced a Holstein cow 'for the good of man,' so it has produced the market system and the patterned process economists refer to as 'competition.'"

35 Biddle (1990: 27f.): "The field of opportunity facing the individual in Commons is analogous to the range of possible genetic variations in Darwin, but while genetic variations occur randomly, variable human practices within the field of opportunity are fashioned, through trial and error, by an active mind motivated by a purpose. Both theories involve a selection process. In Darwin's theory traits are eliminated through the elimination of the organisms bearing the traits, and traits persist in a population if they increase the probability that their possessors will survive and reproduce. In Commons's theory, a practice persists or disappears according to whether the individuals choose to continue or discontinue the practice." Compare also Biddle (1990: 20).

36 Commons (1950: 91): "Natural selection is just as purposeless when it lets wolves and liars survive as when it lets gazelles and George Washington survive. Success is its only measure of fitness. But artificial, or rather purposeful, selection introduces ethical ideas of fitness – the ethical ideas of rights and duty, goodness and badness, justice and injustice."

37 The generation of variation and the selection of modes of behavior are not two different categories of actions, but different aspects of the same actions. The decision, for example, to imitate behavior observed in others can be seen as an act of selection. Imitation, however, can never be an exact replication and thus there is always newness and variability generated.

38 In this sense, one must strictly distinguish between the question of the intentionality of purposeful selection and the question of preadaptation in the realm of human actions. Without doubt, innovative human actions are carried out, as long as they are undertaken consciously, in the informed expectation, produced by earlier experiences and theoretical insights, that they will result in the desired success. But it is equally true that success is not guaranteed and that, in this sense, human behaviour is not preadapted.

39 Biddle (1990: 20): "Commons's emphasis on purposeful action does not preclude an analysis of the unintended consequences of individual action."

40 Rutherford (1994: 105f.): "The overall process of institutional evolution is one that involves a close interaction between spontaneous processes and those involving

efforts at the institutional design. ... Commons's system is one of interaction between evolution and design."

41 Commons (1934: 239f.): "There are variabilities, of course, as conditions change. It is these variabilities that make possible the evolutionary changes of custom. The common law itself is only the decisions of disputes according to prevailing customs, each decision operating as a precedent. Between the multitude of conflicting precedents there is opportunity for the judges to select, so that the common law changes and 'grows' by 'artificial selection' looking toward future consequences."

42 It may be mentioned here in passing what J. St. Mill stated on the controversy about whether social institutions "grew" or were "created": "It is difficult to decide which of these doctrines would be the most absurd, if we could suppose either of them held as an exclusive theory. ... Let us remember, then, in the first place, that political institutions ... are the work of men, owe their origin and their whole existence to human will. ... In every stage of their existence they are made what they are by human voluntary agency. ... We cannot make the river run backwards, but we do not therefore say that water mills 'are not made, but grow.'" (Mill 1972: 176f., 182).

43 Ramstad (1994: 87) remarks with regard to Hayek's ideas: "Nonetheless, the presumption is clear that there is in the nature of things a natural or brute process through which social order obtains." For a comparison between Hayek's and Commons's evolutionary approach, see Leathers (1989).

44 Vanberg (1994a) seeks to construct the relevant arguments from Hayek's writings.

45 Biddle (1990: 46): "Commons's portrayal of social evolution as the outcome of a process of artificial selection served as an argument that the purposeful guidance of social development was not only a hope for the future, but also a historical reality."

46 Biddle (1991: 86): "By the end of his career, Commons had a vision of a new political economy: an evolutionary social science that would unite the study of law, economics, and ethics to facilitate constructive solutions to social problems."

47 Commons (1924: 383) quotes in agreement what Pound said about the task of designing the legal framework: "The task is one of satisfying human demands, of securing interests or satisfying claims or demands with the least of friction and the least of waste, whereby the means of satisfaction may be made to go as far as possible." Commons refers to the same issue when he remarks in another context: "So it is with legislation and judicial decisions. They do nothing but proportion inducements, and individuals do the rest. But they may waste the common wealth by bad proportioning, may enlarge it by good proportioning" (Commons 1924: 330).

48 Rutherford (1994: 145): "Commons attached importance to the bargaining and negotiation between the affected parties themselves in determining a reasonable solution to conflicts of interest. Commons was deeply suspicious of the tendency of 'experts', including economists, to claim to know best. ... Experts could help in the process of negotiation, but they could not attempt to impose solutions, but provide information."

49 Ramstad (1990: 98, fn. 66): "The proper role of the economist is ... to identify from among existing practices the 'good' modifications of working rules that promise to more satisfactorily effectuate the purposes embraced by principals themselves."

7 The market as a creative process

1 An earlier version of this paper was presented at a Liberty Fund Conference on "An inquiry into liberty and self-organizing systems," 26–29 April, 1990, Rio Rico, Arizona, USA. We received helpful comments on previous drafts from Hartmut Kliemt, Karen Vaughn, Jack Wiseman and an anonymous referee.

2 Prigogine and Stengers (1984: 177): "Whenever we reach a bifurcation point, deterministic description breaks down. The type of fluctuation present in the system will lead to the choice of the branch it will follow. Crossing a bifurcation point is a stochastic process, such as the tossing of a coin."

3 Prigogine (1985: 117): "[W]e come to a world which is open, in which the past is present and cumulative, in which the present is there but the future is not. ... The future does not exist yet, the future is in construction, a construction which is going on in all existing activities."

4 The critical importance of individual diversity and variation from an evolutionary perspective is similarly stressed by biologist E. Mayr, who uses in this context the term "population thinking": "Population thinkers stress the uniqueness of everything in the organic world. What is important for them is the individual, not the type... There is no 'typical' individual, and mean values are abstractions. ... The differences between biological individuals are real, while the mean values which we may calculate in the comparison of groups of individuals (species, for example) are man-made inferences" (Mayr 1982: 46f.). Mayr contrasts "population thinking" with "essentialist thinking": "Adoption of population thinking is intimately tied up with a rejection of essentialist thinking. Variation is irrelevant and therefore uninteresting to the essentialist. Varying characters are 'mere accidents,' in the language of essentialism" (ibid.: 487).

5 As P. M. Allen (1985: 268f.) points out, one has to realize "that there is a critical difference between asking whether a system *obeys* the laws of physics, or whether its behavior can be predicted from a knowledge of those laws." For non-linear systems, Allen (ibid.: 270) argues, "the first can be the case without the second being possible, due to the mixture of deterministic and stochastic aspects of non-linear systems." Allen's argument parallels K. R. Popper's (1982: 48) remark in his *The Open Universe*: "[C]ausality has to be distinguished from determinism, and our world of uniqueness is – unlike Kant's noumenal world – in space and, even more important, in time; for I find it crucially important to distinguish between the determined *past* and the open *future*." In reference to Prigogine's work, Popper (1982: 174) argues in the same treatise: "We must not ... blind us to the fact that the universe that harbours life is creative in the best sense: creative in the sense in which the great poets, the great artists, the great musicians have been creative, as well as the great mathematicians, the great scientists, and the great inventors."

6 I. Prigogine (1986: 503): "Clearly, a social system is by definition a non-linear one, as interactions between the members of the society may have a catalytic effect. At each moment fluctuations are generated, which may be damped or amplified by society. An excellent example of a huge amplification ... is the acquisition of knowledge. ... Instead of seeing human systems in terms of 'equilibrium' or as a 'mechanism', we see a creative world of imperfect information and shifting values, in which different futures can be envisaged."

7 This similarity has been explicitly noted by U. Fehl (1986); see also U. Witt (1985).

8 There are other versions of "economic subjectivism" that could be distinguished from both its "radical" and "Austrian" variety, in particular the "opportunity cost approach" that has been systematically stated by one of the present authors (Buchanan 1969; 1987). This version, as well as others that could be identified, will, however, not be discussed as such in the present chapter.

9 P. M. Allen (1985: 269): "The response to this question of 'choice', which makes modeling and predicting difficult, can be of two kinds. Either we can suppose that choice is an illusion and that the mechanical analogy is in fact legitimate, or we must find some new scientific paradigm in which 'choice' really exists."

10 S. C. Littlechild stresses the same point when he summarizes the "radical subjectivist" view as implying that the "as-yet-undetermined actions of other agents" (Littlechild 1986: 31) make for "the essential open-endedness or creativity" (ibid.) in human affairs, that "the future is not so much unknown as it is non-existent or indetermined at the time of decision" (ibid.: 29).

11 Wiseman (1990: 103): "Mainstream economics deals with unknowability by assuming it away. In the simple model, this is done by assuming perfect knowledge of the future. ... The more sophisticated models assume knowledge of the possible number of future states of the world ... They assume that *someone* has a knowledge of the future that no-one can possibly have." See also Wiseman 1989: 159.

12 Wiseman (1989: 268): "*The future* has not yet happened. About it, men can have only *opinions*, related to past experience (learning). Since men can (must) choose how to act, their chosen acts, together with the evolution of the physical world, are continuously creating the emerging future. If this is so (as it must be), then the future cannot be known 'now' (that is, in the continuous present)."

13 As a summary of Shackle's position Littlechild (1979: 33) states: "Choice ... represents an origin, a beginning. ... [I]t does have a sequel. It makes a difference to what comes after. This sequel cannot be foreknown, because subsequent events will depend partly upon other such choices yet to be made."

14 Shackle (1981: 60): "[I]f we had *all the data there are or could be* about the *present*, we might still not be able to infer what the sequel of any action now chosen would be. ... If history, past and to come, is all one book already written at the beginning of time, what is choice? ... But if choice is fertile, effective, truly *inceptive*, then there can be no foreknowledge. History-to-come, in that case, is not only unknown but *not yet existent*."

15 We use the term "teleological" here in a more general sense than that of an explanation in terms of intended ends or purposeful design. We classify as "teleological" all theoretical perspectives that explain processes in terms of some predeterminable end-point toward which they are supposed to move, rather than in terms of explicitly specified forces and principles that actually "drive" them. It is in this sense that we classify as "teleological" an equilibrium theory which describes economic processes in terms of "where they are going," i.e. their end-point equilibria, but does not provide an explicit explanatory account of the dynamics of these processes themselves.

16 Littlechild (1983: 48f.): "[F]or G. L. S. Shackle the relevance of the whole concept (of general equilibrium) is in question. Every act of choice embodies the chooser's creative imagination of the future. The market therefore follows a 'kaleidic' process,

with moments of order interspersed with disintegration into a new pattern. The economy is changing and developing, but in no sense does it have a single goal."

17 Lachmann (1977: 90): "The impossibility of prediction in economics follows from the fact that economic change is linked to change in knowledge, and future knowledge cannot be gained before its time. Knowledge is generated by spontaneous acts of the mind."

18 Wiseman (1989: 227): "But if what is assumed away is the essence of the problem, then greater complexity will generate not greater insights but more sophisticated confusion."

19 I. Kirzner (1985: 11): "I claim, indeed, that the 'alertness' view of entrepreneurship enables us to have the best of both worlds: we *can* incorporate entrepreneurship into the analysis without surrendering the heart of microeconomic theory." Stated differently, Kirzner claims to avoid the neo-classical orthodoxy's failure to account for "the creative entrepreneur" (Kirzner 1985: 13) without falling "into the seductive trap offered by the opposite extreme" (ibid.), i.e. by the radical subjectivist position.

20 G. P. O'Driscoll's and M. J. Rizzo's (1985) exposition of a modern Austrian subjectivist economics is, in a similar way, characterized by a tension between the acceptance of basic tenets of radical subjectivism and the attempt to maintain "an appropriately revised idea of equilibrium" (O'Driscoll and Rizzo 1985: 79).

21 Kirzner (1985: 30f.): "In the course of this entrepreneurial process, new products may be introduced, new qualities of existing products may be developed, new methods of production may be ventured, new forms of industrial organization, financing, marketing, or tackling risk may be developed. All these ceaseless churning and agitation of the market is to be understood as the consequence of the never-ending discovery process of which the market consists."

22 Kirzner (1985: 12): "I postulate a continuous discovery process – an entrepreneurial discovery process – that in the absence of external changes in underlying conditions, fuels a tendency toward equilibrium."

23 Kirzner (1985: 64): "What market entrepreneurship accomplishes is a tendency for transactions in different parts of the market (including the market at different dates) to become coordinated."

24 Kirzner's (1985: 62f.) crucial argument, in this context, is worth quoting at some length: "When we introduce the passage of time, the dimensions along which mutual ignorance may develop are multiplied. Market participants in one part of today's market may not only be imperfectly aware of the transactions available in another part of the market; they also may be imperfectly aware of the transactions that will be available in next year's market. Absence of consistency between different parts of today's market is seen as a special case of a more general notion of inconsistency that includes also inconsistency between today's transactions and those to be transacted next year. ... It is still the case, as noted, that the entrepreneurial function is that of bringing about a tendency for transactions in different parts of the market (conceived broadly now as including transactions entered into at different times) to be made in greater mutual consistency. But whereas in the case of entrepreneurship in the single-period market (that is, the case of the entrepreneur as arbitrageur) entrepreneurial alertness meant alertness to present facts, in the case of multiperiod entrepreneurship alertness must mean alertness to the future.

25 A well-known classical statement of the argument that we simply cannot anticipate future knowledge and, therefore, cannot predict future human choices which will be affected by such future knowledge can be found in Popper's Preface to his *The Poverty of Historicism* (1957).

26 The same kind of tension between Kirzner's chosen theoretical framework and his attempt to incorporate the notion of entrepreneurial inventiveness in the creation of new products and new ways of doing things is also visible in his more recent discussion on the subject (Kirzner 1989: 84ff.). In her review of this book, Karen Vaughn (1990) comments on Kirzner's attempts to account for "the creative aspects of entrepreneurship" while retaining "his earlier language": "It has become obvious to this reviewer that the old language no longer fits his new theoretical insights."

27 Kirzner (1985: 63f.) indirectly refers to this issue without, however, discussing it: "In particular the futurity that entrepreneurship must confront introduces the possibility that the entrepreneur may, by his own creative actions, in fact *construct* the future as *he* wishes it to be. In the single-period case alertness can at best discover hitherto overlooked current facts. In the multi-period case entrepreneurial alertness must include the entrepreneur's perception of the way in which creative and imaginative action may vitally shape the kind of transactions that will be entered into in future market periods."

28 And, by implication, one could argue that the "equilibrium" toward which intertemporal co-ordination – as it is promoted by entrepreneurial discovery of error – tends to gravitate can only be some final state of universal enlightenment, at the end of all times. Support for such, admittedly exaggerated, interpretation may be seen in statements such as this: "My view, therefore, sees initial market ignorance indeed as an inescapable feature of the human condition in a world of change, but also as subject to continual erosion ... [Entrepreneurs] discover where existing decisions were in fact mistaken. Here lies the source for any equilibrating tendencies that markets display" (Kirzner 1985: 13).

29 The discussion here, and elsewhere in this paper, is related, at least indirectly, to a criticism of Michael Polanyi advanced by one of us (Buchanan) in two related papers. Polanyi conceptualized the scientific process as exploration or discovery, and he argued persuasively that decentralized organization of the scientific enterprise would insure more rapid advance in "solving" the "jigsaw puzzle." From this conceptualization of the scientific process, Polanyi supported, by analogy, the spontaneous ordering properties of decentralized market processes. Buchanan's criticism suggested that, even if the discovery–exploration metaphor remains applicable to the enterprise of the physical sciences, such a metaphor is misleading when applied and extended to economic or political interaction among freely choosing individuals. See Buchanan (1977; 1986).

30 The Simons's syllabus was circulated only in mimeographed form. Gordon Tullock, himself a student of Simons in the 1940s, edited and published a somewhat incomplete version (Tullock 1983).

31 This paper was the title essay in the volume *The Logic of Liberty* (Polanyi 1951).

32 For a commentary on Barry's essay, see Buchanan (1982).

33 Although the thrust of his work clearly supports the vision of the market as a creative process, Hayek's (1978a) illuminating discussion on "Competition as a discovery procedure" is not entirely free of the ambiguities which the concept of

discovery tends to invoke when applied to the market process. Potentially misleading are, in this regard, his comparison between the discovery processes in science and in the market (ibid.: 181), and some of his comments on the problem of measuring market performance (ibid.: 185f.).

8 A constitutional economics perspective on international trade

1 The "constitutional approach" has much in common with the theoretical perspective of German ordo-liberalism (Vanberg 1988). For contributions from the latter perspective to the issue of the international economic order, see Gröner and Schüller (1989), Molsberger and Kotios (1990), and Oppermann and Conlan (1990).

2 With reference to the discussion in economics on potential "legitimate exceptions to free trade," Irwin (1991: 207) notes: "Identification of possible exceptions to free trade by economic theorists means neither that such circumstances can be isolated and identified in practice nor that such exceptions would constitute sound economic policy. If the past is any guide, new theories related to strategic trade policy will indeed provide important economic insights, but will not fundamentally challenge the belief of economists in free trade."

3 D. Snidal refers to this view as the "realist position" (Snidal 1986: 35) in the game theory of international politics, and he claims that "[t]his conception of nation-states as interdependent, goal-seeking actors lies at the heart of strategic game analysis" (ibid.: 25).

4 For a critique of a Hobbesian interpretation of international relations, see Kratochwil (1992). Schmidt-Trenz and Schmidtchen (1991: 331) suggest a useful distinction between two notions of a "state of nature": "International trade is any trade between economic agents belonging to different 'protective states' or 'private law communities'. International trade, so defined, suffers from a 'state of nature of type 2', a kind of state of nature that may be conceived of as a residue of pure anarchy (i.e. the 'state of nature of type 1')."

5 Schmidtchen and Schmidt-Trenz speak of the "constitutional uncertainty in international trade" (Schmidtchen and Schmidt-Trenz 1990: 52) as an inhibiting factor in border-crossing commerce. Their focus is on the role that the spontaneous forces "iteration, reputation, and a private–autonomously created potential for sanctions" (Schmidt-Trenz and Schmidtchen 1991: 336) play in overcoming this problem, and they emphasize the fact "that foreign trade is dominated by long-term business relationships" (ibid.: 337). It has, they argue, little in common with an "anonymous market" but is built on mutual trust (ibid.). Although Schmidtchen and Schmidt-Trenz are certainly right in their emphasis on what has been called the "discipline of continuous dealings," as indicated in the above discussion of North's argument, such discipline has its obvious limits beyond which potentially beneficial trades would remain unexploited. The relevance of the utilization of domestic enforcement systems in international trade, as described above, lies in its capacity to extend the market beyond such limits.

6 See also Petersmann (1988: 250) and Willgerodt (1989: 403).

7 Petersmann (1988: 243), quoting a GATT publication, notes that it was an original purpose of GATT to protect governments from rent-seeking activities within their own polities. He contrasts a mercantilist and a constitutional interpretation

of GATT. In the "mercantilist" perspective (ibid.: 246), GATT is an instrument for international trade diplomacy, dealing with alleged international conflicts of interest. The constitutional interpretation views GATT as primarily concerned with intranational conflicts of interest (ibid.: 251). A critique of the mercantilist view is also voiced by Gröner and Schüller (1989: 436) and Molsberger and Kotios (1990: 282).

8   In continuation of the above quote, Tumlir argues: "This reasoning leads to the conclusion that national courts, rather than diplomacy, can and should provide the necessary authoritative interpretation of the international commitments governments undertake in matters of economic policy" (Tumlir 1983: 83).

9   Breton (1987: 268) notes about the "marriage" of parliamentary democracy and competitive federalism: "[P]arliamentary government combined with federalism gives the citizens of a country a more effective set of institutions for reflecting their will, preferences and aspirations."

10   For an interesting excursion into the history of the theoretical discussion on the issue of "movable property and its exit as a restraint on the state," see Hirschman (1981: 253ff.). Hirschman is somewhat critical about the role of the exit mechanism that – as he phrases it – "some quarters have celebrated ... as far more 'efficient' than the 'cumbersome' political process for the redress of people's grievances or the fulfillment of their demands" (Hirschman 1981: 252). Without entering into a discussion of Hirschman's critique, I would like, at least, to note that his main concern – namely that the "voice mechanism" be given proper recognition – deserves to be taken seriously. Both mechanisms should be viewed as complementing each other rather than as exclusive alternatives. To mention only one aspect: The voice mechanism may be a more suitable tool for achieving partial and marginal adjustments in the political environment as the exit mechanism is, by its very nature, a choice among inclusive packages.

11   Sinn (1989: 31): "We share skeptical views arguing against increased international policy coordination. The case for maintaining and fostering competition among politicians is equivalent to the case for maintaining and fostering competition among firms." Vaubel (1990: 74) notes similarly: "Die Intensivierung der weltwirtschaftlichen Interdependenzen hat die nationalen Wirtschaftspolitiker unter einen sich verstärkenden internationalen Wettbewerbsdruck gesetzt, dem sie sich durch Absprachen zu entziehen suchen." The problem of collusion is also a major issue in the discussion on the concept of "cooperative federalism" (Breton 1987: 274; Kincaid 1991).

12   Kincaid (1991: 89f.) distinguishes between two dimensions of federal competition – namely "inter-governmental" or "vertical" competition, i.e. competition between different levels of government (federal governments versus states, states versus local governments, etc.), and "interjurisdictional" or "horizontal" competition, i.e. competition between governments with similar powers, such as interstate and interlocal competition. In the present context, the latter is of systematic interest.

13   Wiseman (1990: 121f.) notes about "the potential importance of federal arrangements as an additional instrument for curbing Leviathan": "It also facilitates *exit* at low opportunity–cost because migration between federal subregions is less difficult than migration between separate countries, and competition between such regions stimulated by the possibility of such migration

is a potentially valuable substitute for (supplement to) the use of constitutional rules."

14 Kincaid (1991: 98): "At base, a federal democracy is a voluntary association of persons and jurisdictions. The right of persons to emigrate is fundamental. However, because emigration is costly, citizens must have effective choices within the polity."

15 Breton (1987: 281) notes on "competitive federalism": "But competitive behaviour is not unconstrained or anarchical behaviour ... . Indeed competitive behaviour is restrained and disciplined behaviour."

16 An example for detrimental competition that critics of competitive federalism like to point to is the use "of special tax incentives and subsidies to recruit businesses from other jurisdictions" (Kenyon and Kincaid 1991: 27). This may indeed be an example where constraints on competition would be appropriate.

17 Sinn (1989: 25): "The importance of capital mobility for policy competition goes beyond curbing harmful policies. It is also assumed to be a way of finding the optimal tax rate and the optimal supply of public goods."

18 It would create what Willgerodt (1989: 422) describes as "competition of judicial and political systems." On this issue, see also Vanberg (1990).

19 See, for instance, the apparent difficulties that Watrin (1991) faces in his attempt to present a liberal outlook at the immigration issue.

Bibliography

Albert, H. (1979) "The economic tradition. Economics as a research program for theoretical social science," in Brunner, K. (ed.) *Economics and Social Institutions*. Boston: Martinus Nijhoff.

Alchian, A.A. (1977) *Economic Forces at Work*. Indianapolis: Liberty Press.

Allen, P.M. (1985) "Towards a new science of complex systems," in Aida S., Allen, P., Atlan, H., Boulding, K., *et al.* (eds) *The Science and Practice of Complexity*, pp. 268–97. Tokyo: The United Nations University.

——(1988) "Evolution, innovation and economics," in Dosi, G., Freeman, Ch., Nelson, R., Silverberg, G., and Soete L. (eds) *Technical Change and Economic Theory*, pp. 95–119. London: Pinter; distributed by Columbia University Press.

Anderson, P., Kenneth, W., Arrow, J., and Pines, D. (eds) (1988) *The Economy as an Evolving Complex System*. New York: Addison-Wesley.

Arthur, W.B. (1990) "Positive feedback in the economy," *Scientific American* 262, 92–99.

Axelrod, R. (1984) *The Evolution of Cooperation*. New York: Basic Books.

Barry, N. (1982) "The tradition of spontaneous order," *The Literature of Liberty* 5, 7–58.

Barry, N.P. (1994) "The road to freedom – Hayek's social and economic philosophy," in Birner, J., and van Zijp, R. (eds) *Hayek, Co-ordination and Evolution – His Legacy in Philosophy, Politics, Economics and the History of Ideas*, pp. 141–63. London: Routledge.

Baumol, W., and Benhabib, S. (1989) "Chaos: significance, mechanism, and economic applications," *Journal of Economic Issues* 3, 77–106.

Becker, G.S. (1976) *The Economic Approach to Human Behavior*. Chicago: The University of Chicago Press.

Benson, B.L. (1990) *The Enterprise of Law – Justice Without the State*. San Francisco: Pacific Research Institute for Public Policy.

Berman, H.J. (1983) *Law and Revolution: The Formation of the Western Legal Tradition*. Cambridge, MA: Harvard University Press.

Bernholz, P. (1992) "Constitutional aspects of the European integration," in Borner, S., and Grubel, H. (eds) *The European Community of 1992. Perspectives from the Outside*, pp. 45–60. Basingstoke: Macmillan.

Bernholz, P., and Faber, M. (1988) "Reflections on a normative economic theory of the unification of law," in Gwartney, J.D., and Wagner, R.E. (eds) *Public Choice and Constitutional Economics*, pp. 229–49. Greenwich, CT: JAI Press.

186 *Bibliography*

Bhagwati, J. (1989) *Protectionism*. Cambridge, MA: The MIT Press.

Biddle, J.E. (1990) "Purpose and evolution in Commons's institutionalism," *History of Political Economy* 22, 9–47.

——(1991) "The ideas of the past as tools for the present: the instrumental presentism of John R. Commons," in Brown, J., and Keuren, D.K.V. (eds) *The Estate of Social Knowledge*, pp. 84–105. Baltimore: The Johns Hopkins University Press.

Böhm, F. (1933) *Wettbewerb und Monopolkampf – Eine Untersuchung zur Frage des wirtschaftlichen Kampfrechts und zur Frage der rechtlichen Struktur der geltenden Wirtschaftsordnung*. Berlin: Carl Heymann (reprinted in 1964; excerpts in English translation published as Böhm 1982).

——(1937) *Ordnung der Wirtschaft*. Vol. 1. *Die Ordnung der Wirtschaft als geschichtliche Aufgabe und rechtsschöpferische Leistung*, Böhm, F., Eucken, W., and Großmann-Doerth, H. (eds). Stuttgart: W. Kohlhammer.

——(1950) "Die Idee des Ordo im Denken Walter Euckens," *ORDO* 3, XV–LXIV.

——(1960) *Reden und Schriften*. Karlsruhe: C. F. Müller.

——(1961) "Democracy and economic power," in *Kartelle und Monopole im modernen Recht*, Vol. 1, pp. 25–45. Karlsruhe: C. F. Müller.

——(1980) "Freiheit und Ordnung in der Marktwirtschaft," in Mestmäcker, E.-J. (ed.) *Freiheit und Ordnung in der Marktwirtschaft*. Baden-Baden: Nomos.

——[1982 (1933)] "The non-state ('natural') laws inherent in a competitive economy," in Stützel, W., Watrin, C., Willgerodt, H., and Hohmann, K. (eds) *Standard Texts on the Social Market Economy*, pp. 107–13. Stuttgart: Gustav Fischer.

——(1989) "Rule of law in a market economy," in Peacock, A. and Willgerodt, H. (eds) *Germany's Social Market Economy: Origins and Evolution*, pp. 46–67. London: Macmillan (English translation of "Privatrechtsgesellschaft und Marktwirtschaft," in Böhm 1980, pp. 105–68).

Böhm, F., Eucken, W., and Grossmann-Doerth, H. (1989) "The Ordo manifesto of 1936," in Peacock, A. and Willgerodt, H. (eds) *Germany's Social Market Economy: Origins and Evolution*, pp. 15–26. London: Macmillan (originally published in German as "Unsere Aufgabe" in Böhm 1937, pp. VII–XXI).

Böhm-Bawerk, E. von (1881) *Rechte und Verhältnisse vom Standpunkte der volkswirtschaftlichen Güterlehre*. Innsbruck: Wagner.

Brennan, G., and Buchanan, J.M. (1980) *The Power to Tax – Analytical Foundations of a Fiscal Constitution*. Cambridge: Cambridge University Press.

Breton, A. (1987) "Towards a theory of competitive federalism," *European Journal of Political Economy* 3, 263–329.

Breyer, S., and MacAvoy, P.W. (1987) "Regulation and deregulation," in *The New Palgrave – A Dictionary of Economics*, Vol. 4, pp. 128–34. London: Macmillan.

Buchanan, J.M. (1969) *Cost and Choice – An Inquiry in Economic Theory*. Chicago: Markham Publishing Company.

——(1975) *The Limits of Liberty – Between Anarchy and Leviathan*. Chicago: The University of Chicago Press.

——(1977) *Freedom in Constitutional Contract – Perspectives of a Political Economist*. College Station: Texas A & M University Press.

——(1977a) "Politics and Science," in Buchanan, J.M. (ed.) *Freedom in Constitutional Contract – Perspectives of a Political Economist*, pp. 64–77. College Station: Texas A & M University Press.

——(1978) "From private preferences to public philosophy: the development of public choice," in *The Economics of Politics*, pp. 1–20. London: Institute of Economic Affairs.

——(1982) "Order defined in the process of its emergence," *The Literature of Liberty* 5, 5.

——(1986) *Liberty, Market and State – Political Economy in the 1980s*. New York: New York University Press.

——(1986a) "The potential for tyranny in politics as science," in Buchanan, J.M. (ed.) *Liberty, Market and State – Political Economy in the 1980s*, pp. 40–54. New York: New York University Press.

——(1986b) "Rights, efficiency, and exchange: the irrelevance of transaction costs," in Buchanan, J.M. (ed.) *Liberty, Market and State – Political Economy in the 1980s*, pp. 92–107. New York: New York University Press.

——(1990a) "The domain of constitutional economics," *Constitutional Political Economy* 1, 1–18.

——(1990b) "Europe's constitutional opportunity," in Buchanan, J.M., Pöhl, K.O., Curzon Price, V., and Vibert, F. (eds) *Europe's Constitutional Future*, pp. 1–20. London: Institute of Economic Affairs.

——(1991) *The Economics and the Ethics of Constitutional Order*. Ann Arbor: The University of Michigan Press.

——(1991a) "Economists and the gains from trade," in Buchanan, J.M. (ed.) *The Economics and Ethics of Constitutional Order*, pp. 109–23. Ann Arbor: The University of Michigan Press.

——(1991b) "The contractarian logic of classical liberalism," in Buchanan, J.M. (ed.) *The Economics and Ethics of Constitutional Order*, pp. 125–35. Ann Arbor: The University of Michigan Press.

——(1991c) "The foundations of normative individualism," in Buchanan, J.M. (ed.) *The Economics and the Ethics of Constitutional Order*, pp. 221–9. Ann Arbor: The University of Michigan Press.

——(1992) "An American evaluation of Europe's constitutional prospects," George Mason University: Center for the Study of Public Choice.

——(1993) "How can constitutions be designed so that politicians who seek to serve 'public interest' can survive and prosper?" *Constitutional Political Economy* 4, 1–6.

Buchanan, J.M., and Congleton, R.D. (1998) *Politics by Principle, not Interest – Toward Nondiscriminatory Democracy*. Cambridge, MA: Cambridge University Press.

Buchanan, J.M., and Lee, D.R. (1991) "Cartels, coalitions, and constitutional politics," *Constitutional Political Economy* 2, 139–61.

Buchanan, J.M., and Vanberg, V. (1988) "The politicization of market failure," *Public Choice* 57, 101–13.

Buchanan, J.M., Tollison, R.D., and Tullock G. (eds) (1980) *Toward a Theory of the Rent-Seeking Society*. College Station: Texas A & M University Press.

Chamberlain, N.W. (1963) "The institutional economics of John R. Commons," in Dorfman, J., Ayres, C.E., Chamberlain, N.W., Kuznets, S., and Gordon, R.A. (eds) *Institutional Economics – Veblen, Commons, and Mitchell Reconsidered*, pp. 63–94. Berkeley: University of California Press.

Coase, R.H. (1975) "Economists and public policy," in Weston, J. (ed.) *Large Corporations in a Changing World*. New York: New York University Press.

Commons, J.R. (1924) *Legal Foundations of Capitalism*. Madison: The University of Wisconsin Press.

——(1931) "Institutional economics," *American Economic Review* 21, 648–57.

——(1934) *Institutional Economics – Its Place in Political Economy*. Madison: The University of Wisconsin Press.

——(1936) "Institutional economics," *American Economic Review* 26 (Suppl.), 237–49.

——(1950) *The Economics of Collective Action*. New York: The Macmillan Company.

Cooter, R., and Ulen, T. (1995) *Law and Economics*, 2nd edn. Reading, MA: Addison-Wesley.

Darwin, C. [1972 (1875)] *The Variation of Animals and Plants Under Domestication*, 2nd edn. New York: AMS Press.

Debreu, G. (1959) *Theory of Value – An Axiomatic Analysis of Economic Equilibrium*. Charles Foundation Monograph No. 17. New York: Wiley.

Demsetz, H. (1995) *The Economics of the Business Firm – Seven Critical Commentaries*. Cambridge, MA: Cambridge University Press.

Donges, J.B., Engels, W., Hamm, W., Möschel, W., Neumann, M.J., and Sievert, O. (1992) *Einheit und Vielfalt in Europa – Für weniger Harmonisierung und Zentralisierung*. Frankfurt: Frankfurter Institut für wirtschaftspolitische Forschung, Schriftenreihe: Band 25.

Dye, T.R. (1990a) *American Federalism: Competition Among Governments*. Lexington, MA: D. C. Heath.

——(1990b) "The policy consequences of inter-governmental competition," *Cato Journal* 10, 59–73.

Ekelund, Jr., R.B., and Tollison, R.D. (1982) *Mercantilism as a Rent-Seeking Society: Economic Regulation in Historical Perspective*. College Station: Texas A & M University.

——(1994) *Microeconomics*, 4th edn. New York: Harper Collins College Publishers.

Epstein, R.A. (1985) *Takings – Private Property and the Power of Eminent Domain*. Cambridge: Harvard University Press.

——(1986) "An outline of takings," *University of Miami Law Review* 41, 3–19.

——(1995) *Simple Rules for a Complex World*. Cambridge, MA: Harvard University Press.

Eucken, W. (1932) "Staatliche Strukturwandlungen und die Krise des Kapitalismus," *Weltwirtschaftliches Archiv* 36, 297–323.

——(1938) "Die Überwindung des Historismus," *Schmollers Jahrbuch* 62, 63–86.

——(1940) "Wissenschaft im Stile Schmollers," *Weltwirtschaftliches Archiv* 52, 468–506.

——(1942) "Wettbewerb als Grundprinzip der Wirtschaftsverfassung," in Schmölders, G. (ed.) *Der Wettbewerb als Mittel volkswirtschaftlicher Leistungssteigerung und Leistungsauslese*. Berlin: Duncker & Humblot (Schriften der Akademie für Deutsches Recht, Gruppe Wirtschaftswissenschaft, Vol. 6).

——(1948) "On the theory of the centrally administered economy. An analysis of the German experiment," *Economica, New Series* 15, 79–100 (Part I), 173–93 (Part II).

——(1950) *The Foundations of Economics – History and Theory in the Analysis of Economic Reality* (translated by T. W. Hutchison). London: William Hodge.

——(1951) *This Unsuccessful Age*. Edinburgh: William Hodge.

——(1952) *Grundsätze der Wirtschaftspolitik*. Tübingen: J. C. B. Mohr (Paul Siebeck).

——(1982) "A policy for establishing a system of free enterprise," in Stützel, W., Watrin, C., Willgerodt, H., and Hohmann, K. (eds) *Standard Texts on the Social Market Economy*, pp. 115–31. Stuttgart: Gustav Fischer.

——[1989a (1939)] *Die Grundlagen der Nationalökonomie*, 9th edn. Berlin: Springer (English translation: Eucken 1992).

——(1989b) "What kind of economic and social system?" in Peacock, A. and Willgerodt, H. (eds) *Germany's Social Market Economy: Origins and Evolution*, pp. 28–45. London: Macmillan.

——[1990 (1952)] *Grundsätze der Wirtschaftspolitik*, 6th edn. Tübingen: J. C. B. Mohr (Paul Siebeck) (excerpts in English translation published as Eucken 1982).

——(1992) *The Foundations of Economics – History and Theory in the Analysis of Economic Reality*. Berlin: Springer (reprint of the first English edition published 1950 by William Hodge, London).

Fehl, U. (1986) "Spontaneous order and the subjectivity of expectations: a contribution to the Lachmann–O'Driscoll Problem," in Kirzner, I.M. (ed.) *Subjectivism, Intelligibility, and Economic Understanding*, pp. 72–86. New York: New York University Press.

Frey, B. (1984) *International Political Economy*. Oxford: Basil Blackwell.

Frey, B.S., and Eichenberger, R. (1999) *The New Democratic Federalism of Europe – Functional, Overlapping and Competing Jurisdictions*. Cheltenham: Edward Elgar.

Gerber, D.J. (1994) "Constitutionalizing the Economy: German Neoliberalism, Competition Law and the 'New' Europe," *The American Journal of Comparative Law* 42, 25–84.

Goldberg, V.P. (1976a) "Regulation and administered contracts," *Bell Journal of Economics* 7, 426–48.

Goldberg, V.P. (1976b) "Commons, Clark, and the emerging post-Coasian law and economics," *Journal of Economic Issues* 10, 877–93.

Gray, J.N. (1982) "F. A. Hayek and the rebirth of classical liberalism," *Literature of Liberty* 4, 19–66.

Gröner, H., and Schüller, A. (1989) "Grundlagen der internationalen Ordnung: GATT, IWF and EG im Wandel – Euckens Idee der Wirtschaftsverfassung des Wettbewerbs als Prüfstein," *ORDO* 40, 429–63.

Grossekettler, H.G. (1989) "On designing an economic order. The contribution of the Freiburg School," in Walker, D.A. (ed.) *Perspectives on the History of Economic Thought*. Vol. 2. *Twentieth-Century Economic Thought*, pp. 38–84 (selected papers from the History of Economics Society Conference 1987). Aldershot: Edward Elgar.

Großmann-Doerth, H. (1933) *Selbstgeschaffenes Recht der Wirtschaft und staatliches Recht*. Freiburg i.Br.: Fr. Wagner'sche Universitätsbuchhandlung.

Gruchy, A.G. (1947) "The collective economics of John R. Commons," in Gruchy, A.G. (ed.) *Modern Economic Thought – The American Contribution*, pp. 135–243. New York: Prentice-Hall.

Habermann, G. (1990) "Die deutsche Handwerksordnung als Relikt der Gewerbebindung," *ORDO* 41, 173–93.

——(1996) "Der Liberalismus und die 'Libertarians,'" *ORDO* 47, 121–48.

Hartwell, R.M. (1995) *A History of the Mont Pelerin Society*. Indianapolis, IN: Liberty Fund.

190 *Bibliography*

Hauser, H., Moser, P., Planta, R., and Schmid, R. (1988) "Der Beitrag von Jan Tumlir zur Entwicklung einer ökonomischen Verfassungstheorie internationaler Handelsregeln," *ORDO* 39, 219–37.

Hayek, F.A. (1939) *Freedom and the Economic System*. Gideonse, H.D. (ed.) Public Policy Pamphlet No. 29. Chicago: The University of Chicago Press.

——(1944) *The Road to Serfdom*. Chicago: The University of Chicago Press.

——(1948) *Individualism and Economic Order*. Chicago: The University of Chicago Press.

——(1948a) "'Free' enterprise and competitive order," in Hayek, F.A. (ed.) *Individualism and Economic Order*, pp. 107–18. Chicago: The University of Chicago Press.

——(1948b) "The economic conditions of interstate federalism," in Hayek, F.A. (ed.) *Individualism and Economic Order*, pp. 255–72. Chicago: The University of Chicago Press.

——(1952) *Individualismus und wirtschaftliche Ordnung*. Erlenbach-Zürich: Eugen Rentsch Verlag.

——(1952a) *The Sensory Order – An Inquiry into the Foundations of Theoretical Psychology*. Chicago: The University of Chicago Press.

——(1952b) *The Counter Revolution of Science*. Glencoe: The Free Press.

——(1956/7) "Über den Sinn sozialer Institutionen," *Schweizer Monatshefte* 36, 512–24.

——(1959) "Liberalismus (1) – Politischer Liberalismus," in *Handwörterbuch der Sozialwissenschaften*, Vol. 6. Göttingen:Vandenhoek & Ruprecht.

——(1960) *The Constitution of Liberty*. Chicago: The University of Chicago Press.

——(1964) "Kinds of order in society," *New Individualist Review* 3, 3–12.

——(1967) *Studies in Philosophy, Politics and Economics*. Chicago: The University of Chicago Press.

——(1969) *Freiburger Studien. Gesammelte Aufsätze*. Tübingen: J. C. B. Mohr (Paul Siebeck).

——(1969a) "Rechtsordnung und Handelnsordnung," in Hayek, F.A. (ed.) *Freiburger Studien. Gesammelte Aufsätze*, pp. 161–98. Tübingen: J. C. B. Mohr (Paul Siebeck).

——(1969b) "Der Wettbewerb als Entdeckungsverfahren," in Hayek, F.A. (ed.) *Freiburger Studien. Gesammelte Aufsätze*, pp. 249–65. Tübingen: J. C. B. Mohr (Paul Siebeck).

——(1971) *Die Verfassung der Freiheit*. Tübingen: J. C. B. Mohr (Paul Siebeck).

——(1973) *Law, Legislation and Liberty*, Vol. 1. London: Routledge & Kegan Paul.

——(1976a) *Law, Legislation and Liberty*, Vol. 2, London: Routledge & Kegan Paul.

——[1976b (1944)] *The Road to Serfdom*. Chicago: The University of Chicago Press.

——(1977) *Drei Vorlesungen über Demokratie, Gerechtigkeit und Sozialismus*, Walter Eucken Institut, Vorträge und Aufsätze 63. Tübingen: J. C. B. Mohr (Paul Siebeck).

——(1978) *New Studies in Philosophy, Politics, Economics and the History of Ideas*. Chicago: The University of Chicago Press.

——(1978a) "Competition as a discovery procedure," in Hayek, F.A. (ed.) *New Studies in Philosophy, Politics, Economics and the History of Ideas*, pp. 179–90. Chicago: The University of Chicago Press.

——(1979a) *Law, Legislation and Liberty*, Vol. 3. London: Routledge & Kegan Paul.

——(1979b) *Wissenschaft und Sozialismus*, Walter Eucken Institut, Vorträge und Aufsätze 71. Tübingen: J. C. B. Mohr (Paul Siebeck).

——(1988) *The Fatal Conceit – The Errors of Socialism*. London: Routledge.

——(1991) *The Collected Works of Friedrich August Hayek*. Vol. 3. *The Trend of Economic Thinking – Essays on Political Economy and Economic History*. Chicago: The University of Chicago Press.

——(1992) "Opening address to a conference at Mont Pelerin," in *The Collected Works of Friedrich August Hayek*. Vol. 4. *The Fortunes of Liberalism – Essays on Austrian Economics and the Ideal of Freedom*, pp. 237–48. Chicago: The University of Chicago Press.

Hirschman, A.O. (1970) *Exit, Voice, and Loyalty – Responses to Decline in Firms, Organizations, and States*. Cambridge: Harvard University Press.

——(1981) "Exit, voice, and the state," in Hirschman, A.O. (ed.) *Essays in Trespassing – Economics to Politics and Beyond*, pp. 246–65. Cambridge: Cambridge University Press.

Holcombe, R.G. (1993) "Federal funding and the cartelization of state governments," mimeograph, Florida State University.

Irwin, D.A. (1991) "Challenges to free trade," *The Journal of Economic Perspectives* 5, 201–8.

Johnson, D. (1989) "Exiles and half-exiles: Wilhelm Röpke, Alexander Rüstow and Walter Eucken," in Peacock, A. and Willgerodt, H. (eds) *Germany's Social Market Economy: Origins and Evolution*, pp. 40–68. London: Macmillan.

Jones, E.L. (1987) *The European Miracle: Environments, Economies, and Geopolitics in the History of Europe and Asia*, 2nd edn. Cambridge: Cambridge University Press.

Kasper, W., and Streit, M. (1993) *Lessons from the Freiburg School. The Institutional Foundations of Freedom and Prosperity*. Australia: The Center for Independent Studies.

Kenyon, D.A., and Kincaid, J. (1991) "Introduction," in Kenyon, D.A., and Kincaid, J. (eds) *Competition among States and Local Governments – Efficiency and Equity in American Federalism*, pp. 1–33. Washington, DC: The Urban Institute Press.

Kerber, W. (1991) "Zur Entstehung von Wissen: Grundsätzliche Bemerkungen zu Möglichkeiten und Grenzen staatlicher Förderung der Wissensproduktion aus der Sicht der Theorie evolutionärer Marktprozesse," in Oberender, P., and Streit, M.E. (eds) *Marktwirtschaft und Innovation*, pp. 9–52. Baden-Baden: Nomos.

Kincaid, J. (1991) "The competitive challenge to cooperative federalism: a theory of federal democracy," in Kenyon, D.A., and Kincaid, J. (eds) *Competition among States and Local Governments – Efficiency and Equity in American Federalism*, pp. 87–114. Washington, DC: The Urban Institute Press.

Kindleberger, C.P. (1986) "International public goods without international government," *American Economic Review* 76, 1–13.

Kirzner, I.M. (1985) *Discovery and the Capitalist Process*. Chicago: The University of Chicago Press.

——(1985a) "The perils of regulation: a market-process approach," in Kirzner, I.M. (ed.) *Discovery and the Capitalist Process*, pp. 119–49 and 175–9. Chicago: The University of Chicago Press.

——(1989) *Discovery, Capitalism, Distributive Justice*. New York: Basil Blackwell.

——(1994) "The limits of the market: the real and the imagined," in Möschel, W., Streit, M.E., and Witt, U. (eds) *Marktwirtschaft und Rechtsordnung*, pp. 101–10. Baden-Baden: Nomos.

Knight, F.H. [1982 (1947)] *Freedom and Reform – Essays in Economics and Social Philosophy*. Indianapolis, IN: Liberty Press.

Kratochwil, F.V. (1992) "International order and individual liberty: a critical examination of 'realism' as a theory of international politics," *Constitutional Political Economy* 3, 29–50.

Krueger, A.O. (1990) "Asymmetries in policy between exportables and import-competing goods," in Jones, R.W., and Krueger, A.O. (eds) *The Political Economy of International Trade*, pp. 161–78. Cambridge, MA: Basil Blackwell.

Kukathas, C. (1990) *Hayek and Modern Liberalism*. Oxford: Clarendon Press.

Lachmann, L.M. (1976) "From Mises to Shackle: an essay on Austrian economics and the Kaleidic Society," *Journal of Economic Literature*, 14, 54–62.

——(1977) "Professor Shackle on the economic significance of time," in Lachmann, L.M. (ed.) *Capital, Expectations, and the Market Process*, pp. 81–93. Kansas City: Sheed Andrews and McMeel.

Leathers, C.G. (1989) "New and old institutionalists on legal rules: Hayek and Commons," *Review of Political Economy* 1, 361–80.

Lenel, H.O. (1989) "Evolution of the social market economy," in Peacock, A., and Willgerodt, H. (eds) *Germany's Social Market Economy: Origins and Evolution*, pp. 16–39. London: Macmillan.

Littlechild, S.C. (1979) "Comment: radical subjectivism or radical subversion," in Rizzo, M. (ed.) *Time, Uncertainty, and Disequilibrium: Exploration of Austrian Themes*, pp. 32–49. Lexington, MA: Lexington Books.

——(1983) "Subjectivism and method in economics," in Wiseman, J. (ed.) *Beyond Positive Economics*, pp. 38–49. London: Macmillan.

——(1986) "Three types of market process," in Langlois, R.N. (ed.) *Economics as a Process – Essays in the New Institutional Economics*, pp. 27–39. Cambridge: Cambridge University Press.

Lowenberg, A.D., and Yu, B.T. (1992) "Efficient constitution formation and maintenance," *Constitutional Political Economy* 3, 51–72.

Magee, S.P., Brock, W.A., and Young, L. (1989) *Black Hole Tariffs and Endogenous Policy Theory – Political Economy in General Equilibrium*. Cambridge: Cambridge University Press.

Marlow, M.L. (1992) "Inter-governmental competition, voice and exit options, and the design of fiscal structure," *Constitutional Political Economy* 3, 73–88.

Mayr, E. (1982) *The Growth of Biological Thought – Diversity, Evolution, and Inheritance*. Cambridge, MA: Harvard University Press.

Medema, S.G. (1992) "Transactions, transaction costs, and vertical integration: a re-examination," *Review of Political Economy* 4, 291–316.

——(1994) "Ronald Coase and American institutionalism," in Samuels, W.J. (ed.) *Research in the History of Economic Thought and Methodology* 14, 51–92.

Milgrom, P., and Roberts, J. (1992) *Economics, Organization and Management*. Englewood Cliffs, NJ: Prentice Hall.

Mill, J.S. (1972) "Considerations on representative government," in Mill, J.S. (ed.) *Utilitarianism, On Liberty, and Considerations on Representative Government*, pp. 173–393. London: J. M. Dent.

von Mises, L. (1940) *Nationalökonomie – Theorie des Handelns und Wirtschaftens*. Genf: Editions Union.

——(1949) *Human Action – A Treatise on Economics*. New Haven: Yale University Press.

——(1985) *Liberalism in the Classical Tradition*, 3rd edn. San Francisco: Cobden Press.

Molsberger, J., and Kotios, A. (1990) "Ordnungspolitische Defizite des GATT," *ORDO* 41, 273–95.

Moser, P. (1990) *The Political Economy of the GATT – With Applications to U.S. Trade Policy*. Grüsch, Switzerland: Verlag Rüegger (Schweizerisches Institut für Außenwirtschafts-, Struktur- und Regionalforschung an der Hochschule St. Gallen, Band 22).

North, D.C. (1987) "Institutions, transaction costs and economic growth," *Economic Inquiry* 25, 419–28.

Nozick, R. (1974) *Anarchy, State, and Utopia*. New York: Basic Books.

O'Driscoll, G.P., and Rizzo, M.J. (1985) *The Economics of Time and Ignorance*. New York: Basil Blackwell.

Olson, M. (1982) *The Rise and Decline of Nations*. New Haven: Yale University Press.

Oppermann, T., and Conlan, P. (1990) "'Principles' – legal basis of today's international economic order?" *ORDO* 41, 297–313.

Oye, K.A. (ed.) (1986) *Cooperation under Anarchy*. Princeton, NJ: Princeton University Press.

Peacock, A. and Willgerodt, H. (1989) "Overall view of the German liberal movement," in Peacock, A. and Willgerodt, H. (eds) *German Neo-Liberals and the Social Market Economy*, pp. 1–15. London: Macmillan.

——(eds) (1989a) *German Neo-Liberals and the Social Market Economy*. London: Macmillan.

——(eds) (1989b) *Germany's Social Market Economy: Origins and Evolution*. London: Macmillan.

Perlman, M. (1986) "Subjectivism and American institutionalism," in Kirzner, I.M. (ed.) *Subjectivism and Economic Understanding – Essays in Honor of Ludwig Lachmann on his Eightieth Birthday*, pp. 268–80. London: Macmillan.

Petersmann, E.-U. (1988) "Handelspolitik als Verfassungsproblem," *ORDO* 39, 239–54.

Polanyi, M. (1951) *The Logic of Liberty*. Chicago: The University of Chicago Press.

Popper, K.R. (1957) *The Poverty of Historicism*. Boston: The Beacon Press.

——(1972) *Objective Knowledge – An Evolutionary Approach*. Oxford: Clarendon Press.

——(1982) *The Open Universe – An Argument for Indeterminism*. Totowa, NJ: Rowan and Littlefield.

——(1997) "Tribute to the life and work of Friedrich Hayek," in Frowen, S.F. (ed.) *Hayek: Economist and Social Philosopher: A Critical Retrospect*, pp. 311–12. London: Macmillan.

Prigogine, I. (1985) "New perspectives on complexity," in Aida, S., Allen, P., Atlan, H., Boulding, K., *et al*. (eds) *The Science and Praxis of Complexity*, pp. 107–18. Tokyo: The United Nations University.

——(1986) "Science, civilization and democracy," in *Futures* 18, 493–507.

Prigogine, I., and Stengers, I. (1984) *Order out of Chaos – Men's New Dialogue with Nature*. Toronto: Bantam Books.

Radzicki, M.J. (1990) "Institutional dynamics, deterministic chaos, and self-organizing systems," *Journal of Economic Issues* 24, 57–102.

Ramstad, Y. (1990) "The institutionalism of John R. Commons: theoretical foundations of a volitional economics," *Research in the History of Economic Thought and Methodology* 8, 53–104.

——(1994) "On the nature of economic evolution: John R. Commons and the metaphor of artificial selection," in Magnusson, L. (ed.) *Evolutionary and Neo-Schumpeterian Approaches to Economics*, pp. 65–121. Boston: Kluwer Academic Publishers.

Röpke, W. (1942) *Die Gesellschaftskrisis der Gegenwart*, 4th edn. Erlenbach-Zürich: Eugen Rentsch Verlag.

——(1949) *Civitas Humana – Grundfragen der Gesellschafts- und Wirtschaftsreform*, 3rd edn. Erlenbach-Zürich: Eugen Rentsch Verlag.

——(1960) *A Humane Economy – The Social Framework of the Free Market*. South Bend, IN: Gateway Editions.

——(1961) "Blätter der Erinnerung an Walter Eucken," *ORDO* 13, 3–19.

——(1963) *Economics of the Free Society*. Chicago: Henry Regnery Company.

Rosenberg, N., and Birdzell, Jr., L.E. (1986) *How the West Grew Rich: The Economic Transformation of the Industrial World*. New York: Basic Books.

Rothbard, M.N. (1956) "Toward a reconstruction of utility and welfare economics," in Sennholz, M. (ed.) *On Freedom and Free Enterprise – Essays in Honor of Ludwig von Mises*, pp. 224–62. Princeton, NJ: D. van Nostrand.

——(1970) *Man Economy and State – A Treatise on Economic Principles*, Vols I and II. Los Angeles: Nash Publishing.

Rutherford, M. (1983) "J.R. Commons's institutional economics," *Journal of Economic Issues* 17, 721–44.

——(1990) "Introduction to the transaction edition," in Commons, J.R. (ed.) *Institutional Economics – Its Place in Political Economy* (with a new introduction by Malcolm Rutherford), pp. xiii–xxxvii. New Brunswick: Transaction.

——(1994) *Institutions in Economics – The Old and the New Institutionalism*. Cambridge: Cambridge University Press.

Sally, R. (1996) "Ordoliberalism and the social market: classical political economy from Germany," *New Political Economy* 1, 233–57.

Schmidtchen, D. (1984) "German 'Ordnungspolitik' as institutional choice," *Zeitschrift für die gesamte Staatswissenschaft* 140, 54–70.

Schmidtchen, D., and Schmidt-Trenz, H.-J. (1990) "The division of labor is limited by the extent of the law – a constitutional approach to international private law," *Constitutional Political Economy* 1, 49–71.

Schmidt-Trenz, H.-J., and Schmidtchen, D. (1991) "Private international trade in the shadow of the territoriality of law: why does it work?" *Southern Economic Journal* 58, 329–38.

Schuknecht, L. (1990) "Protectionism – an intra-national prisoners' dilemma," *Aussenwirtschaft* 45, 39–55.

Shackle, G.L.S. (1979) *Imagination and the Nature of Choice*. Edinburgh: Edinburgh University Press.

——(1981) "Comment," in Shand, A.H. (ed.) *Subjectivist Economics – The New Austrian School*, pp. 59–67. The Pica Press.

——(1983) "The bounds of unknowledge," in Wiseman, J. (ed.) *Beyond Positive Economics*, pp. 28–37. London: Macmillan.

Sinn, S. (1989) "Economic models of policy-making in interdependent economies: an alternative view on competition among policies," mimeograph, The Kiel Institute of World Economics.

——(1992) "The taming of Leviathan: competition among governments," *Constitutional Political Economy* 2, 177–96.

Smith, A. (1981) *An Inquiry into the Nature and Causes of the Wealth of Nations*, 2 Vols. Indianapolis, IN: Liberty Classics (reprint of the 1976 Oxford University Press edition).

Snidal, D. (1986) "The game theory of international politics," in Oye, K.A. (ed.) *Cooperation Under Anarchy*, pp. 25–57. Princeton, NJ: Princeton University Press.

Streit, M. (1992) "Economic order, private law and public policy – the Freiburg School of law and economics in perspective," *Journal of Institutional and Theoretical Economics* 148, 675–704.

——(1994) "The Freiburg School of law and economics," in Boettke, P.J. (ed.) *The Elgar Companion to Austrian Economics*, pp. 508–15. Aldershot: Edgar Elgar.

Stützel, W., Watrin, C., Willgerodt, H., and Hohmann, K. (eds) (1981) *Grundtexte zur Sozialen Marktwirtschaft*. Stuttgart: Gustav Fischer (translated in 1982 as *Standard Texts on the Social Market Economy*, Stuttgart: Gustav Fischer).

Tiebout, C.M. (1956) "A pure theory of local expenditures," *Journal of Political Economy* 64, 416–24.

Trakman, L. (1983) *The Law Merchant and the Evolution of Commercial Law*. Colorado: Fred Rothman.

Tullock, G. (ed.) (1983) *The Simons' Syllabus – Henry Calvert Simons*. Blacksburg, VA: Polytechnic Institute and State University.

Tumlir, J. (1983) "International economic order and democratic constitutionalism," *ORDO* 34, 71–83.

——(1989) "Franz Böhm and the development of economic–constitutional analysis," in Peacock, A. and Willgerodt, H. (eds) *German Neo-Liberals and the Social Market Economy*, pp.125–41. London: Macmillan.

Vanberg, V. (1986) "Spontaneous market order and social rules," *Economics and Philosophy* 2, 75–100; reprinted as Ch. 5 in Vanberg (1994b).

——(1988) "'Ordnungstheorie' as constitutional economics – the German conception of a 'Social Market Economy,'" *ORDO* 39, 17–31.

——(1989) "Carl Menger's evolutionary and John R. Commons' collective action approach to institutions: a comparison," *Review of Political Economy* 1, 334–60; reprinted as Ch. 9 in Vanberg (1994b).

——(1990) "Vom Wettkampf der Systeme zum Wettbewerb von Ordnungen," in *Neue Zürcher Zeitung* no. 173, 28–29 July, p. 35.

——(1991) "Review of *ORDO* vols 40 and 41, 1989 and 1990," *Constitutional Political Economy* 2, 397–402.

——(1992) "Innovation, cultural evolution, and economic growth," in Witt, U. (ed.) *Explaining Process and Change – Approaches to Evolutionary Economics*, pp. 105–21. Ann Arbor: The University of Michigan Press.

——(1993) "F. A. Hayek," in Hodgson, G., Tool, M. and Samuels, W. (eds) *Handbook on Institutional and Evolutionary Economics*. Aldershot: Edgar Elgar.

——(1994a) "Cultural evolution, collective learning, and constitutional design," in Reisman, D. (ed.) *Economic Thought and Political Theory*, pp. 171–204. Boston: Kluwer Academic Publishers.

——(1994b) *Rules and Choice in Economics*. London: Routledge.

——(1997) "Die normativen Grundlagen von Ordnungspolitik," *ORDO* 48, 707–26.

——(1998a) "The Freiburg School of law and economics," in Newman, P. (ed.) *The New Palgrave Dictionary of Economics and the Law*, Vol. 2, pp. 172–9. London: Macmillan; in an extended version reprinted as Ch. 3 in the present volume.

——(1998b) "Menger, Carl (1840–1921)," in Newman, P. (ed.) *The New Palgrave Dictionary of Economics and the Law*, Vol. 2, pp. 635–41. London: Macmillan.

——(1998c) "Buchanan, James M," in Davis, J.B., Hands, D.W., and Mäki, U. (eds) *The Handbook of Economic Methodology*, pp. 40–44. Cheltenham: Edward Elgar.

——(1998d) "Constitutional political economy," in Davis, J.B., Hands, D.W., and Mäki, U. (eds) *The Handbook of Economic Methodology*, pp. 69–75. Cheltenham: Edward Elgar.

Vanberg, V., and Buchanan, J.M. (1988) "Rational choice and moral order," *Analyse & Kritik* 10, 138–60; reprinted as Ch. 4 in Vanberg (1994b).

——(1989) "Interests and theories in constitutional choice," *Journal of Theoretical Politics* 1, 49–62; reprinted as Ch. 10 in Vanberg (1994b).

——(1991) "Constitutional choice, rational ignorance and the limits of reason," in *Jahrbuch für Neue Politische Ökonomie* 10, pp. 61–78. Tübingen: J. C. B. Mohr (Paul Siebeck); reprinted as Ch. 11 in Vanberg (1994b).

Vanberg, V., and Kerber, W. (1994) "Institutional competition among jurisdictions: an evolutionary approach," *Constitutional Political Economy* 5, 193–219.

Vaubel, R. (1985) "Von der normativen zu einer positiven Theorie der internationalen Organisationen," in Giersch, H. (ed.) *Probleme und Perspektiven der weltwirtschaftlichen Entwicklung*, pp. 403–21. Berlin: Duncker & Humblot.

——(1990) "Korreferat zum Referat Wohlfahrtsgewinne durch international koordinierte Wirtschaftspolitik," in Kantzenbach, E. (ed.) *Probleme der internationalen Wirtschaftspolitik*, pp. 71–7. Berlin: Duncker & Humblot.

——(1992) "Die Politische Ökonomie der wirtschaftspolitischen Zentralisierung in der Europäischen Gemeinschaft," in *Jahrbuch für Neue Politische Ökonomie* 11, pp. 30–65. Tübingen: J. C. B. Mohr (Paul Siebeck).

Vaughn, K.I. (1990) "Profits, alertness and imagination," (review of I. M. Kirzner's "Discovery, capitalism, and distributive justice") *Journal des Economistes et des Etudes Humaines* 1, 183–8.

Vousen, N. (1990) *The Economics of Trade Protection*. Cambridge: Cambridge University Press.

Walras, L. [1954 (1874)] *Elements of Pure Economics or the Theory of Social Wealth* (translated by W. Jaffé). Homewood, IL: Richard D. Irwin.

Watrin, C. (1991) "Liberale Toleranz auf dem Prüfstand," in *Das Flüchtlingsproblem – eine Zeitbombe?*, pp. 101–20. Chur/Zürich: Verlag Rüegger.

Weck-Hannemann, H. (1989) "Protectionism in direct democracy – an empirical assessment," mimeograph, Faculty of Economics and Statistics, University of Konstanz, Germany.

West, E.G. (1990) *Adam Smith and Modern Economics*. Aldershot: Edgar Elgar.

Wicken, J.S. (1987) *Evolution, Thermodynamics, and Information – Extending the Darwinian Paradigm*. Oxford: Oxford University Press.

Wildavsky, A. (1990) "A double security: federalism as competition," *Cato Journal* 10, 39–58.

Wilhelm, M.M. [1991 (1972)] "The political thought of Friedrich A. Hayek," in Wood, J.C., and Woods, R.N. (eds) *Friedrich A. Hayek, Critical Assessments*, Vol. 2, pp. 158–77. London: Routledge.

Willgerodt, H. (1989) "Staatliche Souveränität und die Ordnung der Weltwirtschaft," *ORDO* 40, 401–27.

Willgerodt, H., and Peacock, A. (1989) "German liberalism and economic revival," in Peacock A., and Willgerodt, H. (eds) *Germany's Social Market Economy: Origins and Evolution*, pp. 1–14. London: Macmillan.

Williamson, O.E. (1975) *Markets and Hierarchies – Analysis and Antitrust Implications*. New York: The Free Press.

——(1985) *The Economic Institutions of Capitalism*. New York: The Free Press.

Wiseman, J. (ed.) (1983) *Beyond Positive Economics*. London: Macmillan.

——(1989) *Cost, Choice, and Political Economy*. Aldershot: Edward Elgar.

——(1990) "Principles of political economy – an outline proposal, illustrated by application to fiscal federalism," *Constitutional Political Economy* 1, 101–24.

Witt, U. (1985) "Coordination of individual economic activities as an evolving process of self-organization," *Economie Appliquée* 37, 569–95.

——(1994) "The theory of societal evolution – Hayek's unfinished legacy," in Birner, J., and van Zijp, R. (eds) *Hayek, Co-ordination and Evolution*, pp. 178–89. London: Routledge.

von Witzke, H., and Livingston, M.L. (1990) "Public choice in international pollution," mimeograph, University of Minnesota, Department of Agricultural and Applied Economics.

Author index

Subject index

For Product Safety Concerns and Information please contact our EU
representative GPSR@taylorandfrancis.com
Taylor & Francis Verlag GmbH, Kaufingerstraße 24, 80331 München, Germany